T0354353

# THE
# FIDELITY
# FACTOR

# THE
# FIDELITY
# FACTOR

### EXPLORING THE KEY THAT WILL DRIVE
### YOUR CHURCH GROUP TO REVIVAL

# DR. S. SAGOE-NKANSAH

## THE FIDELITY FACTOR
## EXPLORING THE KEY THAT WILL DRIVE YOUR CHURCH GROUP
## TO REVIVAL

iUniverse books may be ordered through booksellers or by contacting:

iUniverse
1663 Liberty Drive
Bloomington, IN 47403
www.iuniverse.com
1-800-Authors (1-800-288-4677)

ISBN: 978-1-5320-2536-5 (sc)
ISBN: 978-1-5320-2811-3 (hc)
ISBN: 978-1-5320-2537-2 (e)

Library of Congress Control Number: 2017911150

Print information available on the last page.

iUniverse rev. date: 05/08/2017

*In the US, write:*
*Living Waters Evangelistic Association*
*14555 Macbeth Drive*
*Silver Spring, MD 20906*

*In Ghana, write:*
*Living Waters Evangelistic Association*
*PO Box SK 152*
*Sakumono Estates*
*Community 13*
*Tema, Ghana*

*Email Address: sagoe.nkansah@gmail.com*

To the memory of my daughter Sybil

The ultimate measure of a man is not where he stands in moments of comfort and convenience, but where he stands at times of challenge and controversy.

—Martin Luther King Jr.

# CONTENTS

# FOREWORD

The dawning of a new day is upon us as Christians. The clarion call of the Holy Spirit has sounded throughout the world. This is a serious notice to Christians everywhere that the imminent return of our Lord Jesus Christ is just ahead in this twenty-first century. This call includes instructions on how Christians should prepare themselves. Our Lord Jesus is coming for His church, which has made herself ready with the assistance of the Holy Spirit. Truth, integrity, and fidelity are at the center of this preparation. Jesus is coming for the Church, which is His bride, who has made herself ready by putting on her white garments of righteousness.

One of the aspects of preparation is fidelity. Men and women who are sensing the call to join the ranks of leadership are experiencing the prompting of the Holy Spirit to take up the pen and become ready writers. The Holy Spirit is directing them to sound the alarm for God's people, saying, "People, get ready! Jesus is coming!" These are servants of God who have paid the price to join the ranks of the high calling of God in these last days. They are being given true revelations concerning preparing for this spectacular event known as the Rapture, the catching away of the bride of Christ.

Fidelity is at the heart of the message of the Holy Spirit. Fidelity is at the heart of the preparation. Transparency must be seen in God's children as we approach the Rapture. Many books have been written about different subjects. However, only a few books are written about fidelity. The Holy Spirit raised up a servant in Ghana, West Africa, with knowledge and the ability to write a much-needed book about this subject, fidelity. His name is Bishop S. Sagoe-Nkansah. He senses the heartbeat of Jesus Christ our Lord in writing this book. Bishop Sagoe-Nkansah wrote a book that is an inspiration to Christians everywhere to rise up and become active members of the body of Christ, which is His bride. Bishop Sagoe-Nkansah is truly a dedicated man of God who embodies a life of holiness, truth, integrity, and fidelity. As you read this book, *The Fidelity Factor*, I am sure that you will be blessed, and you will also agree that fidelity is the heartbeat of Jesus Christ our Lord. People get ready because Jesus is soon returning to this earth to catch away His bride.

—Archbishop Charles E. Henderson, PhD,
Director of Foreign Division, AEGA Ministries Int. Inc.

# ACKNOWLEDGMENTS

My special thanks go to: The Holy Spirit, who inspired the writing of this book; without His counsel and anointing, this writing would have been impossible. To Adelaide, my life partner and co-laborer in the ministry—being there was enough to get me going. It's hard for me to put into words my gratitude when it comes to Archbishop Charles E. Henderson, who committed his precious time in writing the foreword to this book; may your voice of mentoring keep echoing around the globe. To senior territorial bishop in AEGA Ghana, Dr. Albert A. Saah, may God richly bless you for taking the time out of your busy schedule to read this manuscript and give me much encouragement. My gratitude goes to Mr. and Mrs. Ephraim Osabutey, whose supportive prayers came in very handy. Now to Mr. Franklin Kyei—your willingness to assist in editing this manuscript took a huge load off my shoulders; you are such a blessing. Michael, Dad appreciates your taking the time to glance through portions of the manuscript; your suggestions were very useful. My appreciation goes to Mr. Baffour Senkyere Ababio of Elim Pentecostal Church, Brockley, for spending his precious time to help shape the introduction to this book. How can I forget the wonderful staff of iUniverse? Check-in coordinator Mars Alma, editorial consultant Joseph Long, publishing consultant Arvie Fernandez, and marketing consultant Rey Tome: your persistence with me has paid off. To Miss Veronica Gates, I can only say—may God be with you wherever you are. Most of all, I am grateful for the prayers of the IFC Board of Governors, the Living Waters Evangelistic Association, the School of World Missions, and Pistis House, who bore the heavy weight of ministerial responsibility with me so I could find the time and seclusion to write.

# INTRODUCTION

# THE UPPER ROOM

November 27, 2013

"Who wrote the letter?" a voice blurted out. A nervous silence fell across those who'd gathered on the compound, brief but long enough for its meaning to sink in.

"Who wrote the letter?" resounded another, emboldened, it seemed, by the first. In the ensuing minutes, these words swept across the gathering in the bungalow's yard like a mantra amid muffled giggles. The letter under scrutiny that evening had dealt a death blow to our Christian group, ultimately disbanding it. This was quite a dedicated bunch; after all, it had birthed a worldwide spiritual renewal some decades back.

Those present, were there partly out of curiosity and partly because their spiritual pedigree was tied to this historic movement. The overarching reason that rallied this erstwhile fellowship though, was to commemorate a father figure. He'd just passed, and we all felt he was owed that much.

Our nostalgia ran deep, as far back as the first quarter of 1982. You can do the math: These folks go a long way back.

We were all fervently hopeful then. Visions and prophecies were being given on a daily basis about what God was going to do with this youthful group. The euphoria was palpable.

But thirty years down the line, many felt differently. They thought they'd been hoodwinked. Some fellow among us had signed a letter, supposedly written by the group's leader, to excommunicate certain key members—an act that sowed sufficient discord to terminate the momentum of our spiritual revival. Nobody ever took responsibility for the mischief. Decades had passed, and the mystery hadn't still been resolved. Was the fellow who'd done this dastardly deed present among us, or was he not? If you could slightly imagine the havoc it had wreaked within many relationships, careers, and lives, maybe the cry to figure this out will make some sense to you.

Through spending countless hours in counseling with others, I've learned the hard way that regardless of how infidelity comes—be it in marriage, organizations, relationships, or our spirituality—its effect on its victims is basically the same. Trust is broken, and hearts are traumatized.

Perhaps you are wondering how I'd gotten myself entangled with this conundrum. It was a few months into my freshman year in college, and I had barely gotten myself immersed into the humdrum of academic life.

"You've got to see this group!" someone said. The look in his eyes said it all. This was Martin, my new friend, and the bug those "folks" had, had surely bitten him. But in the next few days his exuberance nudged me enough to overcome my reluctance.

Being part of a small spirit-filled group of charismatic enthusiasts the nature of whose Pentecostal activity had quickly grabbed my fascination, I bought the whole kit and caboodle and took my first baby steps toward revivalism. In the basement where they met each dawn, my life became visibly shaken to the core as the Lord met me in a very significant way.

What the Holy Spirit did there had me mesmerized beyond my understanding; and the group's campus leader, an instrument of God's power, kept bragging about their place of worship in the capital. The suburb was Caprice.

Though a resident of Accra for many years, I had a faint idea of that part of town. Aching to find things out for myself and satisfy my intrigue, I made my way there. Honestly, upon my arrival and with very little conception of what the fuss was really all about, I had a bit of a suspicious attitude.

*After all, this guy could have been making it all up,* I thought, but I was floored. Pentecostalism in its rawness was at a feverish pitch when I arrived. Prayer in tongues went on for hours, being interspersed occasionally with songs of worship and prophetic utterance; the atmosphere was charged with some kind of invisible electricity. I was enthralled by what I saw and "got in the game," as some say. The brethren, as they called themselves, had been at it for several months on end. Till then, my perception about Pentecostalism had been that, its patronage derived from the fringes of society. However, the brethren were an exception. They were an unusual mix of personalities, ranging from an aeronautic engineer to high school kids. And to my pleasant surprise, most of those kids were very articulate in English.

Throughout the holidays, they squeezed into a small living room upstairs in a single story—their "upper room"—for stormy prayer meetings. This became my haunt. As I interacted with the brethren about their drive, they all without exception felt absolutely called to their vision of a global revival, and this was the bedrock of their unwavering fidelity to their cause.

I quietly came to a solid conclusion that: unbroken fidelity, vision, fervent and united prayer was the secret behind unleashing God's supernatural power. The power that had completely upended my life on the university campus.

Nonetheless, the mysterious letter episode did occur a couple of years later. And I came to two unavoidable conclusions that totally changed my life and ministry. First, regardless of how hungry a group is for spiritual revival, their goal will remain an illusion until they resolve infidelity among themselves. And second, finding a corporate attitude of unbroken fidelity is the only way any group can participate in an upcoming move of God.

Without being preached to, the significance of these principles became etched in my mind. And this is what I gathered—should any group walk through them, be they educated or uneducated, noble or ignoble, they'll surely experience an outpouring of the Holy Spirit. In a nutshell, I coined the term *fidelity factor* for this crucial element I would become an advocate of, for its reliability.

During my decades of ministry, I've been privileged to pioneer and work with numerous local churches, para-church groups, and fellowships—groups very much like yours.

Some have gone forward and become very successful, while others have floundered and failed completely. As I worked as a trainer of church leaders and provided oversight to a plethora of Christian organizations, I used this unique opportunity to study ministry groups. I've observed that the single most important factor separating the groups that advanced for decades in the move of God and those that become fragmented along the way is the fidelity factor.

What is the fidelity factor? When my wife stays up late waiting for my safe return, that's the fidelity factor at work. When my dad drove through some mountain to get me provisions, because, out of my childish zeal, I'd forgotten to notify him I would be away at a youth camp, that was the fidelity factor at work. The fidelity factor affects our daily lives in many ways. It is an active, *innate* human sense that binds an individual's action in devotion to another person, group, agreements, contracts, institutions, or code of ethics.

It can be highly developed or be subject to arrested development in specific individuals. Its level differs from person to person. It goes to the core of who we are as individuals, whether we perceive within ourselves the need to stay dedicated to certain persons or not. When the fidelity factor is highly developed, groups hold together, and when it is not, they fall apart.

I wrote this book because I absolutely believe the world is at a historic precipice and the church is at the cusp of an unprecedented move of God. In 1913, William Seymour, the pioneer of the Azusa Street Revival, and Maria Woodworth-Etter, a major Pentecostal revivalist, both prophesied on separate occasions that in one hundred years, a major move of God would shake the globe, except this time, the Holy Spirit would be poured out in greater power than ever before (Cauchi 2016). The question however is; are they believable?

This foretelling of revivals isn't unique; it has an authentic historical precedent. For example, Martin Luther's Protestant reformation and revival was prophesied by Jan Huss one hundred years earlier.

If these prophetic words were anything to go by, then 2013 shouldn't have been the beginning of a normal season for you and me. There are two critical points, though. First, the Azusa street revival ended in 1916, exactly one hundred years ago. What that means is, 2013 began a season that will authenticate the prophecy of Seymour and Woodworth- Etter. Second, Katherine Kuhlman, the protagonist of the charismatic movement, died in February 1976, exactly forty years ago (Liardon 1996). Both the one-hundred-year and forty-year anniversaries are significant milestones in human history. Abraham's *Isaac* prophecy occurred on his hundredth birthday. The children of Israel's *milk and honey* prophecy was birthed on their fortieth anniversary in the wilderness. Moses's anointing worked and completed its assignment within those forty years. King Saul reigned over Israel, and King David replaced him in his fortieth year. King David reigned over Israel, and King Solomon assumed the throne in *his* fortieth year. The anointing on Saul worked for forty years; the Davidic anointing worked for forty years; and the Solomonic anointing also worked for forty years.

What's my take? The anointing of the charismatic movement has, after forty years, finished its work. The church is at the threshold of another great anointing, and your group cannot be exempted.

The problem I'll be the first to admit is that, the charismatic movement led the body of Christ into vast and uncharted spiritual territory. Its impact on culture and society was virtually seismic. But, with this groundbreaking era also came acts of sabotage, like our *notorious* letter episode, that fractured and disrupted the global community of believers.

The residue of "Spirit-led" church splits, and combative attitudes in the name of God produced deep-seated mistrust. Spiritual infidelity has left the church today with more trust issues than I can remember. Without resolving the widespread infidelity we've been laden with, many groups like yours and mine will fail in their readiness for another major move of God. I wrote *The Fidelity Factor* to deal with this collective quagmire we find ourselves in.

*The Fidelity Factor* is a step-by-step guide for groups like yours that are hungry for spiritual revival yet struggle daily with the inhibitions of spiritual infidelity within their ranks. It is time to apply the message of this book and get your group ready for the next move of God.

There will be those who straddle the fence, do business as usual, and play by their religious playbook. They will hang onto their dilemma like a dog with a new pan till the season of divine visitation is over. However, there will be also folks like your kind who are clearly hungry for more. To these, nothing is going to keep them away from the next item on God's menu. They long to see their fellowships, cell groups, youth bands, prayer warriors, or home Bible study groups commit with ardent loyalty till the fires of revival are ignited.

*The Fidelity Factor* is a book that encapsulates the principles that will lead your group, fellowship, cell, chapter or prayer band out of the labyrinth of frustration—out of the angst of crying out to God for months and years, desperately yearning for a move of His Spirit, yet being bogged down by group attitudes of unfaithfulness, vacillation, uncertainty and mistrust.

I can recall time and again working with a group that battled with a lukewarm culture, without the slightest idea they were at the edge of stepping into a rare moment of divine glory. Yet through what we will be sharing in this book, they have surprised themselves and everyone else by launching citywide revivals.

Believe it or not, your group can be next in line for an unprecedented move of the Holy Spirit. Are you ready to hit the road? Let's go then.

# THE CALLING

## Step 1: The sons rally to their calling

Paul, a servant of Jesus Christ, called to be an apostle, separated unto the gospel of God. (Rom. 1:1)

I'd run away from God much of my teenage life, and that brought me nothing but depression. I'd come to psych myself into thinking that perhaps the novel experience of college life might be the ultimate turnaround I needed. That didn't happen. Then, out of the blue, I decided to try a Christian meeting. It was already past eight, and I had no clue which spiritual activity the campus had going on. I stuck my *Gideon's New Testament Bible* in my pocket and went church hunting. I felt frustrated after a while and thought that maybe this might not be "the night." I opted to take a shortcut to my residence along a dark, lonely road behind one of the halls.

There, my ears picked up the sound of vocal harmonies and acoustic guitar strings that slowly approached me down the slope. My curiosity got me peering through the dimly lit, shadowy lane to view the singers.

"Hey, where are you heading to around this time?" one of the gentlemen, a six-foot fellow, bellowed.

*Who might that be?* I wondered. He sensed my uncertainty and called my name.

*That voice sounded familiar*, I thought.

A few strides forward confirmed my suspicions. These guys were freshmen from my faculty. The tall one was Martin.

"Oh, just going to an all-night." That's what we called the prayer vigils run by churches.

"What a coincidence," he said. "That's exactly where we're going. Care to join us?"

I gave them my consent with a shrug.

I hadn't been in such a meeting for a long time. It wasn't my favorite pastime; to say it was gut-wrenching might be a good way to describe it. I always felt sinful, guilty, and nervous all rolled into one when I got involved. As difficult as that night was, it began my long journey back to God.

I rededicated my life to the Lord close to midnight and went to bed in the morning feeling like a child of God. To make a long story short, through Martin, God led my footsteps to the brethren, who had a campus group going. And this became my local church.

Basically, a Christian local church is the gathering of spiritual sons and daughters at a specific place and time to fellowship with their heavenly Father and one another. That night made me one of them.

The Greek word translated as church is *ecclesia,* a word borrowed from the secular Hellenistic society that means "called-out ones." Thus, when a people are called out from the generic society to gather for a specific reason, be it secular or spiritual, they are a church. Therefore, the key word that brings a local church into being is *calling.* It presupposes that, for anyone to gather with others to worship God, that individual must necessarily be called. I had been called at that prayer vigil. At approximately eleven thirty on the night of October 10, 1982, God used two guitar-strumming Christian brothers to call me into spiritual son-ship.

God's individual call of the apostle Paul occurred on the road to Damascus; this is a well-documented fact (Acts 9:1–8). There are those individual callings that, like Paul's, are very spectacular, and there are those that are far less so and yet no less spiritual. This to me is noteworthy for not all of us will, in our calling to serve God, have the same face-to-face encounter that Paul had.

Though the divine calling of a group of believers might be to collectively birth a citywide revival, each member would have to embrace it individually. The embrace of this individual or personalized calling can occur in a myriad of ways. Many might find the radio and TV announcements, billboards, handbills, signboards, or newspaper ads to be what God uses to call them to a specific assembly.

Some members of the brethren at Caprice testified to sensing their individual calls through the daily tongue-speaking heard in the upper room. I've heard cases of individuals being directed by angels to embrace their calling to a specific local church or group. The authenticity of the calling of the spiritual sons who belong to a specific fellowship is critical to their fidelity.

The collective fidelity of a group to its *cause* should be traceable to the genuineness of their individual callings to *join.*

> They went out from us, but they were not of us; for if they
> had been of us, they would no doubt have continued with
> us: but they went out, that they might be made manifest
> that they were not all of us. (1 John 2:19)

*Action:* Let each member of your fellowship or local church, settle the issue of the authenticity of his or her divine calling to continue with you.

## Step 2: Obey the calling of a servant

I had taken literally Jesus's call to enter the closet for prayer—though I don't fault anyone for seeing the closet as a metaphor. Now at home for a long break from school work, brimming with a renewed zest for getting intimate with God, I found the wardrobe the most cloistered space for a spiritual tête-à-tête. In the first place, it was dark in there, and that did help in my concentration. Second, it gave me the necessary quietude I needed to meditate.

I had been praying in tongues entirely that morning at my usual place and had loved every minute of it. My dad found the tongues and wardrobe combination quite an annoyance. However, we tolerated each other on that score. After all, finding religion can do strange things to people.

Usually, the prayer was interspersed with moments of silence and singing. Maybe it helped to emote musically and catch my breath momentarily during a lengthy prayer session. I did so on one occasion, and my silence was broken by a voice.

*It couldn't be from that lonely space or without,* I thought. The difference though was that, it came with a rush of God's presence. I knew that presence from the time I had spent with the brethren. It was peaceful, authoritative, and endearing at the same time.

"Rise up, and go outside," it said. I obeyed almost instantly. Outside at the veranda of our home, the same voice spoke with the same rush of God's presence.

"Look," it instructed. "Look at the area."

I looked, and there from my home, situated on a low hill, was a shallow valley that sprawled with a middle-class neighborhood.

"Will you reach them for me?" it asked. Much was being requested here, and I needed to be totally sure about who this "master" was. Thus, I went back in and prayed some more. And after a while, the voice called again, repeating its instruction and request.

On the third occasion, I had it settled: this was God speaking. Under my breath, I answered the proposal "yes, Lord." And with that, the rest was history. Decades of nonstop spiritual service have followed.

The Lord's call of Samuel perhaps indicates to us that His call of individuals is directly tied to their servanthood. In that story, God calls Samuel, but because the young man doesn't know Him yet, he misunderstands the calling. "Now Samuel did not yet know the Lord, neither was the word of the Lord yet revealed unto him" (1 Sam. 3:7). Samuel thought it was a human calling when actually it was a divine call. When we misinterpret the divine calling as a human calling, we tend to be focused on men when we ought to be focusing on God. Samuel became focused on a man, the high priest, Eli. The reason it is easy to misunderstand God's calling as a human call is that God uses a human voice and a human language to call humans to Himself. The voice Samuel heard was the voice of Eli, so he went to Eli.

I have sometimes heard from some folks who obviously were called to serve under certain leaders say to them things like "You know, I have served you all these years and have helped you build this ministry." The reason people called by God talk this way is because they heard their divine calling as a human call. These folks thought they were answering the calling of a man when in reality they were supposed to be answering the calling of God. They thought they were serving a man when, actually, they were serving God.

Then, there are leaders who look to their followers for their provision in fulfilling their divine calling. I once heard one pastor complain bitterly about his congregants saying, "These folks do not know how to appreciate their pastor. Considering how my wife and I have served them, they should have bought me a car by now." I've never looked to any church I've shepherded to provide for my calling. I had to settle this with God very early in my ministry, that if it was He who called me to do what I'm doing then it'll be He who'll provide for my calling, not man. Like Oral

Roberts once said, "God is your source of total supply, man is not your source, man is only an instrument" (Roberts 1999). Hence, I always had to look to God for His supply; "Faithful is he that calleth you, who also will do it" (1 Thess. 5:24). Any attempt to see man as my benefactor has left me disappointed and wounded.

Samuel kept going to Eli to confirm his calling, until on the third occasion, Eli figured it all out. God was actually calling the young man. God the caller had to instruct Samuel based on the essence of the calling. Eli definitely knew that God had to be calling Samuel to serve, hence the young man had to respond based on his identity as a servant. Samuel had to answer the calling properly.

> Therefore Eli said unto Samuel, "Go, lie down: and it shall
> be, if he call thee, that thou shalt say, Speak, Lord; for thy
> servant heareth ..." (1 Sam. 3:9)

Notice the words *thy servant*. Clearly, God's calling targets His servants to serve. We might have to serve under a man, but the call to serve *came* from God.

> And Moses verily was faithful in all his house, as a servant,
> for a testimony of those things which were to be spoken
> after. (Heb. 3:5)

In a similar way, Moses was called individually on Mount Horeb to serve in God's house as a servant and a prophet. But how did he do it? He did it with fidelity. The awareness of an individual's divine calling is the key to true fidelity. Moses was faithful as a servant of God because he was conscious of His heavenly calling as a prophet. In Hebrews 3:1–2, Moses's fidelity to his calling is compared to that of Jesus. They were both loyal to the house of God because they were completely aware that it was God who called them to serve there.

Why will an individual acknowledge that he is a member of a specific local church yet be unreliable in handling the basic tasks of running the ministry there? I believe that is a shame. This only occurs because such individuals live as Christians while being totally oblivious of their calling to serve the house of God. Your responsibility to serve God in His house begins from the very first day of your membership in the body of Christ.

To serve God faithfully implies serving reliably, dutifully, devotedly, and consistently.

> I therefore, the prisoner of the Lord, beseech you that
> ye walk worthy of the vocation wherewith ye are called.
> (Eph. 4:1)

The only way to walk worthy of any calling is to be faithful to it. Fidelity has the capacity to honor a call from God; in the military, it is referred to as the call of duty. When our heavenly duty calls, we must answer—that is, being devoted to it and consistent without complaining. This is what the apostle refers to as "with longsuffering" (Eph. 4:2). It does not matter if no one appreciates your service there. It is true that it hurts to serve in some places, but to continue serving God in the purity of heart, you cannot afford to let the un-Christlike responses of others poison your attitude.

> And whatsoever ye do, do it heartily, as to the Lord, and
> not unto men; knowing that of the Lord ye shall receive
> the reward of the inheritance: for ye serve the Lord Christ.
> (Col. 3:23–24)

Serving God is in many ways similar to financial giving. They both involve giving to the Lord. Financial giving is as valuable to God as the attitude in which it is done: "God loves a cheerful giver" (2 Corin. 9:7). That means that giving to the Lord should be done with the right attitude, just as serving in God's house should be done with the right attitude. The right attitude in serving faithfully is to serve heartily. The original Greek words for *heartily* is *ek psuche*, which actually means "from the soul." This means that walking worthily of your calling implies serving God's call with a mental focus, an emotional attachment, and a willing attitude to perform the Lord's duty. The mind, emotion, and will are the vital components of the human soul.

Fidelity will automatically emerge out of the awareness of a divine call and an emotional attachment to it. Whenever we perform our ministerial duties "as to the Lord," we will walk worthily of our calling; we will dignify our duty with the right attitude because the wrong attitudes of unappreciative people will have no effect on us.

> Unless God raised you up for this very thing, you will be worn out by the opposition of man and devils. But if God be for you, who can be against you? (Wesley 1791)

Never forget that in offering your fidelity to your calling, you'll receive "the reward of the inheritance." (Col. 3:24) According to Revelations 2:10, this is an eternal "crown of life."

> You are born again in a day, but for the rest of your life you'll serve God for your eternal crown.

Can a person miss his reward by serving without fidelity and in the wrong attitude? Absolutely.

> Because you did not serve Jehovah your God with joyfulness and with gladness of heart for the abundance of all things, and you shall serve your enemies whom Jehovah shall send on you, in hunger, and in thirst, and in nakedness, and in lack of all things. And He shall put an iron yoke on your neck until He has destroyed you. (Deut. 28:47–48)

Certainly, poverty, bondage and destruction can never be the reward God promised His *faithful* children.

*Action:* Let all the members of your group who believe they're called to continue with you seek God for clarity in their area of service to the Lord there.

## Step 3: Make the prophetic connection

The awareness of an individual's divine calling is the key to true fidelity. This is a truism. How this thread got woven into the fabric of my life's story still amazes me.

Dragging me out of bed for prayer at dawn would probably get me irate more than anything in the world. And this was another pressing request from Martin.

*I don't need this extreme kind of Christianity*, I thought, looking condescendingly at him. I ironically felt sorry for his desperation. A glance at the scene indicated that perhaps he rather needed a huge favor from me. He was on his knees at this time.

"All right, all right. We'll go, okay?" And so we did. In the basement, I ran into a gaggle of charismatic folks vehemently talking in tongues. It sounded like a garage full of old Ford Model T engines running concurrently at full throttle.

"Urgh," I cringed. *It's not morning yet, so what the heck are they yelling about?* I fumed inside. This was a far cry from my quieter kind of childhood churchliness.

The energetic prayer time soon concluded. Judging from my wristwatch, it had been an hour long.

"Whew!"

We were quickly requested to sit for a meeting of sorts. I grabbed a chair nearby like the others and waited for God knows what.

A young gentleman strutted in front of us with a Bible in hand.

*This might be the guy Martin's been raving about*, I mused. I'd been getting quite a review of their leader's teaching prowess from my friend. My thoughts raced, trying to accommodate what might be next.

But nothing could have prepared me for what was about to happen. In the midst of a riveting lesson, the most surreal thing occurred. I didn't know then what it was, but I do now: the glory of God took over the ambience in the room, and I was sucked as it were into another world.

I remained strapped to this dimension by an unseen force till the lesson ended. Returning to my "flesh" seemed like awakening from a world of glory. I couldn't fully tell what exactly it was, yet my life was radically changed forever.

I went to Martin and said, "Please don't come for me tomorrow at dawn." He reciprocated with an ambivalent look, and I quickly added, "I'll come myself." He heaved a sigh of relief.

And so it happened that, for the next several years, yours truly and this revival group became an item; we were inseparable. I was blessed with two consecutive years of visions and angelic visits. I cried as I witnessed God's mercy on this poor soul of mine.

Without a shadow of doubt, I had come to the full persuasion that the brethren and I had our destinies tied. It was a prophetic connection. I served faithfully in that place till my ministry completely unfolded, and the fellowship got fragmented.

God prophetically connected Jacob to "the house of God," changing his life's story.

> And Jacob went out from Beersheba, and went toward Haran. And he lighted upon a certain place, and tarried there all night, because the sun was set; and he took of the stones of that place, and put them for his pillows, and lay down in that place to sleep. And he dreamed, and behold a ladder set up on the earth, and the top of it reached to heaven: and behold the angels of God ascending and descending on it. And, behold, the Lord stood above it, and said, I am the Lord God of Abraham thy father, and the God of Isaac: the land whereon thou liest, to thee will I give it, and to thy seed; And thy seed shall be as the dust of the earth, and thou shalt spread abroad to the west, and to the east, and to the north, and to the south: and in thee and in thy seed shall all the families of the earth be blessed. And, behold, I am with thee, and will keep thee in all places whither thou goest, and will bring thee again into this land; for I will not leave thee, until I have done that which I have spoken to thee of. And Jacob awaked out of his sleep, and he said, Surely the Lord is in this place; and I knew it not. And he was afraid, and said, How dreadful is this place! this is none other but the house of God, and this is the gate of heaven. (Gen. 28:10–17)

In this passage, the phrases *this place* and *this land* refer to the house of God. God spoke, saying, "The land whereon thou liest, to thee will I give it … and will bring thee again into this land." Obviously, Jacob's life was prophetically linked to the house of God.

How did that occur? A weary Jacob, running from his twin brother, stumbled at sundown on a place called Luz. There, God gave him a prophetic understanding of Bethel or the house of God, in this town called Luz. *Bethel* means "the house of God" in Hebrew. Jacob's decision to rest at this place was not an accident. God had ordered his steps there because his destiny was hooked to it. He might have "lighted upon a certain place," but this place was hinged to his destiny. This "certain place" is Bethel, the house of God. His life's journey was prophetically magnetized to the house of God.

How he found that out was through the prophetic dream he had in the house of God. Jacob's calling was prophetically interwoven with the house of God. God told him that He wasn't going to let him go till he had returned to fulfill his purpose in this place. Since God wasn't going to let go, Jacob couldn't run away from this place; he had a prophetic responsibility to it.

You can't find your spiritual rest at any other place than the specific house of God you were destined to serve. This is because God ordered your steps to that very spot. It might be a fellowship, prayer team, Bible study group, home cell or local church. You are yoked to this spot by divine sovereignty.

Like Jacob, none of us find ourselves in the house of God, fellowship, ministry, mission or group by accident. The house of God came into our lives by divine arrangement. Our destinies were wired to it, and there was little we could have done about it. Our individual prophetic visions and understanding of God's house are critical to this fact, that there are certain places we can't run away from. We can't untie ourselves from the places God has prophetically connected us to and not be badly hurt.

However, fidelity to the house of God cannot be developed without a clear inner conviction; you'll need an undeniable conviction that God has specifically called you to that group, fellowship or church. The apostolic team of Paul and Barnabas had such a prophetic connection.

> Now there were in the church that was at Antioch certain
> prophets and teachers; as Barnabas, and Simeon that was
> called Niger, and Lucius of Cyrene, and Manaen, which
> had been brought up with Herod the tetrarch, and Saul
> [Paul]. As they ministered to the Lord, and fasted, the
> Holy Ghost said, Separate me Barnabas and Saul [Paul]
> for the work whereunto I have called them. (Acts 13:1–2,
> brackets added)

Paul and Barnabas knew they were jointly and prophetically *called* to this *work*. Fidelity is faithfulness, and this means "full of faith." Hence, you have to be full of faith in the corporate dream of your Bethel, God's house—your place of worship or local church. The prophetic dream of Jacob was significant because it enabled him see the image of faith about the house of God. This image of faith that was given to Jacob at Luz did make him full of faith for the house of God, and it's in this same faithful spirit that we are to serve in God's house.

> And there was one Anna, a prophetess, the daughter of
> Phanuel, of the tribe of Aser: she was of a great age, and
> had lived with an husband seven years from her virginity;
> And she was a widow of about fourscore and four years,
> which departed not from the temple, but served God with
> fastings and prayers night and day. (Luke 2:36–37)

Here, Anna's individual call to serve in the place of worship is identified. She was called by God to serve Him in the capacity of a prophetess. In the middle of a generic call to worship in the temple, Anna knew she was called specifically by God to serve Him with fastings and prayers night and day. Anna was what we call an intercessory prophet—called to pray the prophecy of God's house into reality. Thus, her individual call was one to loyally serve God in His house as His intercessor.

> And Moses verily was faithful in all his house, as a servant,
> for a testimony of those things which were to be spoken
> after; But Christ as a son over his own house; whose house

are we, if we hold fast the confidence and the rejoicing of the hope firm unto the end. (Heb. 3:5–6)

Moses and Christ were faithful to the house of God because they were filled with the image and zeal of faith about the house of God. Moses built the tabernacle based on a vision he had. Jesus called the house of God the place of prayer for all nations after He had zealously cleaned it out (John 2:14–17). These men faithfully served God as a critical part of their calling. God gives us dreams to produce faith in us. God makes us full of faith to spiritually produce fidelity and a commitment that cannot be shifted regardless of how bad things get. People who know their prophetic connection to the house of God cannot allow their mouths to speak contrary to its vision because that would be spiritual suicide. It would be equal to killing your own destiny. It is in your best interest to keep speaking in line with the vision till it comes to pass. You must always operate in the spirit of faith.

You must only testify of what you have spiritually seen (John 3:11). Fidelity can be revealed in what you say and what you do. It is this fidelity that moves God to build the dream of His house or Bethel, into becoming the majestic edifice filled with the glory of God. God builds His house out of our spiritual dream and by the confession of our lips. The prophetic connection of the Hebrew people to this place paid off, and King Solomon was able to build the magnificent building called Solomon's Temple. Solomon himself did this out of pure fidelity to his father David's dream.

> Then he called for Solomon his son, and charged him to build an house for the Lord God of Israel. And David said to Solomon, My son, as for me, it was in my mind to build an house unto the name of the Lord my God. (1 Chron. 22:6–7)

We also can be people of faith and fidelity, holding on to our confession in spite of the opposing circumstances, till the dreams and visions we first saw become a reality. God does not change His mind like we do because He says what He means and means exactly what He says. As children of God, we need to imitate Him as our Father. We need to say what we mean and mean what we say. When we say we are committed to our Bethel, local church or group, we should mean it. When we make such a commitment, we should make it out of our dreams and visions. Commitments made out of a prophetic revelation should not change in spite of what happens in the future. This is because we have made a prophetic connection to our place of worship—our Bethel. This is true fidelity. Once you make such a commitment, you cannot allow death or life, or angels, or things present, or things to come, or principalities, or powers, or thrones, or dominions, or height, or depth, or demons, or men to separate you from the divine love you have for the place of your prophetic connection (Rom. 8:37–39).

*Action:* Let all members of your group pray consistently for the spirit of revelation to give them prophetic convictions, visions and dreams about its destiny.

# MILESTONE 2

# THE GATHERING

## Step 1: Gather the sons

> Gather the people, sanctify the congregation, assemble the
> elders, gather the children, and those that suck the breasts:
> let the bridegroom go forth of his chamber, and the bride
> out of her closet. (Joel 2:16)

By the time I'd been affected by the brethren in October 1982, they'd been gathering on almost a daily basis for hours of prayer since January. Can a group of believers gather on a daily basis for that long? Yes, they can, if the gathering is a faithful response to an authentic call of God.

The gathering of spiritual children should be a direct response to the call of God. For the most part, God will call a person and ask him or her to "call" an assembly. Thus, it will be the call of God sounding a "trumpet" through the call of humans. Faithfulness to the call will ultimately produce the gathering of a congregation. Some of these gatherings can continue for days, weeks, months, and maybe even years. As we'll come to find out, it could, through the power of fidelity, endure for decades. Its objective is to bring a new generation into the move of God.

Two scriptures align with the concept of the local church, fellowship, group, band, or ministry team. Jesus said, "For where two or three are gathered together in my name, there am I in the midst of them" (Matt. 18:20). This highlights the gathering for spiritual reasons as being a church thing. And then, "No man can come to me, except the Father which hath sent me draw him" (John 6:44). In these scriptures lie the ideas of "drawing" and "gathering" as being behind the existence of any local church. The heavenly Father draws His sons, and they in response gather together in His presence in the name of His Son Jesus Christ. The local church is thus, a spiritual family gathering.

Some folks would assume they attended a church service because they were invited by a friend or neighbor. What Jesus is saying is simply that, people gather to worship as a local church only because there has been a supernatural "drawing" of each individual by the heavenly Father. Hence, God calls and draws His children each Sunday morning to gather for spiritual fellowship, the time and place of worship notwithstanding.

Making the upper room my haunt wasn't a human orchestration. I was so enthralled by my experience with the Holy Spirit that I could hardly recall when I washed down, got into a pair of jeans and found my way to the gathering. My hunger for God overrode all my sensibilities.

My family watched me with amazement, wondering about the change that had swept through my life. Within the prayer fraternity, I was very relatable, but at home I had become a hermit. I was being helplessly drawn like a moth to the flame of *God's presence*. It's hard to explain the magnetism that produced those faithful gatherings. Though the local church can only gather to worship in spirit and in truth because of the generic call of God, it is critical to note that no one can join the ranks of the "called-out ones" unless the heavenly Father specifically draws him or her to Himself. This is the individual call of the spiritual son as compared to the general call of the local church: "Wherefore, holy brethren, partakers of the heavenly calling" (Heb. 3:1).

The Father does call and draw, yet He asks, "Gather my saints together unto me" (Ps. 50:5). I later found out that these magnetic drawings by the heavenly Father and the gathering of His children to spend prolonged periods in His presence were a global phenomenon—the charismatic movement.

In January 1983, a very similar movement began in Argentina. Argentines like Ed Silvoso have this documented in their writings.

> Not forsaking the assembling of ourselves together, as the
> manner of some is; but exhorting one another: and so much
> the more, as ye see the day approaching. (Heb. 10:25)

In the season of divine visitation, God by His sovereign will, calls out a people to a specific place. The faithful response to this call will produce a gathering; call it a local church, fellowship, ministry or group. However, not all who have been called to gather do obey: "they forsake the assembling." This is "the manner of some." Those referred to as "some" can't include you my friend, because you'll obey the rallying voice of the Spirit like I did.

Was the decision to overcome that inward rebellion and override my doubts, fears, and excuses easy? No, but I'm glad I did and joined the brethren.

Due to this likely threshold or limitation to be crossed, the apostle Paul, like my good friend Martin, urged, "I beseech you therefore, brethren, by the mercies of God, that ye present your bodies a living sacrifice, holy, acceptable unto God, which is your reasonable service" (Rom. 12:1).

My faithfulness to that call put me into my "reasonable service"—the ministry and the revival gathering.

> And I thank Christ Jesus our Lord, who hath enabled me, for that he counted me faithful, putting me into the ministry. (1 Tim. 1:12)

Like the apostle Paul, all faithful responders to the call who gather and serve are always grateful in the long run. In the 1980s, the response came in a plethora of ways: retreats, camp meetings, prayer band meetings, seminars and miracle services. But aren't we grateful? Certainly, for the Holy Spirit's breeze came and swept through our gathering.

*Action:* As led by the Holy Spirit, gather for retreats, camp meetings, prayer warrior meetings, seminars and miracle services.

## Step 2: See the vision

My eyes scanned the living room upon entering. It was full of youngsters, at least most of them, with some seated on the floor. They had been giving the speaker their rapt attention.

An empty seat at the left-hand corner caught my attention, so I made a beeline. Once I got comfortable in the chair, I noticed that it looked more like an aircraft seat, something that gave me the idea that the owner most certainly had a liking for aviation. Then, I focused my attention on the speaker like the others.

"I'll stand on the platform of holiness and power!" he passionately said. He was seated on a chair, surrounded by books that lay on the floor about him. The aura of authority he exuded was exacerbated by his neatly tucked-in, short-sleeved shirt over brown cotton pants.

I took in the visage of this copper-colored gentleman.

*Oh, this is most likely the spiritual dad of our campus leader,* I surmised. Certainly, his reputation went ahead of him. His words seared my heart with a strange heat. The vision he described got me animated.

The apostle Peter does quote Joel's prophecy on the day of Pentecost.

> And it shall come to pass in the last days, saith God, I will pour out of my Spirit upon all flesh: and your sons and your daughters shall prophesy, and your young men shall see visions and your old men shall dream dreams. (Acts 2:17)

And most definitely, this young man had seen a vision.
*I want to hear more of this,* I thought.

The following weeks saw his revelation of global evangelism completely transform my worldview.

> But ye shall receive power, after that the Holy Ghost is come upon you: and ye shall be witnesses unto me both in Jerusalem, and in all Judaea, and in Samaria, and unto the uttermost part of the earth. (Acts 1:8)

For the worldview of a revival group, fellowship, evangelistic team, prayer band or Bible study cell to radically change, it should receive a fresh revelation of the Lord's vision. The Lord's vision is the worldwide witnessing of the gospel of His kingdom. For out of the Lord's vision, we can all find out our individual visions by the Spirit's outpouring.

When the Spirit comes upon us, "in thy [His] light shall we see light" (Ps. 36:9, brackets added). In the light of His generic vision, we shall see the light of our individual visions. And this becomes the key to our *prophetic connection* to the revival group, fellowship, evangelistic team, prayer band, Bible study cell or local church.

The vision of the Lord called the disciples to a deeper fidelity for reaching the nations. The Greek word for *witness* is *martur,* out of which we got the English words *martyr* and *martyrdom.* The disciples were to be legal witnesses of the Lord's resurrection even at their own peril. And they were to do this "unto the uttermost part of the earth." In their fidelity to the

Lord's vision, they stepped into the move of God. The Lord wouldn't pour out His Spirit upon a group that had proved itself disloyal to His vision.

In this current season and time, we're seeing evidence of the closing stages of the last days. God's Spirit moved in several cycles during the twentieth century; now in the twenty-first century, God is most likely going to pour out His Spirit upon all flesh again.

The year 2018, with all that is going on, seems a good time to experience a new breeze of the Holy Ghost around the world. You can't have that without an unflinching fidelity of individuals to groups, ministries, local churches, and fellowships. Such unbroken loyalty can't occur without a prophetic connection to the ministry. Prophetic connections to a group are a direct product of individual visions.

As the leader of the brethren spoke those fiery and visionary words into my spirit, my light bulb got turned on in the upper room. A few months later, God gave me a six-hour vision that got me tenaciously hooked to the revival group.

> And the LORD answered me, and said, Write the vision, and make it plain upon tables, that he may run that readeth it. (Hab. 2:2)

As a group, do you want to know the direction of the Holy Spirit's wind so you "may run" with it? Watch the visions given by the Holy Spirit.

*Action:* The vision of the group hungry for revival must be written, read, spoken and lived daily.

## Step 3: Connect with the invisible

Over the year 1984, the fellowship on campus grew. The newcomers demonstrated an unusual hunger for the move of God.

"You know, a strange thing happened," one newcomer named Marian said. "I looked into my book a few days ago, and all I could see were souls." Like the others, she had begun seeing visions of souls on the mission field. These visions provided "the evidence of things not seen"—at least not yet seen in the group's experience.

> Now faith is the substance of things hoped for, the
> evidence of things not seen (Heb. 11:1)

They were connecting with the invisible evangelistic pedigree of the brethren.

The crowd of unsaved souls seen in their books quickly gave me a flashback to the voice of our spiritual dad in the upper room saying, "I'll stand on the platform of holiness and power." In the realm of visions, these newcomers were standing where he stood and seeing what he saw. This looked pleasantly bizarre when you understand that they'd never met or heard him before. But what's the surprise? It's the same Holy Spirit, isn't it?

Now, they believed what he believed.

It made complete sense when those on campus began speaking and acting in a similar fashion as the brethren at Caprice. They were connecting to the same invisible source of faith.

> We having the same spirit of faith, according as it is
> written, I believed, and therefore have I spoken; we also
> believe, and therefore speak. (2 Corin. 4:13)

Since real faith deals with things not seen, it's the fulcrum of real faithfulness. They—faith and faithfulness—deal with the same spirit, "the spirit of faith." True fidelity is faithfulness "in spite of," *not* faithfulness "because of." It really doesn't make sense in real life.

True fidelity means sticking it out with a group both in the good times and the bad times, the up seasons and the down seasons, in times of sorrow and in times of joy. To do this, you will have to connect with things not seen—the invisible.

But there were those among these new kids on the charismatic block that gave me much concern. They were ready to abandon their privileged education in the university if need be, to pursue the visions they'd seen.

*Now what in the world am I going to do?* I thought. I had mentored a number of them, and their recent disinterest in academia had presented an enigma to me. I had heard it said that faith is an act, and I couldn't fault them for wanting to act on what they believed, could I? The few revivals we had conducted in some neighboring high schools had gotten them all fired up. This vision of *souls on the mission field*, they might have been thinking, "was for real."

Beyond that, the lecturers, assignments, tests, and the whole nine yards of other mundane pressures didn't make this any easier. But the invisible *vision* implies the unseen *future* and the unseen *potential* that lie behind the difficulties of the present time and the painfulness of the current circumstance.

These Johnny-come-lately protégés of mine had seen the invisible potential of the campus group and believed it hook, line and sinker. Now they were ready to die for it.

Fidelity was churning within their hearts. I once overheard one sage of a preacher say, "What you aren't ready to die for, you aren't ready to live for." Isn't that true?

True fidelity is proven by not being moved by what you see and hear. You are not moved because you are anchored in something beyond the visible.

Now, come hell or high water, these campus disciples were ready to pay the price to see the upcoming move of God. Were they even ready to forgo their hard-won scholarships? That got me edgy and nervy for a while just thinking of it. However, thank God, in the long run some truce was arrived at. *They decided to stay and study.* I couldn't stomach any supposed pyrrhic victory when some concerned parent got on my case and blamed me for the other option. However, by faith, their true fidelity had been demonstrated. They had proved their mettle; they were totally sold out for the group's vision.

The unbreakable connection they had made with the invisible in spite of the contrary visible circumstance is called *spiritual faith*.

***Action:*** All the members of your group should together make a commitment to pay the price for a move of the Holy Spirit in their generation.

# THE UNDERSTANDING

## Step 1: Initiate fidelity

I once heard this narration from a bishop about a pastor who bumped into his good friend in town.

"How's the ministry going, buddy?" his friend quizzed.

"Oh, we've now grown to about five hundred," he answered.

"Wow! That's wonderful. Now how did that happen?" he said with amazement in his voice, shaking the pastor's hand.

"Don't bother about all of that," the pastor retorted, looking rather crestfallen and unexcited.

"Why?" the friend asked, peering into his eyes.

"Because they're all crooks," he said.

In case you'd didn't get the joke, I deduced thoughtfully after the bishop told me this, that *it's not just a bunch of people that make visions come alive; it's rather a specific kind of people that do.*

An unfaithful bunch will frustrate any vision, but a people of fidelity will take it from obscurity to notoriety. I believe there are thousands of heavenly visions waiting for a people of fidelity who could birth them into the earth. The problem is, there are not that many such folks in the earth.

> Most men will proclaim everyone his own goodness: but
> a faithful man who can find? (Prov. 20:6)

All the moves of the Holy Spirit have been characterized by heightened periods of spiritual fidelity. It is the fidelity of God's people that has mostly triggered the seasons of revival and spiritual restoration throughout church history.

Among the brethren, I discovered this reality. When the Holy Spirit and faithful people do find each other, it's a match made in heaven. With that, I can easily predict a move of God.

*Fidelity,* according to Webster's 1913 dictionary, doesn't just mean "faithfulness," but also "a careful and exact observance of duty or performance of obligations." It also means "loyalty or a firm adherence to a person or party with which one is united or to which one is bound." Put simply, we need fidelity for groups and relationships to thrive.

It's always taken a few faithful people dedicated to praying through, till the fires of revival began to blaze across a particular geographical territory. On my college campus, the group in the basement were only five in number when I joined, but didn't they pray and weren't they faithful to a fault?

Without fidelity to a single cause, no revolution, whether religious or secular, can be realized. I'm convinced that a vision without a people of pure fidelity will fail.

King Solomon wrote, "Where there is no vision, the people perish" (Prov. 29:18). On the flipside, *where there are no people, the vision will perish.* I will quickly add also that, where there are no people of fidelity, the vision will surely perish.

In my view, it's not just a group that makes visions and dreams come alive, but rather a faithful people who do. It's not a beautiful couple that will make a marriage work; rather, their acts of fidelity do. Great things have always happened within the church when a God-inspired people of fidelity worked with His vision.

***Action:*** Every member within your group must be measured against a touchstone, which is an exact, persistent and consistent observance of duty or performance of their obligations.

## Step 2: Understand the fidelity factor

Of all the milestones that a group preparing for the next move of God should respond to, I believe the most critical is the "understanding" milestone. As Solomon said, "With all thy getting, get understanding" (Prov. 4:7).

I would lay down many nights—countless nights—thinking, wondering and analyzing, sometimes teary eyed and sick to my stomach about what was going on within the global church or my congregation. I've had some time to do some introspection, questioning the why, how, when and who of it all. Have I in any way assisted in this anomaly called infidelity?

*What for instance went wrong with our beloved evangelistic association called the brethren?* I mused. These musings weren't happenstance; I had been hit badly most recently.

"Honey? Honey, what's wrong?" My wife had been querying me for days about my strange silence. I had been sitting on my bed with my gaze awkwardly fixated on the video deck's blinking timer.

Some forty-eight hours later, her constant prodding finally got me to break my silence. It was the church. One of our satellite campuses had suffered a split. We had recently entrusted the congregation to a pastor recommended by one of my mentees within the central ministry. He had raved about him with glowing words, but in hindsight, we had overlooked several red flags. All the symptoms of latent infidelity had been there, staring us right in the face. I had unconsciously turned a blind eye to it all to give some months of my attention to some writing I was engrossed with.

Now, through conspiring with some of our stalwarts on that campus, he had formed a new congregation—his congregation. I was dumbfounded and stayed shell-shocked for days. Nothing throughout my leadership journey had prepared me for such a discovery. It was mind-boggling and mind-blowing at the same time.

The apostle Paul wrote,

> Exhort servants to be obedient unto their own masters, and to please them well in all things; not answering again; Not purloining, but shewing all good fidelity; that they may adorn the doctrine of God our Saviour in all things.
> (Titus 2:9–10)

"Good fidelity"? I like the connotation. The fact that the apostle connotes fidelity with *good* indicates the presence of the *bad* kind. My ministry had been enjoying some semblance of a move of God. But, we'd now become victims of bad fidelity. My fault was that I had misunderstood and downplayed the significance of the fidelity factor in birthing revivals, sustaining it, and even aborting its future.

The word *fidelity* in the Greek is *pistis*, which is the exact word translated as "faith." The Hebrew word translated as "faithful" speaks of loyalty or trustworthiness. To rehash the facts; from the word *faithful*, we know that the fidelity factor is inextricably interwoven with faith.

Faith and faithfulness are basically joined at the hip. To be faithful, you need not only possess this spiritual virtue called faith; you also need to be *full* of it.

In the New Testament, the word *faithful* is originally in the Greek, *pistos,* which according to Strong's Concordance, means exactly what it does in the Old Testament—"trustworthiness." In this way, it takes *pistis* (faith) to be *pistos* (faithful), which means it takes faith to be a trustworthy or a faithful person.

Therefore, to understand the fidelity factor, we need to understand what faith is. I do quite clearly recall our campus leader defining for me what faith is. As a matter of fact, I first heard this in his teaching in the basement. He said, "Faith believes in God's Word even in the face of contrary natural evidence."

Faith believes in the invisible God even in the face of contradictory natural evidence. I also heard Dr. Morris Cerullo say, "Faith is loyalty to God." So to be faithful or loyal means to be full of faith. The fidelity factor is a faith factor.

Loyalty as a character trait, is deeply rooted in an individual's faith. In my life's journey, I have met hundreds and perhaps thousands of Christians, but I can make a finger count of how many I can with certainty call full of faith.

Maybe this is the reason King Solomon asked, "Most men will proclaim everyone his own goodness: but a faithful man [who firmly adheres to duty] who can find?" (Prov. 20:6, brackets added). The fullness of faith, in my view, is a rare human trait that "who can find?"

The fidelity factor is actually the trustworthiness factor. This is a character issue in God's economy. *How much trust could be reposed in a person by a group must be based on the demonstrated fidelity of the individual.*

> And the things that thou hast heard of me among many witnesses, the same commit thou to faithful men, who shall be able to teach others also. (2 Tim. 2:2)

According to the apostle Paul, trusted principles must be entrusted to trustworthy men only. He calls these trusted principles, faithful sayings.

In Numbers 12:7, God calls Moses faithful; someone who is morally true or certain, in whom trust could be invested.

The biblical question "A faithful man who can find?" (Prov. 20:6) is one demanding an answer from the fallen human race. The reality is that the answer to this question will take a lifetime to be discovered. For many betrayed husbands, wives, managers, pastors, leaders, and community organizers, the answer has yet to become obvious. For anyone to answer this question, the fidelity factor has to be properly understood. For instance, are there loyal humans in this world? If so, how do we define them?

If Christianity has trudged along this far, it is because of its faithful men and women. Your group isn't an exception. The fidelity factor is truly a critical factor.

*Action:* Your group must have a retreat to study the subject of Christian fidelity and its application to its vision.

## Step 3: Stand on the three pillars of fidelity

I believe there are many questions that an individual might ask in his or her lifetime, but there will be a few that will forever stay in his or her memory.

A lady cried, or should I say, wailed out her disappointment. She had just witnessed the crumbling of an entire ministry. I caught her from the corner of my eye where she sat. She had been sitting on the stairs leading to the nightclub where our services were held on Saturdays. She had been let down by her mentors.

I received the fallout with much mixed feeling. After all, all the combatants were my brethren—"the brethren." There were no sides to choose from. We'd all failed to hold up our fidelity to a common vision.

The question loomed high and large over our heads; however, how was all this going to play out within the current move of the Holy Spirit? I guess no one had thought about that.

The bigger question was, did God see these feuding human proclivities in us and still call us to this assignment in spite of its ability to unravel like this? I don't think so.

In Acts 1:21–22, those who qualified to participate in the next move of God were being identified, their track records being examined. The men who were qualified to testify about the Lord's resurrection were being elected. The criterion for selection was based on the proof of their fidelity.

Their fidelity had to span the three and a half years of Jesus's ministry. Their continuous visible presence everywhere the Lord went was key. Why? Because these men were being selected to occupy the place of an unfaithful disciple—Judas Iscariot. Judas betrayed the Lord on the night of His arrest, becoming a guide to His enemies. Thus, this deserter had to be replaced with a faithful character. The unfaithful spirit of Judas Iscariot ceded vital ground for Satan within the ministry of Jesus (John 13:27).

To ensure that spiritual infidelity was not perpetuated in their midst by one unfaithful person replacing another of the same demeanor, the apostles measured themselves with the rod of proven fidelity. Spiritual fidelity to them was a critical factor for birthing the next move of God: on the day of Pentecost. In a nutshell, God called them, but the apostles had a sacred standard to protect—their touchstone for fidelity that prevented infidelity from dismantling the ministry of Jesus Christ. Without an understanding of the faith pillars on which the standards of good fidelity stand, failure will be inevitable. Infidelity among and within groups, fellowships, ministries and local churches will greatly inhibit the move of the Holy Spirit.

The fidelity factor operates by three faith pillars: faith in God, faith in a vision, and faith in other humans. Without faith in the reliability of God, faith in a vision from God, and faith in the fellow human being, the fidelity factor will fail to advance the move of the Holy Spirit. The reason the fidelity factor flounders in certain organizations is because the men and women who labor there do not have the faith, the inner conviction or the certainty that: first, God placed them where they are; second, the vision being pursued will surely come to pass without fail; and third, the men and women working alongside them are ready to die for what they are working for.

The reason for understanding these faith pillars is crucial, for the agents of Satan have planted seeds of infidelity among groups, fellowships, ministries and local churches. In the experience of the brethren, it was a letter penned by an anonymous writer.

Some groups do not trust each other though they minister in the same territory. Within many groups, fellowships, ministries and local churches, restless political wars between pulpit and pew, leadership and laity have turned God's house into a spiritual war zone.

Several revival movements have failed to endure simply because unfaithful men entering into its ranks weren't connected to its vision. The fidelity factor must exist to bind the spiritual leaders to their spiritual sons and the spiritual brethren to one another.

The Apostle Jude wrote of this long ago.

> For there are certain men crept in unawares, who were before of old ordained to this condemnation, ungodly men, turning the grace of our God into lasciviousness, and denying the only Lord God, and our Lord Jesus Christ.

> Likewise also these filthy dreamers defile the flesh, despise dominion [leadership authority], and speak evil of dignities. (Jude 1:4, 8, brackets added)

The result of this restless political wrangling and its termination of certain significant moves of God is the watered-down manifestations of the Spirit we see today. There's the emergence of a present generation of evangelical Christians who are asking the Gideon question.

> And Gideon said unto him, Oh my Lord, if the LORD be with us, why then is all this befallen us? and where be all his miracles which our fathers told us of, saying, Did not the LORD bring us up from Egypt? but now the LORD hath forsaken us, and delivered us into the hands of the Midianites. (Judges 6:13)

This present crop of believers is asking, "Where are all the miracles we read about in the revivals of the bygone era? Where are those creative miracles plus strange signs in the heavens and the earth?" Why are they asking these questions? Because they see so much spiritual defeat in their groups and local churches at the hands of the secular humanists. The moral compromise both in the pulpit and pew has caused many to question the reality of the power of God. At the very root of all this spiritual degradation, is the compromise of the fidelity factor or the Judas syndrome—that is, infidelity to the word of God, the living Christ and His Holy Spirit.

*Action:* Your group must clearly define the standard of fidelity that will ready it for the next move of God.

# THE DRIVERS

## Step 1: Serve God with the soul

I've found it quite puzzling why some members of fellowships, groups, local churches and ministries are unflinchingly faithful to the call upon the worship houses they serve in, while others aren't.

"So see you tomorrow!" I shouted as I drove off. We had just had an intense prayer meeting—our Saturday evening intercessory time. Dropping off some of the ministry team members was my lot.

"Okay, tomorrow." My ears picked the sister's faint reply in the distance as we drove off. She was our praise and worship leader.

The next morning, I asked one brother where our sister was. The Sunday morning service was already in session, and I was sitting on tenterhooks. The brother shook his head, and that didn't help my nerves.

Without her input, the service wasn't as top notch as it should have been. But we got by somehow.

*Maybe she fell ill last night or she's been involved in some domestic accident,* I thought. My mind reeled, looking for answers. So we visited her residence right after the service.

As we stood in the living room, my jaw dropped to the floor — I couldn't believe my eyes; I'd miscalculated. The praise and worship leader, with much gaiety in her eyes, looked up at us. Her fingers were busy. She had been eating a homemade meal, picked from our traditional carte du jour with soup. Her capriciousness had led to taking the day off without the slightest tinge of her conscience to inform us.

Despite the fragmentation of our evangelistic association, I kept its kind of ministry as a touchstone of sterling Christian fidelity—my sacred standard. Now, that wouldn't come across as a reason for some self-inflicted injury, but it was. I helplessly tried to duplicate their fidelity in other groups: others who didn't know what the brethren knew or feel what they felt. And so was the case with this praise and worship leader. My pitting her fidelity against that of the brethren didn't help.

Severally, this left me bemused, frustrated and occasionally desperate. Then, I had my aha moment. The fidelity such as was witnessed among the brethren wasn't a spontaneous expression. It was driven by certain drivers. Those who served with good fidelity were supernaturally driven by these drivers.

As a result of being driven, good fidelity will yield three fruits: first, fidelity to the God who strategically called their group together; second, fidelity to the vision being pursued; and third, fidelity to the men and women who serve in the group.

Moses's congregation, "the Church in the Wilderness," was formed by the Hebrew ex-slaves called out of Egypt. Their vision was to possess a land flowing with milk and honey—Canaan. Moses and a few men were faithful to that call, but not all.

*Fidelity to God*

Those who were like Joshua and Caleb demonstrated genuine fidelity to the God who called them. Read God's testimony about Caleb:

> Because all those men which have seen my glory, and my miracles, which I did in Egypt and in the wilderness, and have tempted me now these ten times, and have not hearkened to my voice; Surely they shall not see the land which I sware unto their fathers, neither shall any of them that provoked me see it: But my servant Caleb, because he had another spirit with him, and hath followed me fully, him will I bring into the land whereinto he went; and his seed shall possess it. (Num. 14:22–24)

*Fidelity to the Vision*

Caleb demonstrated genuine fidelity to the vision being pursued. Read where he expressed his fidelity:

> As yet I am as strong this day as I was in the day that Moses sent me: as my strength was then, even so is my strength now, for war, both to go out, and to come in. Now therefore give me this mountain, whereof the Lord spake in that day; for thou heardest in that day how the Anakims were there, and that the cities were great and fenced: if so be the Lord will be with me, then I shall be able to drive them out, as the Lord said. (Josh. 14:11–12)

*Fidelity to the Men and Women Who Serve*

Caleb demonstrated his fidelity toward Moses by having his back. He stilled the fearful voices of his colleagues, the ten spies. He was ready to stick with Moses through thick and thin.

> And Caleb stilled the people before Moses, and said, Let us go up at once, and possess it; for we are well able to overcome it. But the men that went up with him said, We be not able to go up against the people; for they are stronger than we. (Num. 13:30–31)

The gravity of Caleb's fidelity to Moses's church was visible. It became obvious when he stilled the voices of the ten spies. Their rebellion had taken hold of the entire congregation.

> And Joshua the son of Nun, and Caleb the son of Jephunneh, which were of them that searched the land, rent their clothes: And they spake unto all the company of the children of Israel, saying, The land, which we passed through to search it, is an exceeding good land. If the Lord delight in us, then he will bring us into this land, and give it us; a land which floweth with milk and honey. Only rebel not ye against the Lord, neither fear ye the people of the land; for they are bread for us: their defence is departed from them, and the Lord is with us: fear them not. (Num. 14:6–9)

When the voices of rebellion did finally spread within the church, Moses's life was placed in danger. For "all the congregation bade stone them with stones. And the glory of the Lord appeared in the tabernacle of the congregation before all the children of Israel" (Num. 14:10).

By being driven by the supernatural drivers, a person will be in a position to walk worthily of his calling (Eph. 4:1). According to Paul, we all have a calling to fulfill within our fellowship, group, ministry or local church (Rom. 12:4–8).

How do we serve God worthily? By serving Him heartily (Col. 3:23–24). The word *heartily* in the Greek is *ek psuche*, which means "out of the soul." Biblically, three words have been attached to the soul—this is the mind or imagination (Acts 14:2); the emotion or passion (Matt. 26:38); and the will or willpower (Eph. 6:6). The Greek word *psuche* was translated in these three verses as *mind* or *imagination, passion,* and *willpower*.

The following is one verse that deals with the mind or imagination:

> But the unbelieving Jews stirred up the Gentiles, and made their minds [psuche] evil affected against the brethren. (Acts 14:2, brackets added)

Serving God with the imagination produces a vision. God will enlighten an imagination that will serve Him.

> The Father of glory, may give unto you the spirit of wisdom and revelation in the knowledge of him: The eyes of your understanding being enlightened. (Eph. 1:17–18)

The emotion or passion is evident in this verse:

> Then saith he unto them, My soul [psuche] is exceeding sorrowful, even unto death: tarry ye here, and watch with me. (Matt. 26:38, brackets added)

Serving God with the emotion or passion produces zeal and compassion. God will inspire an emotion that will serve Him.

> And his disciples remembered that it was written, The zeal of thine house hath eaten me up. (John 2:17)

> And Jesus went forth, and saw a great multitude, and was moved with compassion toward them, and he healed their sick. (Matt. 14:14)

The following is regarding will or willpower:

Not with eyeservice, as menpleasers; but as the servants
of Christ, doing the will of God from the heart [psuche].
(Eph. 6:6, brackets added)

Serving God with willpower produces boldness. God will empower
the will that serves Him.

And when they had prayed, the place was shaken where
they were assembled together; and they were all filled with
the Holy Ghost, and they spake the word of God with
boldness. (Acts 4:31)

Hence, the difference between my praise and worship leader and the
brethren was a fidelity that was driven to serve God with the soul—a soul
completely yielded in service to God.

*Action:* Your group should, through frequent fasting and prayer, serve
God with their souls.

## Step 2: Serve God heartily from the imagination

Have you ever heard that *FEAR* can be an acronym for "False Evidence
Appearing Real?" Well, talk about feeling creepy with a sudden rush of
goose pimples.

"Look," the pastor said, pointing into the distance. "Over there, near
that hotel building, you'll find a white calico-clad tree. That's it."

We had been riding to town on a bus, and I had been getting quite a
lecture about mysterious twin babies coming out of a pit with gold nuggets.
A tree worshipped as a fetish had been uprooted decades ago, and the hole
left behind had produced this weird legend. Eerily, after being removed
by an earth-moving machine one afternoon, the tree appeared back in its
place, roots and all, by the next morning.

My companion had lived in the city during his seaman days. Now,
as a pastor, he was seeing the culture there through a different worldview.

"This city is a highly demonized place," he added. This was in the
1990s, and for some months I had been engaging in a church-planting
effort in this southern port city in my country.

My eyes were filled with terror as I gazed attentively at his face. I felt I had made a mistake. Perhaps I hadn't heard God properly.

Prior to imbibing the fearful narrative, I had to deal with a perplexing array of discouraging issues. Every day came up with some new battle to put me down. I admit, there were days when I wanted to just fold things up and quit.

While praying and musing over my decision on many such occasions, the vision of the ministry's future would enlighten my imagination, and soon a new determination would fill my heart. These visions kept driving into me a sense of fidelity to the mission till the breakthrough finally occurred. King Solomon said, "A desire accomplished is sweet to the soul," (Prov. 13:19). And boy, didn't my day of sweetness come?

It was standing room only in the classroom where we'd met, as the Holy Spirit's presence swept through the place. Those services ended with some still overcome by the ambience, lying on the floor for hours.

In Genesis 11:5–6, the imagination of man is mentioned as a critical key to his dedication to duty. Even God cannot stop people who do things out of their imagination. Fidelity implies an unwavering dedication to duty. We cannot be loyal until we act on our calling out of our imagination. To imagine means to see images with the mind. Those who see the images of their calling with their minds develop a sense of unusual fidelity. How do we see images with our minds? *First* we see images with the eyes of our understanding or hearts.

> That the God of our Lord Jesus Christ, the Father of glory, may give unto you the spirit of wisdom and revelation in the knowledge of him: The eyes of your understanding being enlightened; that ye may know what is the hope of his calling, and what the riches of the glory of his inheritance in the saints. (Eph. 1:17–18)

The prophetic image seen with our understanding is called a vision or revelation (Acts 9:11–12).

> And that having the eyes of your heart full of light, you may have knowledge of what is the hope of his purpose,

what is the wealth of the glory of his heritage in the saints. (Eph. 1:18 ESV)

Then *second*, this becomes an image seen with the eyes of the head or the mind. Ecclesiastes 2:14 says, "The wise man's eyes are in his head." However, there seems to be a correlation between the thoughts of the heart—"the eyes of your understanding"—and the images of the mind or intellect—the imagination.

> And God saw that the wickedness of man was great in the earth, and that *every imagination of the thoughts of his heart* was only evil continually. (Gen. 6:5, emphasis added)

Finally, whatever the eyes of your heart see, the mind or intellect will imagine. Biblically, therefore, humans have three sets of eyes: the eyes of the heart (the spiritual eyes), the eyes of the head (the intellectual eyes), and the eyes of the body (the biological eyes). All of these eyes see images.

Why will God pour out His Spirit upon a man; so he could see only visions? (Acts 2:17)

No, it is so that man can be driven to serve Him heartily out of his imagination. Paul served God by a heavenly vision (Acts 26:19–20). His imagination saw images from heaven about his calling and as a result, he was faithful to the call to be an apostle (Rom. 1:1, 9).

> And I thank Christ Jesus our Lord, who hath enabled me, for that he counted me faithful, putting me into the ministry. (1 Tim. 1:12)

Paul could not be stopped by anything: infirmities, reproaches, necessities, persecutions or distresses. His fidelity was driven by a heavenly vision.

> But none of these things move me, neither count I my life dear unto myself, so that I might finish my course with joy, and the ministry, which I have received of the Lord Jesus, to testify the gospel of the grace of God. (Acts 20:24)

God only gives us visions of our calling because He wants us to be faithful till the end so we can receive an earthly and eternal reward.

> I have fought a good fight, I have finished my course, I have kept the faith: Henceforth there is laid up for me a crown of righteousness, which the Lord, the righteous judge, shall give me at that day: and not to me only, but unto all them also that love his appearing. (2 Tim. 4:7–8)

*Action:* Your group should pray without ceasing till the Holy Spirit's vision of their upcoming revival enlightens their imagination.

## Step 3: Serve God heartily from your passion

The fervency was infectious. I had been spending hours each day praying and worshipping with the brethren in the campus basement. Martin was getting concerned about what he viewed as a penchant for extremist attitudes within the group. I found it laughable because, in all honesty, I was having a ball. Starting each day so inflamed by the Spirit gave me no desire to let up. At its zenith, I could sense passion like electric currents surging through my being.

*What in the world is Martin talking about?* I thought. I ultimately wore out his patience, playing down his fears. He left the group, but I pressed on.

At home, my family felt similarly. Dad did his best with his surliness, but it was to no avail. Staying out of his way, I found an improvised prayer cell among some new housing projects. There, with others of like passion, we emoted in supplication all we wanted.

I witnessed these folks walking for miles to the prayer grounds. They did so each dawn for months, singing with smiles on their faces. Their zeal was palpable. Then, without warning, a revival broke out in the suburb, sweeping in its wake hundreds of teenagers and adults into our meetings.

> Not slothful in business; fervent in spirit; serving the Lord (Rom. 12:11)

The word translated as *fervent* in this verse is the Greek word *zeo*, which means "hot to the boiling point" or "zealous." In the Greek, the word used as *business* in this translation is *spoude;* it means "enthusiasm" or "diligence"; the ESV translates it as *zeal*. We are called upon by the Lord to serve Him faithfully, and this can be done by being zealous in our spirits.

Those who traversed the dirt road each dawn to pray for months certainly were driven, I guess by the same hot-to-the-boiling-point enthusiasm I'd been inflamed with. For nothing else could have kept a group so fixated on purpose as that.

Fidelity requires a certain level of commitment and consistency to duty and no person who is "slothful in business [enthusiasm]" can serve the Lord by it. To be called faithful implies always being there when needed or being available and always reliable. For this to occur, a person needs to be driven spiritually. I've already made it clear that good fidelity is rooted in spiritual faith; therefore, it is a godly behavior. It is divine. God is faithful.

> Thy mercy, O Lord, is in the heavens; and thy faithfulness
> reacheth unto the clouds. (Ps. 36:5)

Fidelity becomes necessary only because this natural life is full of its ups and downs. A faithful person cannot be driven by what goes on around him in the natural; he has to be supernaturally driven. If a person is driven by the events that go on around him, he will despise his efforts in the days of small things (Zech. 4:10).

One of these supernatural drivers is passion or emotion. How are we supernaturally driven by these?

> Of the increase of his government and peace there shall be
> no end, upon the throne of David, and upon his kingdom,
> to order it, and to establish it with judgment and with
> justice from henceforth even forever. The zeal of the Lord
> of hosts will perform this. (Isa. 9:7)

God here speaks about the increase of His government and explains how it will be achieved; He said His zeal "will perform this."

Zeal or jealousy cannot tolerate infidelity, be it in marriage or the house of God.

> But whoso committeth adultery with a woman lacketh understanding: he that doeth it destroyeth his own soul. A wound and dishonour shall he get; and his reproach shall not be wiped away. For jealousy is the rage of a man: therefore he will not spare in the day of vengeance. He will not regard any ransom; neither will he rest content, though thou givest many gifts. (Prov. 6:32–35)

The Hebrew word translated as *jealousy* is *qinah*. It's the exact word translated as *zeal*. These are emotional expressions.

*Zeal*, according to the *Advanced English Dictionary*, is "an excessive fervor to do something or accomplish some end." The fervent spirit produces a jealous emotion.

Since zeal is critical for performance, can fidelity be achieved without it? According to the scriptures, God is faithful, but in His faithful acts, His zeal is a critical supernatural driver. *Zeal* and *jealousy* mean the same thing in the Hebrew and Greek languages. Jealousy is a human emotion. However, according to 2 Corinthians 11:2, there is a godly kind of jealousy. This is a jealousy or zeal that is supernaturally driven. How does godly jealousy or zeal supernaturally drive us in our emotion? Zeal does three things: it demonstrates fidelity, demands fidelity, and repudiates infidelity.

> And the Jews' passover was at hand, and Jesus went up to Jerusalem, And found in the temple those that sold oxen and sheep and doves, and the changers of money sitting: And when he had made a scourge of small cords, he drove them all out of the temple, and the sheep, and the oxen; and poured out the changers' money, and overthrew the tables; And said unto them that sold doves, Take these things hence; make not my Father's house an house of merchandise. And his disciples remembered that it was written, The zeal of thine house hath eaten me up. (John 2:13–17)

The zeal of the Lord within Jesus could not tolerate this, and it began to burn hot and consume His emotions. Matthew narrates this very incident and quotes Jesus.

> And said unto them, It is written, My house shall be called the house of prayer; but ye have made it a den of thieves. (Matt. 21:13)

The vision of the house of God was to be a house of prayer for the nations (Mark 11:17). However, certain thieves who had gained entrance into the fold did not demonstrate fidelity toward the vision of God's house. They made Jesus's "Father's house an house of merchandise."

*Zeal Demonstrates Fidelity*

> And a certain Jew named Apollos, born at Alexandria, an eloquent man, and mighty in the scriptures, came to Ephesus. This man was instructed in the way of the Lord; and being fervent in the spirit, he spake and taught diligently the things of the Lord, knowing only the baptism of John. (Acts 18:24–25)

God is jealous and will not share His glory with anyone (Isa. 42:8). This divine jealousy is zeal that will make God watch over His glory or supernatural wealth and will not leave it to be abused. God is jealous over His children and will not leave them to be abused. He will be there every moment to ensure that they are preserved. His faithfulness is attached to His zeal. The faithfulness of leaders to their followers must be attached to their zeal or divine jealousy (2 Corin. 11:2, Rom. 10:2). Jesus calls this the zeal of God's house. He could not stand for God's house to be abused. His faithfulness to God's house was attached to His zeal. You cannot be faithful to your calling and keep it holy without the zeal of God's house eating you up (John 2:17). We cannot understand the ministry in God's house without understanding the zeal of the Lord.

*Zeal Demands Fidelity from Its Covenant Partner*

God is a jealous God because He demands the highest form of fidelity from His covenant people. He told Israel that He was jealous over them (Exo. 34:14). The zeal that proceeds out of jealousy causes God to be faithful to His covenant people, and in exchange, demand their unquestioned fidelity. God demonstrated His fidelity to humanity by sending His Son to shed His blood and die on the cross for them. In exchange, God demands the same level of fidelity from us when it comes to our readiness to die for Him. When we are fired up by the zeal of the Lord, then we are ready to sacrifice whenever God demands our fidelity. This is why a zealous church will be a sacrificing church. A zealous church understands the jealousy of God, that God has a right to be jealous and demand from them the highest level of fidelity. When I understood that Jesus died on the cross for my sins, from that day to this moment, no sacrifice has been too much for me to offer for the Lord, for He is worthy of my highest fidelity.

*Zeal Repudiates Infidelity*

When we don't give to God our sacrifices and fidelity—rather, giving it to someone or something else—then God gets jealous. His Holy Spirit is grieved, and His zeal then drives Him to withdraw His blessings. The fear of God and all true holiness or consecration is driven by zeal. When the Lord fills us with His zeal, then the fear of God drives us to be ready to die for Him the same way He died for us. The zeal of Jehovah God will cause us to perform acts of sacrifice and fidelity toward Him. You cannot be faithful to God's call upon your life without a fair amount of understanding about the zeal of the Lord.

*Action:* The shortcut to stirring zeal within your group is for everyone to get filled with the Holy Spirit and pray in tongues regularly.

## Step 4: Serve God heartily from your willpower

My family and I had strolled across the cul-de-sac that hugged a colonial building. The regal-looking edifice housed some administrative offices. My wife and I had arrived with our son for his first day in senior high school.

Someone bellowed my name, causing me to turn. And there was a familiar face.

"Nelson!" I said. I was pleasantly surprised at bumping into an old mentee. We had not met in donkey years. He was there for the same reason as I was.

One of my most memorable recollections of him was his miraculous healing in a service. It was organized by the brethren close to my neighborhood. He seemed that day untrammeled, as it were by God's power, into prancing up and down the aisle. He usually walked with a limp from an accident he'd suffered.

He did continue in the faith though, becoming a stalwart. We hugged joyfully, and much of that was owed to our shared memory of events. It didn't take long to get Nelson digging into his bag of memories.

"You know we'd gone out for evangelism that day," he said, referring to an outreach conducted by the brethren. We'd been planting a fellowship together in a bustling intersection within the capital. His partner in this task was a young woman— a fellow sister. Although other parents shuttled back and forth, seeking out the welfare of their wards, he kept on in his narration unfazed.

"We'd entered a house situated by a busy street to reach its people; our surprise though was, it housed a fetish shrine and a shaman," he said. In all honesty, I'd never heard of this, and thus my curiosity was tickled.

"On my first impulse," he said, "I felt we were in the wrong place; we therefore made a U-turn. We turned around and ran into a woman who had just brought in a dead child. She'd come in seeking for some succor from the shaman. He cast a clueless look at the dead child and its hapless mother." At this point, I got ahead myself and asked, "So what did you do?"

"We asked for the child to be handed to us. They obliged. With the dead child in my arms, we prayed. To our surprise, the child came back to life."

"Hallelujah!" I yelled.

"The woman's entire family followed her to the service and got saved," he quickly added.

"Nelson, I'd never heard of this before," I said, gazing at him with delight. I do recall that it was similar acts of Spirit-driven heroism by ordinary people like this that sparked the flames of spiritual revival across my nation.

True courage, if you can tell, is a driver which drives the human will to achieve some amazing feats or acts of great bravado. Fidelity to a spiritual assignment regardless of how daunting it is can fall into this category. In such a case, the driver is supernatural.

Courage is the only force that opposes fear, and fear is a counterforce to faith. It takes faith to be faithful. It takes the spirit of courage to drive a man to undertake acts of faith and faithfulness.

> Be strong and of a good courage, fear not, nor be afraid of them: for the Lord thy God, he it is that doth go with thee; he will not fail thee, nor forsake thee. And Moses called unto Joshua, and said unto him in the sight of all Israel, Be strong and of a good courage: for thou must go with this people unto the land which the Lord hath sworn unto their fathers to give them; and thou shalt cause them to inherit it. (Deut. 31:6–7)

We have already established that Joshua was faithful to Moses's vision to inherit the land of Canaan. He was not to be afraid of giants, battle or dangerous terrain if he had to be faithful just as Moses was. From these verses, it becomes obvious to us what drove Joshua inside to be faithful against all odds. It was courage that became his supernatural driver that drove him to be willing to fight in the face of seemingly insurmountable obstacles.

> I know thy works, and where thou dwellest, even where Satan's seat is: and thou holdest fast my name, and hast not denied my faith, even in those days wherein Antipas was my faithful martyr, who was slain among you, where Satan dwelleth. (Rev. 2:13)

In the church of Pergamos, one man, Antipas, held on to his testimony unto death. He was thus called faithful by Jesus. This man had a spirit similar to those in the church of Smyrna. He was courageous. He faced death without fear. All martyrs are very courageous men and women. As a result, an entire church, despite their spiritually oppressive surroundings—for they dwelt in a city with a satanic government—held fast to Jesus's name and did not deny their faith. The fires of fidelity were stoked in the hearts of the brethren in Pergamos as a result of the martyrdom of Antipas.

> Fear none of those things which thou shalt suffer: behold,
> the devil shall cast some of you into prison, that ye may
> be tried; and ye shall have tribulation ten days: be thou
> faithful unto death, and I will give thee a crown of life.
> (Rev. 2:10)

The church of Smyrna was being asked by the Lord Jesus to be faithful unto death. How were they going to do that? They were not going to fear suffering, imprisonment, and tribulation. In other words, they had to be brave or courageous.

If those in the church of Smyrna had to face suffering, imprisonment, tribulation and death and still remain faithful, they needed to be bold, brave and courageous. Courage and boldness require the ability to face danger, difficulty, uncertainty or pain without being deflected from a chosen course of action.

> And Moses verily was faithful in all his house, as a servant,
> for a testimony of those things which were to be spoken
> after. (Heb. 3:5)

The man Moses is recognized as a man of true fidelity in the scriptures. What was the basis for this fidelity? What was the supernatural driver that drove this kind of faithful attitude? This supernatural driver is called courage.

Through courage, Moses was driven to be faithful as a servant of God when he approached Pharaoh to ask for the freedom of all the Hebrew slaves.

It takes a close examination of Moses's story to appreciate his courage. Prior to God's call, Moses had committed a crime and was being sought by the government of Pharaoh. He had been a fugitive for forty years in the land of Midian. The last place he wanted to be was Egypt, and the last person he wanted to see was Pharaoh. If he had to be faithful to the call upon his life, he had to be driven by an unusually high level of courage. It took God tussling with him and convincing him with several signs and miracles for the right level of courage to be stirred up in his heart. Churches need people of great courage to stand with them in times of great trials. Strong churches are made of faithful people, and these people are driven supernaturally by the spirit of courage.

Earlier in this chapter, we examined Numbers 13:30–31 and Numbers 14:6–9, where Moses's church—the Church in the Wilderness—at some point needed courageous men. Out of the twelve spies sent to survey the land of Canaan, ten came back with an evil report. They stirred up a spirit of fear among the children of Israel. The camp of the Hebrews became filled with awe and trepidation for they had heard that their foes were giants and that the land ate its inhabitants. Caleb stilled the people before Moses and reversed the spirit of fear by declaring words of courage to them.

The apostles overcame the fear of the Jews and prayed for boldness or courage to remain faithful to the divine call upon the church.

> And when they had prayed, the place was shaken where they were assembled together; and they were all filled with the Holy Ghost, and they spake the word of God with boldness. (Acts 4:31)

As Winston Churchill said in November 1954 at the Chateau Laurier in Ottawa,

> We have surmounted all the perils and endured all the agonies of the past. We shall provide against and thus prevail over the dangers and problems of the future, withhold no sacrifice, grudge no toil, seek no sordid gain, fear no foe all will be well. We have, I believe, within us the life—strength and guiding light by which the tormented world around us may find the harbor of safety, after a storm-beaten voyage. (Churchill 1954)

*Action:* This is a moment for true self-examination among your group's members. Each will have to answer these questions: How far do you want

God to take your life? How much are you ready to sacrifice to see God's glory in your generation?

## Step 5: Be supernaturally driven by faith

Have you ever heard the mantra "Faith is an act" before? I'll tell you, hearing it phrased is one thing, but seeing it epitomized is another.

"Brother, you need a car?" a young lady said.

I had been standing on the side of the busy road, trying my darnedest to get some transportation. One of the brethren, a young lady dressed in a pinafore, had perhaps seen the frown on my face.

"Yes," I said with a nod.

It was getting dark, and the taxis were whizzing by. My failed attempts to get one to slow down, let alone pick me up, had left me jaded and frustrated. The prayer session, as always, had lasted throughout the day—almost ten hours. I needed to get home in a jiffy.

The headlights of a car could be seen approaching some fifty meters away.

"In the name of Jesus, stop!" she sternly announced, flagging it down. Much to my amusement, the vehicle slowed and parked beside us. Opening its door, she beckoned my entrance.

"Thank you! Thank you!" I said.

"See you tomorrow," she said, waving.

*Now, that was new,* I thought.

The realization soon came that she wasn't an exception. It was a commonality among the brethren. When faced with obstacles, they proclaimed, "By faith!" Though this was cliché, more often than not, true spiritual faith drove their fidelity. They had an unquestioned belief in the faithfulness of God. The concept is simple: *If God wouldn't fail His word, then there's no need in letting go. I'll hold on till the end.*

Soon, I was inspired to get in the rhythm, and what a ride it has been.

So then they which be of faith are blessed with faithful
Abraham. (Gal. 3:9)

Those who are faith-driven go on to be blessed with faithful Abraham. Abraham's name was tagged to a fidelity rooted in the supernatural dynamic of faith. This was the trajectory of his life; he was fully persuaded by God in Mesopotamia to live a faith-filled life, and this went on to make him faithful in the land of Canaan. None of us can be associated with the blessings of Abraham without understanding the root of it all; his fidelity was the root of his blessing, and his faith was the root of his fidelity. All fidelity is faith-driven or supernaturally driven by faith; hence, we "who also walk in the steps of that faith of our father Abraham" (Rom. 4:12) are beckoned to follow in his path to the blessings of fidelity.

The frequency of walking "in the steps of that faith," Abraham's type of faith, can be seen in corporate acts like giving, prayer, evangelism, worship and fasting.

> And the saying pleased the whole multitude: and they chose Stephen, a man full of faith … And Stephen, full of faith and power, did great wonders and miracles among the people. (Acts 6:5, 8)

To be faithful, one has to be full of faith. Stephen was a man of true fidelity because he was driven by a heart full of faith. Even in the face of the contradiction of sinners, he did not faint in his mind, not for a second (Acts 6:9–14, 7:54–60).

Stephen was driven by faith to demonstrate this high sense of fidelity to the apostolic teaching and vision. It was through this fidelity that he became the first martyr of the church.

In 1 Thessalonians 5:24, God is described as faithful, and this makes fidelity a divine quality. God is looking for a man who shares in this divine quality of life, a man He could work with, and He found Abraham to be that man.

It takes a heart full of faith to supernaturally drive fidelity in any interpersonal relationship.

> Believe in the Lord your God, so shall ye be established; believe his prophets, so shall ye prosper. (2 Chron. 20:20)

Fidelity in an interpersonal relationship with God should be driven by faith.

> But without faith it is impossible to please him: for he
> that cometh to God must believe that he is, and that he is
> a rewarder of them that diligently seek him. (Heb. 11:6)

You'll also need faith to supernaturally drive your fidelity into an interpersonal relationship with a leader (2 Chron. 20:20). A fellowship must collectively believe in its minister or pastor to be faithful to his or her vision, ministry and message to achieve group fidelity. The lack of faith in any person will ultimately lead to infidelity. If you do not believe in a person, you cannot remain faithful to his or her vision, ministry and message. When church folk stop believing in their pastor, they might not say anything, but they will ultimately vote with their feet. Their vote of no confidence or no faith would be seen in their absence from the services.

*Action:* Your group members should be given the opportunity to act on their faith and see the Word work. Conducting miracle services and calling upon individuals to pray for the sick is a great example.

## Step 6: Be supernaturally driven by love

Lying supine on my bed, reclining on my pillow, my gaze got fastened to a scene on the television. A boy carrying another kid on his back showed up. He trudged forward wearily toward an old English-style mansion. I listened.

The weary chap approached an elderly priest, who looked endearingly at them and asked if he was tired from his load. The boy replied, "He ain't heavy, Father; he's my brother." Honestly, these words stayed with me. The title of the movie was *The Boys Town.*

I later found out that, in the 1940s, the words "He ain't heavy, Father; he's my brother" were taken as a slogan for Boys Town children's home by one Father Edward Flanagan. Actually, the story goes way back to 1884, when James Wells, moderator of the United Free Church of Scotland, told in his book, *The Parables of Jesus,* the story of a little Scottish girl carrying a big baby boy. Seeing her struggling, someone asked if she was tired. With surprise, she replied, "No, he's not heavy; he's my brother."

Something within those words seemed to have resonated with common folk such that "He Ain't Heavy, He's My Brother," a popular ballad written by Bobby Scott and Bob Russell, became a worldwide hit for the Hollies in 1969. In subsequent years, it was covered by many artists. Those words weren't powerful because they were set to music; they were weighty words for they evoked the sensibility of family fidelity.

This story resonated with me, perhaps prophetically. For later on, I would see a similar incident play out in my ministry, though not exactly like it.

While checking in on our missionary base in North Africa, the missionary discussed on the phone with me the ailment of a man whose efforts had been key to the growth of their work. Usually, these cases are handled by their ministry team, but this person's condition had persistently defied strenuous medical efforts and prayer. The symptoms involved the swelling of his head, and he went in and out of consciousness. It had all the indications of a terminal disease. I requested that, if it was possible, he be flown over to our ministry base in West Africa to be prayed over.

They agreed, and the traveling arrangements were worked out. A family member of his called, alerting me that they were on their way. I assumed they might arrive in a taxi or some private vehicle. But when they came, a lady was carrying the ailing gentleman on her back. They had walked quite a significant distance. I was clearly taken aback by it all. The lady was obviously exhausted, her feet dirtied by the dusty road she'd trekked with the weight of her unique burden. Why would she suffer that much? She was his younger sister, and having no car of her own, she chose to arduously bring her brother over.

The healing of our good friend came very quickly. His sister wept, knelt and praised God in utter bewilderment. Jumping up and down that afternoon, he gave the idea that those months of suffering had been a fluke. I watched as the two walked away, the gentleman totally unassisted. The lesson that came through to me was the fidelity of this younger sister to her older brother. In my opinion, next to Jesus, she was the hero that day: he wasn't heavy, for he was her brother. That which drove the fidelity of this younger sibling was brotherly love.

> Bear ye one another's burdens, and so fulfil the law of
> Christ … And let us not be weary in well doing: for in due
> season we shall reap, if we faint not. (Gal. 6:2, 9)

We're called to "bear one another's burdens" without being "weary in well doing" and fainting along the way. This could be a tall order if true brotherly love doesn't undergird our efforts. Why brotherly love? The apostle Paul, in the verse preceding the above, begins the sixth chapter by calling the Galatians brethren. The reason they should bear one another's burdens is because they are brethren. The church will do well if it carries its understanding of family fidelity from the natural world into its spiritual relationships. On our way to birthing revivals, we will as brethren have to deal with a lot of flawed personalities. However, in our fidelity toward one another, it doesn't matter how burdensome a Christian brother's or sister's difficulties might be; he or she isn't heavy to carry along, for he or she is our sibling. Groups whose members don't bear one another up run the risk of falling apart and aborting their vision.

The key to strong groups, fellowships, ministries and local churches is fidelity. It's a divine nature, a supernatural nature that must be supernaturally driven.

All strong groups depend on strong relationships. They need strong relationships between the members of those groups and God. They need strong relationships among the members of the local church, fellowship or ministry group —authentic relationships.

One of the indicators of strong spiritual relationships is fidelity. People who walk in strong spiritual relationships are loyal or faithful to one another. The more spiritual a relationship becomes, the more faithful or reliable it becomes. But all relationships face challenges, and some challenges have the capability to destroy them. It is easy to be faithful or loyal to people when they're easy to get along with, but when they are particularly difficult people, then you will need something to keep you loyal to them even in those difficult moments. In Jesus's relationship with His disciples, He faced being denied, betrayed, misunderstood and abandoned, yet, in all these, He remained faithful to His calling to God and to these friends of His. What was the secret behind His tenacious fidelity? The Bible says in John 13:1,

> Now before the feast of the Passover, when Jesus knew
> that his hour was come that he should depart out of this
> world unto the Father, having loved his own which were
> in the world, he loved them unto the end.

The secret is love, divine love. Love drove the fidelity of Jesus. He loved them through thick and thin. This is because love is longsuffering, endures all things, and never fails (1 Corin. 13). True love does not fail friends, brethren, partners or spouses when they need help. Love does not cut and run in the middle of difficult situations. Love does not abandon ship when a relationship gets difficult. Love is faithful to a fault. In God's word, love and faithfulness are found in the same person.

Some church folk feel a certain kind of fidelity toward their earthly siblings more so than toward their spiritual brethren. They will do anything to be there for their biological families, yet they do not mind absenting themselves from participating in church, even when their spiritual brethren desperately need them.

> And he said unto another, Follow me. But he said, Lord,
> suffer me first to go and bury my father. Jesus said unto
> him, Let the dead bury their dead: but go thou and preach
> the kingdom of God. And another also said, Lord, I will
> follow thee; but let me first go bid them farewell, which
> are at home at my house. (Luke 9:59–61)

Obviously, the fidelity of these disciples regarding their earthly families was way above that which they had for Christ and His cause. The church exists for the cause of Christ. A local church must love the Lord enough to be faithful to His cause. As much as we should love our earthly families and be dedicated to them, our fidelity to the Lord, His church, and His cause must far exceed it. Many martyrs through the centuries had to make a choice to be faithful to the cause of Christ even though they knew the detrimental effect that their deaths would have on their biological families.

> And above all things have fervent charity among yourselves:
> for charity shall cover the multitude of sins. (1 Peter 4:8)

We must understand that love without an unwavering fidelity is falsehood. Love covers a multitude of sin. It's a part of fidelity to be able to protect the secrets of our partners, friends, spouses and brethren. When someone discloses information shared in private to the public, especially without our permission, we feel betrayed. Betrayal is an act of infidelity. An unfaithful friend cannot keep a secret. When we love the Lord, His people, and His cause, then it will drive us to stay faithful in spite of how challenging our situation gets.

*Action:* Set a day aside for each member of your group to purchase a gift for his or her brother or sister. This would be a symbol of brotherly love.

# MILESTONE 5

# THE TESTS

## Step 1: Know the testers of genuine fidelity

It had been quite a while, almost a year, since a particular young lady had joined the brethren. She prayed in tongues, cleaned the fellowship premises, and shared the gospel during our outreach meetings.

"I saw a vision about you, and you were preaching at an evangelistic crusade," she said.

"Oh! Thanks," I said. Though quite a rookie in judging prophecies, I had always felt it was sophomoric for some novice to go out on a limb to tell a vision, particularly at a busy bus station. This was my closest encounter to date with her. Sasha (not her real name) had endeared herself to the brethren that way.

We had assumed that, for all intents and purposes, she was this squeaky-clean person who had served with the purest motive and offered our group an exemplary kind of fidelity. This perception probably held till her true purpose was uncovered during an exorcism. Actually, the term bandied about those days for such an event was "deliverance ministration." She had been honest enough with an older lady to tell about some of her nefarious dealings. Our older sister had been jolted by it, hard.

"Where are you running to?" I asked, watching a troupe of young men scurrying out of the warehouse. It was an empty facility we had claimed "by faith" for our services. I had been counseling some visitors that late afternoon and hadn't a clue of the rumpus that had occurred inside.

"No, no, no, this is bizarre," one "escapee" said, shaking his head.

Apparently, an exorcism to cast out the demons in Sasha had been in session. She had been demon-possessed and had practiced witchcraft for years. She had, in the process, developed a reputation for sexually seducing anointed men of God and destroying their ministries. I heard it through the grapevine, if you know what I mean. "Faithful" and relevant service was her way of winning the trust of those unsuspecting church leaders. Some among the brethren had become her latest victims.

The Messiah, the Bible says, will be an anointed leader, "and [the anointing] shall make him of quick understanding ... and he shall not judge after the sight of his eyes, neither reprove after the hearing of his ears" (Isa. 11:3). Anyone judging after the sight of his eyes could have been easily fooled by Sasha, the seduced anointed men included.

If you care to know, the deliverance ministration came to an abrupt end that day, largely due to Sasha's stripping down into her birthday suit—in plain language, she went nude. Whether this was a tactic of demons, pulled off whenever they are between a hammer and an anvil, it's hard to tell.

But it quite explains the escape-for-dear-life event that followed. Real gentlemen cannot view a striptease, can they? I'll tell you this though—Sasha was never seen or heard of again.

The Bible indicates to us that the platform of life will present to each of us events that will test our fidelity or our trustworthiness. The key players in this drama of life are the human being, God and Satan. It's permitted, therefore, within this earthly arena to be tested by people, God and Satan. We will examine a few tests that can easily establish genuine fidelity in any person.

*The Human Test*

> And let these first be put to the test; then let them become Deacons if there is nothing against them. (1 Tim. 3:10 BBE)

> And let them also be tested first; then let them serve as deacons if they prove themselves blameless. (1 Tim. 3:10 ESV)

Both the BBE and the ESV translations of this verse establish that those who serve as deacons within the local church must be tested first. The Greek word translated as *deacon* is *diakoneo,* which means "to serve" or "servant." In this sense, the deacon is a servant of the local church. However, Christ expects all of his servants to serve with a high sense of fidelity.

> His lord said unto him, Well done, thou good and faithful servant: thou hast been faithful over a few things, I will make thee ruler over many things. (Matt. 25:21)

In this way, the apostle Paul admonishes Timothy to test all the servants of the local church to be sure they serve with the purest fidelity, for they have to prove themselves "blameless." This test will ultimately weed out the servants with false fidelity and set aside those with genuine fidelity for service within the spiritual ministry of the fellowship, ministry, group, or local church.

*The Lord's Test*

> Now after these things, God put Abraham to the test, and said to him, Abraham; and he said, Here am I. And he said to him, Take your son, your dearly loved only son Isaac, and go to the land of Moriah and give him as a burned offering on one of the mountains of which I will give you knowledge. (Gen. 22:1–2)

Does God still test the fidelity of His servants? Yes, He does.

> And he came out, and went, as he was wont, to the mount of Olives; and his disciples also followed him. And when he was at the place, he said unto them, Pray that ye enter not into temptation. And he was withdrawn from them about a stone's cast, and kneeled down, and prayed, Saying, Father, if thou be willing, remove this cup from me: nevertheless not my will, but thine, be done. (Luke 22:39–42)

Jesus Christ at the Garden of Gethsemane referred metaphorically to the "cup" of "temptation" as the test by His "Father." The word *temptation* was translated from the Greek word *peirasmos,* the exact word translated as *trial* in 1 Peter 4:12. It means "a putting to the proof," "proving a person," "trial," "test," or "temptation."

> Beloved, think it not strange concerning the fiery trial which is to try you, as though some strange thing happened unto you. (1 Peter 4:12)

The apostle Peter in this verse addressed his fellow Christians as "beloved." Thus, "think it not strange" when a servant of the church is tested today by the God of Abraham.

*Satan's Test*

> Then Jesus was sent by the Spirit into the waste land to be
> tested by the Evil One. (Matt. 4:1 BBE)

If Satan or the "Evil One" ever tested my fidelity, he should find it a
piece of cake *if* he succeeded with Jesus the Son of God. Except, in this
case, the Holy Spirit uses the services of the Evil One; hence the words
"sent ... to be tested."

***Action:*** Your group must ready itself for all kinds of tests as it pursues
the experience of spiritual revival. These tests will ultimately prove the
genuineness of each member's fidelity.


## Step 2: The inconvenience test

There will never ever be an "appropriate" time for serving God. The
planets might never line up for you to say, "This is the season to be
faithful." When the call of God comes knocking at your door, it might
favor your situation or be an inconvenience. This is the reason that some
miss their day of visitation—because they missed their day of fidelity.
Why? Because fidelity was an inconvenient choice when the clarion call
to help birth a move of God came.

"You know, I was once given the opportunity to pastor a church," said
Sam, an elderly gentleman I had often chatted with. He had picked up this
conversation with me after learning I had accepted the call of God and
ministered since my teenage years.

"So what did you do?" I asked.

"Well, I'm sorry to say, I turned it down," he said, sounding remorseful.

"Why?" I asked.

"You know sonny, I came from a very dysfunctional home. Though my
dad was wealthy, he divorced my mum and wouldn't take care of us. As a
result, we were challenged with a lot of poverty. I'd always said to myself
through it all, *I'll be somebody one day*," he said.

"So you see, when that came along, I couldn't help but disappoint
God." His voice sounded sad. Then, with a spontaneous stir of enthusiasm,

he said, "But I built myself a great career in the financial industry, and now I have a wonderful family."

I could literally listen through Sam's façade and decipher the tone of regret. He could have been one of those anointed ministers of his day. I guess we would never know.

> And a certain scribe came, and said unto him, Master, I will follow thee whithersoever thou goest. And Jesus saith unto him, The foxes have holes, and the birds of the air have nests; but the Son of man hath not where to lay his head. And another of his disciples said unto him, Lord, suffer me first to go and bury my father. But Jesus said unto him, Follow me; and let the dead bury their dead. (Matt. 8:19–22)

Fidelity must be tested at inconvenient times and under inconvenient circumstances. I believe that the majority of church folk sincerely want to serve God with fidelity, but they only want to do it at their own convenience. The scribe said, "I will follow thee whithersoever thou goest." This gentleman wanted to join Jesus's ministry, but the Lord quickly reminded him that it would be very inconvenient; some of the inconveniences in their hectic travel schedule would include finding a place to lay their heads. There weren't any Holiday Inns or Sheraton Hotels in the cities, towns and villages they visited. There aren't any convenient circumstances for serving God.

Then there was a disciple who really wanted to pursue the Lord's ministry all the way. He had already joined His team of interns and should have participated in the upcoming opportunities, except it wasn't a convenient time. He wanted to wait and bury his dad first. "Follow me; and let the dead bury their dead," Jesus counseled. In other words, the funeral had to be put on hold in the interest of following his teammates. The reason for this is simple: Jesus conducted his entire earthly ministry within a three-and-a-half-year duration; He had a very tight schedule and no convenient time for mundane activities. It was obvious that bringing in other personal issues would greatly hamper the mission. If you have to follow the Lord with others, you'll have to do it at great personal inconvenience. There is no convenient season for serving the Lord.

> He that observeth the wind shall not sow; and he that
> regardeth the clouds shall not reap ... In the morning
> sow thy seed, and in the evening withhold not thine hand:
> for thou knowest not whether shall prosper, either this
> or that, or whether they both shall be alike good. (Ecc.
> 11:4, 6)

In this way, one has to pass the inconvenience test if fidelity should mark their work in the Lord's vineyard. Those who look out for convenient times and seasons, according to Solomon, "shall not sow." The Lord's work needs one who will commit and "withhold not" his hand "in the morning" and "in the evening." Fidelity requires a very sturdy hand, through the changing seasons and circumstances. "Wisdom and knowledge shall be the stability of thy times" (Isa. 33:6). The Hebrew word translated in this verse as *stability* is *emunah*, which also means "faithfulness," "trustworthiness," or "fidelity." Thus, in the Hebrew language, stability and fidelity are joined at the hip; you cannot separate them. Those who have faithful associates will have stable institutions, churches, corporations and enterprises. Those who want to obey God's call at their own convenience will never be faithful and stable servants of the Lord.

In other words, whenever the call to serve God within your fellowship, ministry, team, local church or group becomes an inconvenience, you're actually being tested—tested by God, humans or Satan.

*Action:* Your group members should watch closely how they each handle the inconveniences of their corporate call. The fidelity of each member must be measured by this.

## Step 3: The money test

"That's mine. All of that's mine!" the minister said, wrestling the offering out of the hands of the ushers. I recall reading these words many years ago. I cringed and thought, *How in the world would a minister do something like that?*

This minister ministered in one of the Full Gospel Businessmen Fellowship meetings. It's been decades. Demos Shakarian, its founder, narrated the story in his book *The Happiest People on Earth* (Shakarian and Sherril 1975).

The money grabbing had occurred right after the offering was taken that day. Shakarian concluded the narrative by telling how this man, many years afterward, looked a far cry from the picture of prosperity. I have never forgotten the lesson I learned from this: that it pays to let the Lord *move* men to bless rather than forcing it out of their hands.

> But Gehazi, the servant of Elisha the man of God, said, Behold, my master hath spared Naaman this Syrian, in not receiving at his hands that which he brought: but, as the Lord liveth, I will run after him, and take somewhat of him ... But he went in, and stood before his master. And Elisha said unto him, Whence comest thou, Gehazi? And he said, Thy servant went no whither. And he said unto him, Went not mine heart with thee, when the man turned again from his chariot to meet thee? Is it a time to receive money, and to receive garments, and oliveyards, and vineyards, and sheep, and oxen, and menservants, and maidservants? (2 Kings 5:20, 25–26).

Fidelity in serving should be driven by a desire for either the supernatural or the natural, but never both. Elisha's fidelity to Elijah was driven by a desire for the supernatural.

> And it came to pass, when they were gone over, that Elijah said unto Elisha, Ask what I shall do for thee, before I be taken away from thee. And Elisha said, I pray thee, let a double portion of thy spirit be upon me. (2 Kings 2:9)

But in the case of Gehazi, the story was a little different. He didn't serve Elisha with a fidelity driven by a desire for the supernatural. His fidelity through the years was driven by a desire for money and material acquisition. The prophetic anointing upon Elisha was a transferable one. Since Elisha received his anointing from Elijah by servanthood (2 Kings 3:11), it stands to reason that "Gehazi, the servant of Elisha" was the next in line for a transference. The principle behind transference is simple: "commit thou to faithful men" (2 Tim. 2:2). So it isn't enough to serve; you'll have to serve with genuine fidelity.

The day for Elisha to find out about Gehazi's fidelity did finally come. It was a money test, and it came by means of a Syrian general called Naaman. The man had every material thing that Gehazi desired, and this stirred up the covetous spirit that had lingered in him all throughout the years of his stewardship. On the surface, it seemed to everyone, Gehazi had served Elisha with genuine fidelity till Naaman got healed and his huge financial donation was declined.

> But Gehazi, the servant of Elisha the man of God, said, Behold, my master hath spared Naaman this Syrian, in not receiving at his hands that which he brought: but, as the Lord liveth, I will run after him, and take somewhat of him. (2Kings 5:20).

Gehazi missed it, for it wasn't the "time to receive money, and to receive garments, and olive yards, and vineyards, and sheep, and oxen, and menservants, and maidservants." His covetous spirit was so contrary to Elisha's that he went against his master's judgment. Gehazi broke faith with Elisha, and everything radically changed from that moment. Gehazi had failed the money test, and his infidelity had tarnished his servanthood. He was disqualified to inherit Elisha's anointing.

I've watched certain ministers treat wealthy people as their financial "big fishes." They view them as those who can fund their appetite for material wealth rather than individuals in need of spiritual help. When it's all said and done, these big fishes feel used and abused. It's the price they paid for following charisma rather than character. There are also the so-called "gifted ministers" who only offer their ministry to the highest financial bidders. Like professional footballers, they are traded for the highest contract fees. Sad, isn't it?

Judas Iscariot failed the money test and didn't live to see the day of Pentecost (Acts 1:14–16).

> Then one of the twelve, called Judas Iscariot, went unto the chief priests, And said unto them, What will ye give me, and I will deliver him unto you? And they covenanted with him for thirty pieces of silver. (Matt. 26:16–18)

Genuine fidelity always serves for something higher than money. The money test comes across as one of the toughest fidelity tests, for we all need money to deal with very important life issues. It is hard to watch your family go without certain necessities of life in the name of fidelity to financial ethics.

At the end of the day, the fidelity to our calling or ministry mustn't be tied to the paycheck; we shouldn't be compelled to minister to individuals, plant churches, accept ministry invitations, author books, and record music or have concerts primarily based on what will be earned. Our call must be tied exclusively to God's supernatural direction. Money shouldn't drive our choices in serving God and His people, but genuine fidelity.

> I have coveted no man's silver, or gold, or apparel. (Acts 20:33)

When our tenure of spiritual stewardship in this world is over, this should be our testimony—after we've passed the money test.

*Action:* Your group members must watch out for corrupt attitudes toward money and hold one another to high standards of financial stewardship. Desires must be set exclusively on the supernatural of the Holy Spirit.

## Step 4: The motive test

Church splits aren't accidental, I believe. They're just an end result of infidelity gone unchecked. But are they avoidable? I believe they are—that is, if we watch out for circumstances that test human motivation and their early test results.

In the late '80s, the ministry I had joined was budding. The brethren were history at this stage. We had started out as a prayer cell in a suburb and gained some spiritual momentum in the process. The surge was actually a ripple from the charismatic movement's euphoria. We were happy to still see some moves of God and were gung ho about it.

Then fidelity test number one came–our pastor was offered a scholarship to study in another African nation. However, he declined due to his fidelity to the ministry. Being one fine gentleman, he had recommended his assistant instead. It was a laudable move. The fellow was, in my opinion, a rather genteel and affable kind.

This was followed by fidelity test number two. The assistant, while away studying, rubbed shoulders with other ambitious leaders and heads of ministries. Several ministry opportunities came up, stroking his ego. His fidelity to the group at home might have been severely tested at this point. After all, he had what it took to strike out on his own—the education, the connections, and the gifting to pull it off.

He returned a different man. While still congenial and brimming with newfound confidence, his demeanor indicated an aggression we had theretofore never known. *What's gotten into him?* I mused.

All this uncertainty came to a head though, in our annual ministry convention. A foreign guest speaker—a friend of his—was invited. He said some divisive things from the pulpit, and we were all left wondering, scratching our heads for answers.

Finally, we figured the conspiracy out. The motive was to oust the pastor and usurp his position.

"What in the world is going on?" Some murmured.

How long this had been in the works was hard to tell. One thing was for sure though: the travel opportunity had tested the motives of the assistant's heart. Perhaps it makes some sense to hear the apostles pray, "Thou, Lord, which knowest the hearts of all men." Wasn't it because they knew how difficult it was to know "hearts of all men"? This is the Most High's department.

Along the way, something within his personality had escaped us. To make a long story short, the new work suffered a split.

> Then saith one of his disciples, Judas Iscariot, Simon's son, which should betray him, Why was not this ointment sold for three hundred pence, and given to the poor? This he said, not that he cared for the poor; but because he was

a thief, and had the bag, and bare what was put therein.
(John 12:4–6)

Judas Iscariot developed an appetite for money. He'd come to love filthy lucre way beyond his love for the Lord and His people. He couldn't be trusted with the ministry's till. The love of money can easily compromise human fidelity and turn a person into a thief. Judas proposed certain ministry projects for the poor. The idea though was to pad the price figures of an alabaster box to be auctioned off. It would be "sold for three hundred pence," with some monies siphoned off for himself. The plan couldn't work out. The donor, a lady, spent it on Jesus (John 12:3). "And from that time he sought opportunity to betray" his mentor just to seize the money he wanted (Matt. 26:10–16): "thirty pieces of silver."

> Then one of the twelve, called Judas Iscariot, went unto the chief priests, And said unto them, What will ye give me, and I will deliver him unto you? And they covenanted with him for thirty pieces of silver. And from that time he sought opportunity to betray him. (Matt. 26:14–16)

Today, an "Iscariot syndrome" has taken over the global church ministry in the form of a corrupted prosperity gospel, and by this, the house of prayer has become a "den of thieves" (Luke 19:46). I cannot recall the numerous times the trust of God's people has been betrayed in this arena and made headline news.

Upon a casual examination of Jesus's ministry, things seem to run like a typical Pentecostal-charismatic organization. Judas was one of the twelve members of the executive board (Luke 10:2–4).

> And when he had called unto him his twelve disciples, he gave them power against unclean spirits, to cast them out, and to heal all manner of sickness and all manner of disease. (Matt. 10:1)

Beneath the surface of ministering to the spiritually oppressed multitudes, was a lurking ulterior motive in the heart of Judas: the financial secretary. This had nothing to do with sick folk and demonized lives. His credibility remained unchallenged till his fidelity was tested. I'll call it the motive test. It appeared to him in the form of a female disciple, Mary.

> Then took Mary a pound of ointment of spikenard, very costly, and anointed the feet of Jesus, and wiped his feet with her hair: and the house was filled with the odour of the ointment. (John 12:3)

Mary had such a pure fidelity and devotion to the Lord, that she saved her salary to have a "very costly" alabaster perfume box. All she wanted to do was to anoint "the feet of Jesus" and wipe "his feet with her hair." Jesus knew the motive behind her fidelity; it was not romantic, corrupt or sinful like the onlookers guessed (Luke 7:39). Her fidelity was driven by pure agape love, a purity the apostle Peter lacked at the time (Matt. 26:69–75).

Wherefore I say unto thee, Her sins, which are many, are forgiven; for she loved much: but to whom little is forgiven, the same loveth little. (Luke 7:47)

Mary's ministry to the Lord was coming from such a pure motivation that it exposed the corrupt motivations of Judas's heart. Mary was not an apostle. She was not one of "the twelve" key leaders of Jesus's ministry; she did not cast out devils or heal diseases. She was just a lady forgiven of her many sins, and her motive for serving the Lord had no ulterior agenda. Her fidelity was way ahead of that of the leaders of Jesus's ministry, and it caused her actions to fall right into divine timing.

> "For in that she hath poured this ointment on my body, she did it for my burial. Verily I say unto you, Wheresoever this gospel shall be preached in the whole world, there shall also this, that this woman hath done, be told for a memorial of her. (Matt. 26:12–13)

Mary was to go down in history as the only person who anointed Jesus's body for burial, and Jesus prophesied about that. Her genuine fidelity has made her a historic figure within the gospel of Jesus Christ. Judas also went down in the New Testament as a historic figure, but for all the wrong reasons. Judas failed the motive test when he met Mary, because pure motives always expose the impure ones. Many public leaders with impure motives have been exposed by the pure motives of ordinary people.

King David proposed a warfare strategy to get rid of Uriah (2 Sam. 11:14–15). The real motive was not to punish him for a crime he had committed but to hide his sexual affair with Uriah's wife (2 Sam. 11:2–5, 26–27). When King David's motive for serving Israel had gone wrong, it took an ordinary officer within his military—Uriah—to expose it; and he did it by his pure motive for serving in the army (2 Sam. 11:6–11). David failed the motive test.

*Action:* Your group members should take an inventory of their motives before the Lord. A prayer meeting asking God to search their hearts will be in order. All must agree to swiftly deal with all revelations of failing the motive test.

## Step 5: The absence test

Joe had spent most of his working years shepherding a church in Europe. It was a thriving church who'd come to love and respect his ministry. Somewhere in the middle of his career, he had sensed a call to return to his home country to begin a new work. He had felt through his years in Europe the assurance of his church's fidelity.

After all, these were his people right?

At face value, the measure of their fidelity was dependable, so he packed up and left for Africa. The work in Africa struggled initially, just as all pioneering efforts would, and Joe had to depend much on the support of his congregation in Europe—his faithful ministry partners.

This arrangement worked out quite well until the pastors he had left behind rebelled against further financing his ministry. They disregarded his instructions and despised his authority. Perhaps their foreign commitments, when juxtaposed with the overhead expenses, had become impractical.

Whatever the reason was, the following months saw the cash streams from Europe to Africa dry up. Joe felt betrayed, stranded and traumatized. Not too long afterward, it was reported that he had suffered a stroke. He never made a full recovery and died in the following months. The trauma he had suffered might have been too much. His protégés failed the absence test.

> Wherefore, my beloved, as ye have always obeyed, not as
> in my presence only, but now much more in my absence,
> work out your own salvation with fear and trembling. For
> it is God which worketh in you both to will and to do of
> his good pleasure. (Phil. 2:12–13)

The zest and obedience exhibited by followers during the absence of their leader is a great indicator of their fidelity. The absence of a leader is therefore a crucial test of fidelity. The apostle Paul not only expected the fidelity of the Philippian church to his instructions during his presence, but he expected fidelity all the more in his absence.

> Do all things without murmurings and disputings: That
> ye may be blameless and harmless, the sons of God,
> without rebuke, in the midst of a crooked and perverse
> nation, among whom ye shine as lights in the world. (Phil.
> 2:14–15)

Paul did expect the church of Philippi to "do all things without murmurings and disputing" during his absence. This was very important, for to found a fellowship, ministry, group, team or local church and entrust its operation to a bunch of unfaithful members is without question a recipe for disaster.

The fidelity of true compatriots should outlive the leader. It'll therefore be prudent to take short leaves of absence for testing your future leaders. You don't need folks who portray a when-the-cat's-away-the-mice-will-play attitude.

> And the Lord said, Who then is that faithful and wise
> steward, whom his lord shall make ruler over his household,
> to give them their portion of meat in due season? Blessed
> is that servant, whom his lord when he cometh shall find
> so doing. Of a truth I say unto you, that he will make him
> ruler over all that he hath. But and if that servant say in
> his heart, My lord delayeth his coming; and shall begin to
> beat the menservants and maidens, and to eat and drink,
> and to be drunken; The lord of that servant will come in a

day when he looketh not for him, and at an hour when he
is not aware, and will cut him in sunder, and will appoint
him his portion with the unbelievers. (Luke 12:42–46)

The absence of his lord tested the fidelity of the unfaithful steward, for he took advantage of his lord's absence and delay "to beat the menservants and maidens, and to eat and drink, and to be drunken." Having failed this test, his infidelity was judged by appointing him his portion with infidels.

*Action:* The members of your group must undergo the absence test. The group leader should agree with them about his standard of fidelity. Afterward, the leader must take various leaves of absence. Your group's fidelity standard before and after these absences must be closely examined.

## Step 6: The copy test

Fidelity can be a strange animal sometimes; on many occasions, it makes no sense whatsoever.

Many years had passed since the upper room, and the circumstances of my life had radically changed. I was ministering in the port city and had gathered a few loyalists, but its growth was challenged. It wasn't what I had expected. I reminisced habitually about the glory of the years gone by.

*What am I going to do?* I mused in the recesses of my heart.

Then I heard, *Do what Captain did.* You see, I knew that voice. And it was the Holy Spirit speaking in His usually inimitable way.

"How?" I replied under my breath. This dialogue began for me months of visions and revelations. They had a hindsight scope. It had been so long that I had forgotten certain simple things I had observed at the upper room. The visions brought them all back, and with a greater clarity.

*Did the Holy Spirit say* Captain? I wondered. He was the leader of the brethren. Interestingly, I had never questioned the origin of his title. I just went along with it.

In snippets and sound bites, the way the leader of the brethren got led by the Spirit became my road map. As the ministry overcame one hurdle after another, we gained some respectable velocity.

This principle of imitation had its own mysterious history. In the upper room, whatever the leader did was for us male disciples to copy. We prayed like he did, preached like he did, and most bizarrely, dressed like he did.

How could one young man have such an effect on other young men? It was the fidelity factor at work.

After Elisha picked up the royal robe of Elijah, he went to the Jordan and crossed it by copying his mentor's style: he "smote the waters."

> And Elijah took his mantle, and wrapped it together, and smote the waters, and they were divided hither and thither, so that they two went over on dry ground ... He [Elisha] took up also the mantle of Elijah that fell from him, and went back, and stood by the bank of Jordan; And he took the mantle of Elijah that fell from him, and smote the waters, and said, Where is the LORD God of Elijah? and when he also had smitten the waters, they parted hither and thither: and Elisha went over. (2 Kings 2:8, 14–15, brackets added)

This showed that Elisha had gotten hooked to Elijah's spirit. In the same way, we young men were prophetically connected to our leader's spirit. Meeting my "Jordan" in a port city, I had been reminded by the Holy Spirit to cross it my mentor's way.

Fidelity to the spirit of a team and its leader is signaled by a *copying* attitude. Those who would do things differently from the team and its leader not only lack their spirit but have failed the copy test.

> But I trust in the Lord Jesus to send Timotheus shortly unto you, that I also may be of good comfort, when I know your state. For I have no man likeminded, who will naturally care for your state. For all seek their own, not the things which are Jesus Christ's. But ye know the proof of him, that, as a son with the father, he hath served with me in the gospel. (Phil. 2:19–22)

The apostle Paul, at the writing of this letter, was expressing his personal opinion about Timothy his spiritual son. It was obvious from his comments that Timothy had gone beyond just following the man of God around; he had grown to the level of being like-minded with him. Timothy had adopted Paul's philosophy or mindset. In the process, they had become kindred spirits.

The apostle had mentored by then, many spiritual sons and daughters, but he said that when it came to like-mindedness, "I have no man." He had no man in his spiritual league except Timothy. What this father-son relationship had reproduced in Timothy was the natural care that Paul had for the Philippian church. The word translated as *naturally* in the Greek is actually the word *genuinely*. The same genuine fidelity and care that Paul—the founder of the Philippian church—had for it, flowed through his spiritual son Timothy.

> Now if Timotheus come, see that he may be with you without fear: for he worketh the work of the Lord, as I also do. (1 Corin. 16:10)

Yes, Timothy did care for the local church in the same genuine manner as the apostle Paul; he did it with the same mindset. In the process of caring, Paul said, "He worketh the work of the Lord, as I also do." He copied his spiritual father in his way of working the work of God because, through the years, he observed and told Timothy, "Thou hast fully known my doctrine, manner of life, purpose, faith, longsuffering, charity, patience," (2 Tim. 3:10).

The apostle Paul found it easy to recommend Timothy to the churches, for he reproduced or copied his style of ministry. Though he wrote this letter from his prison cell, he knew that he could minister vicariously through Timothy. The churches felt Paul's spirit through Timothy.

> "And John answered and said, Master, we saw one casting out devils in thy name; and we forbad him, because he followeth not with us. And Jesus said unto him, Forbid him not: for he that is not against us is for us. (Luke 9:49–50)

According to Jesus, this copying is very critical because it ties directly into the fidelity factor. The one who Jesus's disciples saw copying His style of ministry was "for" them because he wasn't "against" them. You cannot forbid he who copies or emulates you, for it ties into he being on your side. I believe, this is why the apostle Paul said to the Corinthian church, "I urge you, then, be imitators of me" (1 Corin. 4:16), and again, "Be imitators of me, as I am of Christ" (1 Corin. 11:1).

You test followers by assigning them to tasks and watching how they copy your approach; their imitation will show their fidelity to your ministry. Should they however do their own thing, then their fidelity cannot be relied upon. Those who are like-minded always end up "working the work of the Lord, as you also do." Timothy was the only protégé of Paul who passed the copy or imitation test.

*Action:* The leader of your group must test its members by assigning to them specific tasks and observe to see whether they prefer to copy the leader's style of ministry or choose theirs.

## Step 7: The revenge test

If you have never before been hurt by a trusted fellowship, team, church or ministry member, then you have yet to undergo your revenge test. I have.

Among the brethren, this particular man was one of a kind. The buddy of my campus leader was stolid and choleric most of the time, and on a good day he had a wry sense of humor. He brushed aside my comedic alchemy with others as unspiritual. To him, true spirituality was a potpourri of serenity and gravity. I bought into all of Brother R's views, but he using that to keep me miserable got me really irate.

I'd seen him deliberate with my campus leader about me many times; and that really got to me. I suspected, he'd won him to his side. It showed in his beetle-browed attitude. I felt conspired against.

The vacation was over now, and he needed my support to hold the fort. My support? He had to once more find the stone refused by the builder, yours truly's faithful hand, to steer things at the fellowship till he returned from school, right?

*Why wouldn't he call his buddy to fill in for him? Why me?* I thought. *This is my chance to get back at him for keeping me in relegation, for unjustifiably back-benching me.* I could feel the heat rising up inside.

How could I do it? I wondered. Perhaps taking a long rain check would do. Maybe I could let him sweat out his insecurities, wondering till the last minute if I'd even change my mind at all. Blah, blah, blah.

But I didn't. Proverbially, the fierce feuding of two elephants leaves the innocent bushes devastated in their wake. The ministry must go on, the work can't fail, and the love of the people must be priority. I repented and balked.

And that's how I dealt with my revenge test and passed with flying colors. The group survived its fledgling season and the vision of revival became tangible.

David's fidelity to King Saul, in my opinion, was one of the most remarkable Old Testament pictures of human character.

> And the men of David said unto him, Behold the day of which the Lord said unto thee, Behold, I will deliver thine enemy into thine hand, that thou mayest do to him as it shall seem good unto thee. Then David arose, and cut off the skirt of Saul's robe privily. And it came to pass afterward, that David's heart smote him, because he had cut off Saul's skirt. And he said unto his men, The Lord forbid that I should do this thing unto my master, the Lord's anointed, to stretch forth mine hand against him, seeing he is the anointed of the Lord. So David stayed his servants with these words, and suffered them not to rise against Saul. But Saul rose up out of the cave, and went on his way. (1 Sam. 24:4–7)

King Saul had become a schizophrenic and authoritarian leader. The Bible makes it clear that much of this was due to his demonization and personal insecurities (1 Sam. 16:14, 23). David, from the very day of tasting his first military victory, bore the brunt of King Saul's demonic tendencies (1 Sam. 18:10–13).

Though a captain over the Israeli army and a son-in-law of the king, David suffered much within the palace. Through the years, Saul had not shied away from making his intention to assassinate David known. Now the day had finally arrived for David to take Saul out before he achieved his aim. The king was asleep and had no idea of how precarious his situation was. David's lieutenants goaded him on; they even quoted God's word to support the action. This was a perfect situation for revenge; David's oppressor was right in his hands. But somewhere deep within the recesses of his heart, fidelity had driven its principles. So, as he yielded to this most subtle temptation by cutting off Saul's skirt, "David's heart smote him," and he refrained from revenge by listening to his conscience.

In his fidelity, look at the terms David used for King Saul: "my master" and "the Lord's anointed." Fidelity had led David to revere this psychotic person to the extent of restraining his men from doing him harm. Thus, the future king of Israel had passed the test of revenge. Vengeful personalities have failed this crucial test and cannot be considered men or women of pure fidelity. Those who harbor sentiments for repaying evil must repent, or they will fail this important test.

I have had to, through the years, repent numerous times of the vengeful feelings that lingered behind the mask of churchy togetherness. It's sad to say that many church splits are the result of failing the revenge test.

The Los Angeles Azusa Street Revival hit such a snag. Clara Lum, the Azusa Street mission's secretary, was deeply hurt by William Seymour, the revival group leader. Behind her pain was his choice to marry Jennie Evans Moore, the pianist. Some members believed the marriage was a red herring, and Clara was one of them. She couldn't take it and abruptly left.

Some assert that Lum secretly nursed a romantic desire for Seymour. Be that as it may, she did the unthinkable by taking with her the group's entire national and worldwide mailing list. This devastated the revival mission financially (Liardon 1996).

In getting back at Seymour for his choice, Lum failed the revenge test and terminated one of the most significant revival movements of the twentieth century.

***Action:*** Your group members must observe the attitudes of those hurt by others among them. How they handle this in the spirit of love is crucial to identifying the truly loyal members.

## Step 8: The vanity test

The vanity test, in my opinion, is one of the most subtle fidelity tests of these modern times. Many who had been faithful in the ministry during periods of great suffering have miserably failed this test in times of material prosperity.

The man shook his head sadly.

"What?" I asked.

"Bishop, I want to quit my job," he said with a stern look in his eyes.

*This guy is serious,* I surmised.

"You know, one big bishop just visited the church," he continued.

"Yes."

"He said he wasn't happy with the honorarium."

"And how much was that?" I pressed.

"Thousands of dollars," he replied.

"You mean it?" I asked.

This gentleman had been working for an organization headed by a "rising star."

He felt disappointed, for money had engulfed their pursuits. He felt his fidelity to God was in danger of being corrupted just by hanging out with this star—hence his decision to leave. I was concerned.

I personally knew the rising star. He had cut his teeth doing ministry in the heat of the charismatic renewal. Despite the stark poverty of his upbringing, his fidelity was without question. Now, it was another story. He had fallen for the lifestyle of the rich and famous.

> By faith Moses, when he was come to years, refused to be called the son of Pharaoh's daughter; Choosing rather to suffer affliction with the people of God, than to enjoy the pleasures of sin for a season; Esteeming the reproach of Christ greater riches than the treasures in Egypt: for he had respect unto the recompense of the reward. (Heb. 11:24–26)

"By faith Moses" chose "rather to suffer affliction" and avoid "the treasures in Egypt." His lifestyle of affliction was a faith-based choice.

If your primary goal for fasting, praying and seeking God is to attain wealth and affluence, then the attainment of these objectives will corrupt your fidelity to serve God. You're weakened in your fidelity as the vanities of life are placed at your beck and call. Your loyalty is divided.

Worldliness packaged as affluence has done some of the greatest harm, I think, to individual fidelity within the church. People's hearts must be in the right place as they enter the money zone.

Jesus warned about the dire consequences of failing the vanity test.

> For what shall it profit a man, if he shall gain the whole world, and lose his own soul? (Mark 8:36)

He was talking about the wealthy-house-and-empty-soul syndrome from which many rich people suffer. Many have striven hard to get to the top, but when they got there, they found nothing to fill their spiritual appetite.

Whenever your material needs become your primary goal in serving God, then your failure of the vanity test is inevitable. When your spiritual needs become your primary goal in serving God, then your passing of the vanity test is guaranteed.

If your primary goal for fasting, praying and seeking God is to experience the depths of His glory, then the attainment of these objectives will only reignite your fidelity to serve Him. The depths and the riches of God's glory are unfathomable to the human mind.

> For Demas hath forsaken me, having loved this present world, and is departed unto Thessalonica; Crescens to Galatia, Titus unto Dalmatia. (2 Tim. 4:10)

At this stage, certain key leaders within Paul's apostolic ministry team deserted the mission. One of them was Demas. We know of this because of Philemon 1:24, where Paul mentions him as one of his fellow laborers. To be called a fellow laborer by the apostle Paul implied being part of an elite group of global church leaders. These were exceptional clergymen, yet this did not prevent Demas from failing the vanity test. The reason given was that he "loved this present world." What did he find in the world of Thessalonica that instigated his desertion of ministry? The apostle John said,

Love not the world, neither the things that are in the world. If any man love the world, the love of the Father is not in him. For all that is in the world, the lust of the flesh, and the lust of the eyes, and the pride of life, is not of the Father, but is of the world. (1 John 2:15–16)

Demas, this associate of Paul's apostolic team, having "loved this present world"—was quite a loaded statement. If apostle John's writing was anything to go by, then Demas had no more of "the love of the Father"— the heavenly Father—"in him." His love of the Father had been replaced by three spiritually dangerous proclivities: "the lust of the flesh, the lust of the eyes, and the pride of life." Paul uses the term *present world* to refer to the "current trends" of their time: the latest fashion in clothes, housing, jewelry, perfumes, and lifestyle. These elements of opulence and affluence appealed only to the flesh, the eyes, and human pride. Demas had failed the vanity test.

As I look around today, it seems to me that this spiritual virus of vanity has had a field day in corrupting the fidelity of many global church leaders who have loved this present world. Staying faithful to your original call isn't as easy as many make it seem, and countless have gone AWOL because of it. At the end of the day, the temporary rewards of worldly glamour cannot be a substitute for the eternal crown of glory. Think of it.

Your wealth and affluence here are your earthly crown of glory, but your genuine fidelity in serving God secures your eternal crown of glory.

*Action:* Your entire group must resolve to stay true to their pursuit of global revival regardless of how wealthy the ministry becomes, knowing that any segue of their desires into wealth can corrupt their fidelity and kill the move of God they're enjoying.

## Step 9: The suffering test

The shuffling of human feet on the veranda drew my attention to the visitors we had just received in our compound. A firm but gentle knock rattled the wooden door that led to the hall. I had just arrived home that evening from a wonderful, Spirit-filled service and couldn't fathom who it was that had arrived.

In a tired voice, I gave my response, opening the door. It was a middle-aged man. To my recollection, he was a stranger. From where I stood, I could see that he dragged behind him a teenage girl. Her reticence raised a red flag that there was trouble, but the shadows of the unlit porch obscured her visage. Then they both entered, and the light hit her face. It was Tarah, one of our dedicated protégés; I called them my daughters. She had been in the service earlier that evening reveling in the revival atmosphere.

The obviously vexed man introduced himself as her father. What was his reason for such a grand entrance? He wanted to identify and warn the kingpin of the Christian fellowship that his daughter was banned henceforth from attending their meetings.

My attention was quickly drawn to the stick he menacingly held in his right hand. Had he been beating her with that? I was furious. This girl loved the services. I couldn't for the life of me understand punishment for serving God. I told him in no uncertain terms that he shouldn't be beating that child, especially not for worshipping God. He retorted in anger. He said something like "She's my daughter, and I'll do whatever I darn wish!" I'm sorry to say that some altercation ensued—no fisticuffs, though.

He stomped out fuming with rage.

"You wait till I send you out of this country to your mother!" he yelled at her. Tarah's mum lived in England.

Truth be told, I was worried. I wondered if the abuse she had suffered would cause her zeal to wane.

At the next service, my eyes scanned the room anxiously, and *there she was*. This little girl had fought through the fire of persecution to serve God again. Her fidelity to God had been tested and had survived.

> And to him they agreed: and when they had called the apostles, and beaten them, they commanded that they should not speak in the name of Jesus, and let them go. And they departed from the presence of the council, rejoicing that they were counted worthy to suffer shame for his name. And daily in the temple, and in every house, they ceased not to teach and preach Jesus Christ. (Acts 5:40–42)

Throughout church history, persecution has been used to test the fidelity of Christians. God used the fires of persecution to sort out false fidelity from the genuine.

> And Saul was consenting unto his death. And at that time there was a great persecution against the church, which was at Jerusalem; and they were all scattered abroad throughout the regions of Judaea and Samaria, except the apostles. (Acts 8:1)

"All scattered abroad ... *except the apostles.*" In the midst of the cataclysm, the apostles decided to stay. They wouldn't quit and run. They passed the suffering test.

> In February 2000, ravaging Muslim mobs attacked Rehoboth Church in Kaduna, Nigeria burning it nearly to the ground, but church members continued to attend services inside the charred walls of the sanctuary. All the church records, Sunday School material, and Pastor Zakari's books were destroyed in the fire. (Foxe 2001)

Did you notice that? "But church members continued to attend services inside the charred walls of the sanctuary." These Northern Nigerian Christians passed the suffering test.

> I know thy works, and where thou dwellest, even where Satan's seat is: and thou holdest fast my name, and hast not denied my faith, even in those days wherein Antipas was my faithful martyr, who was slain among you, where Satan dwelleth. (Rev. 2:13)

The Pergamos Christians were faithful because *they dwelt,* they did not *run from,* "where Satan dwelleth." They resolved to stay in the fires of persecution. It takes genuine fidelity to pull that off.

*Action:* The members of your group should use their suffering to settle the authenticity of their fidelity. After each storm, the remnant should be given the thumbs up. They've passed the suffering test.

## Step 10: The rejection test

"Come on, come on, boy" the campus leader said, trying his darnedest to get me psyched up. My recent absence from the meetings had troubled these two fellows—the campus leader and his buddy. Since the leader had been approached about it, he now served as the arbiter. I had been rankled by his colleague's attitude. Honestly, I wanted out. I felt fed up.

I considered myself an unnecessary appendage in his grand scheme. Being on a long, unnecessary break from college education had gotten on my nerves, and he not acknowledging my spiritual usefulness didn't help either.

This was the '80s, and a military junta running our national affairs had caused some revulsion from the colleges. We called it an "a luta continua," and were kicked out by the authorities.

At home, the revival group left in my care kept hanging by a thread. This was my ordeal whenever my colleague's high school's vacation was over. After slugging out my challenges with a small leftover group, I was left high and dry and unappreciated. Now, his return had coincided with a bevy of teenagers brimming with their boarding school charismatic adventures. It was home sweet home for them, but for me, I had a lemon in hand, and had to try squeezing out some lemonade.

I could hardly believe it. He had gotten me retired without any apologies. Talk about being peeved on the back bench. That should have been an understatement.

This was my rejection test. Did I pass, though? I think I did.

"Okay, I'll give it a thought," I said calmly, not because I had a choice but really because my unrelenting nature couldn't give up midstream—at least not when I had seen visions of a coming revival.

Looking through life's rearview mirror, I can now say I'm grateful for not biting the bait of rejection. For in the absence of the bossy fellow, the vision came true and a move of God was born. We saw deaf-mutes, blind eyes, and various diseases healed in the services.

Do people who are truly faithful have a level of faith that is totally immune to rejection? I have no idea. What I learned though is that, God specially ordains rejection in the lives of those He wants to participate in His business. He does it to prove them. Those who have false fidelity abandon ship at the slightest sense of rejection. Those who pass the rejection test take a licking and keep on ticking. Consider Elisha:

> And he left the oxen, and ran after Elijah, and said, Let me, I pray thee, kiss my father and my mother, and then I will follow thee. And he said unto him, Go back again: for what have I done to thee? And he returned back from him, and took a yoke of oxen, and slew them, and boiled their flesh with the instruments of the oxen, and gave unto the people, and they did eat. Then he arose, and went after Elijah, and ministered unto him. (1 Kings 19:20–21)

He wouldn't take no for an answer. And the move of the Spirit on the life of Elijah was later inherited by Elisha, all because he had overcome rejection.

The story of fidelity is never complete without painful rejection. Genuine fidelity presses on in spite of rejection. A man who cannot handle rejection has an ego too dangerous for work in God's economy. He cannot stay with a mission till the end. Sooner or later, someone will say or do something he perceives as rejection, which will anger, embarrass, or discourage him. No amount of rejection should be too strong for the genuinely loyal. No leader can trust the fidelity of a man with a rejection complex. He'll fail the group when they least expect it.

*Action:* Your group members should watch out for those with a rejection complex; those who feel rejection at the most benign intentions. They would need the daily assurances of the others to pass their rejection test.

## Step 11: Testing the horse and the mule

"This fellow is ripping off his church."
"Is such an expensive car necessary?"
"Isn't this a show-off?"
The community outside went on and on about it. Their beef was, a rapidly growing congregation had just bought their pastor a Mercedes. These were the years of the military junta in the nation, and the economy was in a downturn. Most churches weren't doing so well financially.

Needless to say, the gesture had drawn some condemnation from the press and the Christian community.

Sometimes it's hard to tell exactly what the motivation for such gossip is. After all, we all need a jalopy to get around, don't we? So why complain if someone's got a nice one?

The reaction, nevertheless continued, and the church got tired of it all, of the tabloid brouhaha, I suppose.

They wrote a rebuttal stating their reasons for the purchase. They made it clear, they had appreciated their pastor's ministry through the years and felt it most appropriate to express their gratitude this way. Now, what really got me was their statement to this effect, which I have paraphrased: "We don't feel remorseful demonstrating our love and appreciation for our pastor in such a costly manner, and should the opportunity ever present itself in the near future, we'll do it again."

This got the wagging tongues to quiet down—at least most of them. In my little reflection, I did get their drift; this gift came out of pure fidelity and devotion from a genuinely grateful people. It was unforced, not coerced, and plainly nobody else's business.

> Don't be like the horse, or like the mule, which have no understanding, Who are controlled [forced] by bit and bridle, or else they will not come near to you. (Ps. 32:9 WEB, brackets added)

Fidelity is never true unless it is unforced and spontaneous. True fidelity cannot help itself; it's a love slave, slaving from the heart without considering a reward. The horse and the mule are used here because they have two diametrically opposed natures. The horse is too eager to go and therefore has to be restrained. On the other hand, the mule is very reluctant to go and therefore has to be forced. These two creatures show the nature of two diverse disciples. One has to be forced to stay, whereas the other has to be dragged to go. The use of any element of force either to restrain or to coerce reveals an unfaithful heart. The bit and the bridle are the elements of force used on creatures that lack the understanding of fidelity to a leader's vision.

Likewise, the use of force to either restrain or to coerce in the service of God indicates the flunking of an important fidelity test. If you have to be forced by men or money to stay with a particular ministry, then you have the infidelity of a horse. If you have to be forced by men or devils to attend church meetings or do the work of God, then you have the infidelity of a mule. Either way, you need a thorough change of heart.

This is the reason horses and mules are "broken" by their trainers; it is to develop a character in them that responds properly to their vision through genuine fidelity.

*Action:* Your group should look out for attitudes among them that need either coercion to follow their vision or restraint to be a team player. These members need a thorough change of heart.

## Step 12: The hard sayings

I had heard the campus leader make some very tough utterances on occasion. At home, I overheard one of the brethren use the phrase "harsh words."

*Now what the heck is that?* I thought.

I got used to them pretty quickly. I needed a tough skin to survive that environment—the tough hide of genuine fidelity.

What I mean by "got used to" is that this way of speaking had become my new normal, so I unconsciously used it on others.

For example, in conversation with a female undergraduate about her romantic situation, I said, "You'll have to give him up," speaking as compassionately as I could.

Most freshmen find that being undergraduates for a few years means more than pursuing a degree. The ladies, especially at that time, found this phase of life quite unsettling. They wanted to be romantically attached to someone, because not finding a boyfriend in college could be threatening to their futures. The prospects of marriage, some thought, became dismal after school.

So these were hard, hard words for any young woman. Sister M had just been saved and filled with the Holy Spirit, and she couldn't be dating some amorous guy while working out her newfound faith. Her fidelity to the group's spirituality was crucial to the revival, so I said it like it was.

> Many therefore of his disciples, when they had heard this, said, This is an hard saying; who can hear it? ... From that time many of his disciples went back, and walked no more with him. (John 6:60, 66)

The brethren knew their intention wasn't to express themselves as hard people but rather to drive home very valuable principles that they wholeheartedly understood. Normally, the leader at the upper room conveyed his cherished values in some short, straight-to-the-point statements, and sometimes he used a much more nuanced approach. Regardless, these could somehow painfully punch your ego.

I determined, *If others have stayed put, then I'll do so as well.*

We stayed persistent in spite of it all, giving our unflinching loyalty. I guess we passed the fidelity test then.

Many, rather than following the leader's heart, end up rejecting his or her words and ministry. Usually, statements way above our understanding can at the first impression sound very hard and controversial. Hard statements can easily offend. You cannot keep being offended by a leader and be genuinely loyal to him or her at the same time.

> When Jesus knew in himself that his disciples murmured at it, he said unto them, Doth this offend you? (John 6:61)

Offense at hard sayings can cause you to murmur in your heart against a leader while going about your daily business. Such a reaction is born out of false fidelity.

These revolting disciples murmured against Jesus just because they were offended; as a result, they failed the fidelity test and left.

*Action:* Your group should observe their members who are offended by the supposed harsh words uttered by a leader or a colleague. Each should watch his or her own verbal or nonverbal murmuring in response to offensive remarks.

## Step 13: The long and difficult journey

"If it's of God, it will stand the test of time," a speaker said. That was a regular refrain that enthusiastic upstarts like us would hear in the upper room. My naïveté then wouldn't permit me to ascertain the full import of this statement.

I always knew that the move of God birthed by the brethren would endure. Upon hindsight, it has. After several decades, the vision of global revival conceived in the upper room has impacted multitudes of groups and local churches.

I wouldn't kid you—the journey has been arduous. I'm sad to say that many couldn't make it this far. But true fidelity has soldiered on through toils and snares carrying the flame of the Spirit.

Both true and false fidelity speak the same language at the beginning; however, false fidelity wouldn't survive the test of time.

> After the king (Pharaoh) had finally let the people go, the LORD did not lead them through Philistine territory, though that was the shortest way. God had said, "If they are attacked, they may decide to return to Egypt." So he led them around through the desert and toward the Red Sea. The Israelites left Egypt, prepared for battle. (Exo. 13:17–18 CEV)

The reason God elongates the journey toward success isn't *always* because the vision doesn't proceed from Him, but rather to sift true fidelity from the false. He may do it to prevent a backsliding from the vision, the decision "to return."

False fidelity doesn't see the end of the journey and would therefore abandon the group, fellowship, ministry or local church midway should it become too long and difficult.

> And wherefore hath the Lord brought us unto this land, to fall by the sword, that our wives and our children should be a prey? were it not better for us to return into Egypt?

And they said one to another, Let us make a captain, and
let us return into Egypt. (Num. 14:3–4)

The Israelites, who left Egypt for Canaan, were tested by the long
journey and its challenges. This separated the falsely faithful from the
genuinely faithful. While the genuinely faithful were set for the full
journey, the falsely faithful said at some point "Let us make a captain,
and let us return into Egypt." But the faithful mentees did stay loyal to
their leader through the decades.

They would be in the wilderness, going around in circles with the
disloyal crowd, for forty years.

And your children shall wander in the wilderness forty
years, and bear your whoredoms, until your carcases be
wasted in the wilderness. After the number of the days in
which ye searched the land, even forty days, each day for
a year, shall ye bear your iniquities, even forty years, and
ye shall know my breach of promise. (Num. 14:33–34)

It's always taken a few faithful people dedicated to praying through,
sometimes for decades, till the fires of revival begin to blaze across a
particular geographical territory.

This was the case of the Moravian prayer chain, which produced the
first and second Great Awakening. Twenty-four men and twenty-four
women covenanted together for praying around the clock. Their fidelity to
the ministry of intercession was passed on and continued by others for an
entire century (Liardon 2008)! The test of time is a crucial test of fidelity.

*Action:* Your group must look out for members who are discouraged
by the lack of instant results. Such wouldn't tolerate the long journey
toward a move of God. They'll fail the test of time.


## Step 14: The open-door policy

Most leaders, I believe, are known occasionally to say things that are
difficult to swallow.

"Those of you from other fellowships can leave if you want to!" the man yelled. Silence pervaded the room; we could hear a pin drop.

He had the habit of speaking like this whenever agitated by something. The swift growth of his ministry had attracted some criticism from fellow Christian leaders and ministries. His angst stemmed from rumors that he was a "sheep thief"—of us followers—and we weren't few.

"I want my own converts," he said sternly. I made a cursory glance at the others behind me. I just needed to know that I wasn't heeding alone. None seemed moved by his brashness.

*That's strange*, I thought. *The harshness of this gentleman's spirit should be enough to set off a mass exodus,* taking a cue from Jesus's ministry.

> From that time many of his disciples went back, and walked no more with him. Then said Jesus unto the twelve, Will ye also go away? (John 6:66–67)

He was pushing an open-door policy by asking who else would go away. Elijah also used this policy on Elisha. It might seem harsh, yet it was a very relevant fidelity test.

> And Elijah said unto Elisha, Tarry here, I pray thee; for the LORD hath sent me to Bethel. And Elisha said unto him, As the LORD liveth, and as thy soul liveth, I will not leave thee. So they went down to Bethel. (2 Kings 2:2)

Elisha knew that by "tarry here," Elijah was asking him to stay while he left. Elisha refused. His fidelity resisted the suggestion.

Jesus opened the exit door for any of His disciples who felt they had had enough of His tough-cookie leadership style. Whenever the exit door is opened, the falsely loyal take advantage of the opportunity to leave. They wanted to leave anyway but couldn't because they were under the impression that they might be misunderstood or seen for who they truly were. Therefore they had gritted their teeth and tolerated the situation until the leader encouraged a departure.

> And she [Naomi] said, Behold, thy sister in law is *gone back unto her people, and unto her gods: return* thou after thy sister in law.
>
> And Ruth said, Intreat me not to leave thee, or to *return* from following after thee: for whither thou goest, I will go; and where thou lodgest, I will lodge: *thy people shall be my people, and thy God my God.* (Ruth 1:15–16, brackets and emphasis added)

Ruth was tested by Naomi's idea but didn't fall for it. Orpah did, however. Her colleague had found it most reasonable to return to her kinfolk, for after all, the old dame had no more sons to offer.

The two young ladies needed new opportunities, both to heal from their bereavement and to find love again. The future looked dismal for these three widows, and frankly, Naomi was not the best company at this stage (Ruth 1). She had become very mean and hurtful.

The open-door policy was actually welcome news, but with the eye of faith, Ruth saw through it all. It was a test. Her vision peered through the pitch-black tunnel to the flickering light at the end. She had conceived a mysterious hope in the midst of such hopelessness.

Ruth's fidelity is legendary, for she had committed her life to the God and people of a bitter, grieving old lady who had begged to be left alone. The situation justified a walkout.

She committed to Naomi's God when, from all indications, it looked like He had failed her abysmally. Honestly speaking, returning to the gods of her childhood looked quite appealing. The exit door had been flung open, but she passed the test nonetheless.

All fellowships, ministries, groups and local churches hungry for revival need men and women with Ruth's kind of fidelity to see them through some of the most difficult seasons. I can guarantee this, though: the forces of darkness and evil agents of Satan will do their utmost to erect roadblocks, stage opposition, and fight to the death if they can. But true, undefiled fidelity will win.

*Action:* At this stage, your group can call for the implementation of the open-door policy. All who doubt the vision should be asked to leave so that the truly faithful will stay.

## Step 15: The high price of the calling

There's a huge price to pay in birthing revivals. Whenever or wherever the onus does fall on us to be God's instrument of the time, there will be major sacrifices to make.

"We beg you in the name of God," came the desperate cry from two young men hungry to see revival but caught in a citywide curfew. The military were policing those days, and like ravenous wolves, they had been roaming the streets for recalcitrant ones. This night it was us. We had been arrested.

We had been seeking transportation out of town for a retreat, but two consecutive days of returning home disappointed had left us frustrated. The buses just weren't available because there were no tires. I guess a shambolic economy will do that to any nation. We had to stay in town, this time overnight.

We felt hidden, camouflaged, and safe behind a wooden kiosk. But I guess we weren't that hidden. Some dude snoring in there like a juggernaut gave us away.

Speaking in tongues didn't help much. With a Kalashnikov bearing down on us, the almighty God's name was the only resort we had that night. I shuddered, with sweat running down my pants. The military personnel crassly yelled at us and made us kneel within a runabout. They treated us like some waifish criminals.

Heaven did finally intervene, and we were let go. Stubborn chaps— you'd think we'd go home and forget it. But no. At the crack of dawn, we did get the transportation. We've got to sacrifice for the revival willy-nilly. Then, with the breeze rushing in my face where I sat in the speeding bus, we set out to unburden our souls in prayer and fasting.

Every vision or dream has a high price tag, and those who fulfill it should count the cost and pay it fully. The men and women who desire a move of God must fully understand the cost of the vision.

Many among the brethren felt the burden to leave all for the sake of the Spirit's will. As I've reiterated, the burden fell on my group at a time that school was still a priority. I was already in college. It was common then to hear young men and women claiming that they had sensed the call to pursue a full-time ministry. Were they wrong? No, they weren't.

> And David longed, and said, Oh that one would give me drink of the water of the well of Bethlehem, that is at the gate! And the three brake through the host of the Philistines, and drew water out of the well of Bethlehem, that was by the gate, and took it, and brought it to David: but David would not drink of it, but poured it out to the LORD, And said, My God forbid it me, that I should do this thing: shall I drink the blood of these men that have put their lives in jeopardy? for with the jeopardy of their lives they brought it. Therefore he would not drink it. These things did these three mightiest. (1 Chron. 11:17–19)

Now, I will let you in on some symbols. In the Old Testament, David was a type of Christ. Water, biblically, is a figure of the Holy Spirit's ministry, and David claimed he was very thirsty. The allegory was that Christ's body desperately needed spiritual ministry. That is your group, fellowship, ministry or local church. But David used the occasion to test the fidelity of his men.

Fidelity, be it in marriage, business or ministry, always comes at a great cost. Faithful service will cost anyone dearly. In a quest to determine the value of the fidelity of his men, David tested them. We know that David's "longing for water" was not a thirst but a deliberate test because he "would not drink it" at the end. Hence, the event is exclusively an allegory. It was purely symbolic.

It's important to test the fidelity of our colleagues from time to time so that we know where they stand with us. The test of David was to announce to these three captains his hugely expensive desire: "Oh that one would give me drink of the water of the well of Bethlehem, that is at the gate!" It was expensive because it could cost them their lives, for the three had to break through the host of the Philistines in the Valley of Rephaim and draw water out of the well of Bethlehem. This was a time of war, and the Philistines were the longtime enemies of the Jewish army.

Before the test at the cave of Adullam, these men were known as a part of thirty military captains, but afterward they became an elite group known as "the three mightiest."

Leaders must merit their position on your team by passing specific fidelity tests. *Never, ever promote an untested leader!*

The term *mightiest* indicates that the thirty captains of David's army were mighty men, but these three surpassed them all. Were they mighty by reason of their courage, heroism, or bravado? Way beyond these, it was their ability to "put their lives in jeopardy" to faithfully serve their leader.

By testing his men in this way, David was able to determine the value of their fidelity. Visions can be fulfilled only when the value of our fidelity is equal to the price quotes on their price tags. David knew that the road to achieving the vision of the kingdom of Israel would cost many lives, and he needed men who were ready to shed their blood.

I can see in all of this the prophetic picture of the apostles of Christ: the Church's mighty men. I can see how fidelity drove them into martyrdom, shedding their blood to see God's kingdom established in the earth.

Through my years of ministry, I've seen many walk into some local church right after Bible school training and expect it to be a walk in a park of roses. Then they'll be tested to the hilt with numerous challenges: hunger, thirst, danger, financial needs, pressures, insults, pain—and the list goes on and on.

After a while, they see the high price tag of the vision. Guess what? Their shadows never again darken the doors of the church. Others, being politer, begin to make all kinds of excuses. There are those, though, who candidly apologize for their simplistic thinking, saying, "I never thought it would be so difficult. I've got to rethink my decision." I believe this is why some ministers jump from church to church; they're seeking someone to butter their bread, but there is no free lunch anywhere. You have to pay the price on the price tag of some vision *somewhere* with a fidelity of huge value.

***Action:*** Your group must gather and resolve in unison to pay the price for ministering to one another and the Lord, and for birthing a revival in their generation.

## MILESTONE 6

# THE DISCERNMENT

## Step 1: Discern the spirit of Egypt

It was 1988, and we were still in the thick of the charismatic movement. I had some maturity under my belt then. Thanks to the brethren, certain things no longer fazed me like they had five years earlier. But I still had some learning to do, honestly. And that I did, for sure.

I had recently been hero-worshipping a hugely influential preacher; his forte was holiness. He spoke about it with such inerrancy that it reminded me of the psalmist's words, "My tongue is the pen of a ready writer" (Ps. 45:1). His words weren't glib like he was sweet-talking anyone. They sounded sincere, and they magnetized me to the TV.

Listening with tear-filled eyes, I mused emotionally, *This man speaks for me like nobody does.* I had soaked in his words and ministry like a dry sponge. A video of his crusade was playing then.

But this wonderful, enthralling ride was to come to a grinding halt one day. The experience left me confused and dizzy. A scandal broke about the preacher on the international news, but I wrote it off. I considered it the residue of a conspiracy gone bad. He'd had a rendezvous with a prostitute, the rumor went.

*His enemies are behind it all*, I anxiously reasoned.

"It can't be him. No, it can't," I soliloquized. I was firm in my stance till a *Newsweek* article about him was printed. The photo showed him behind a pulpit, where his Baton Rouge church watched him cry, "I've sinned."

"No, no, this can't be," I muttered all the way to prayer, and I bawled like I was losing my mind. It took me several years to get over his infidelity. To me, he was a larger-than-life communicator. I'd placed him on a pedestal.

I struggled from that day, viewing every holiness preacher with deep-seated mistrust and suspicion. It was a field day for the media, which did little to end my agony.

If I had ever received any education on spirituality from this Pentecostal preacher, that conduit had been truncated; whatever God intended came to an end. He could no longer feed my spirit. A breach had developed. I'll be less well-off in my spiritual growth without some divine intervention. I learned quickly that seeing the "nakedness" of a revered figure can have harmful consequences, as it did with the descendants of Ham (Gen. 9:24–25).

> And Noah began to be an husbandman, and he planted a vineyard: And he drank of the wine, and was drunken; and he was uncovered within his tent. And Ham, the father of Canaan, saw the nakedness of his father, and told his two brethren without. And Shem and Japheth took a garment, and laid it upon both their shoulders, and went backward, and covered the nakedness of their father; and their faces were backward, and they saw not their father's nakedness. (Gen. 9:20–23)

The spirit of Egypt could be genealogically traced to Ham, the father of the Egyptians. It is an attitude that saw and revealed the nakedness of one who was supposed to be revered (Gen. 9:20–22).

Ham, the patriarch of the Egyptians, had a spirit that mocked the nakedness of his pioneering father, Noah. He was the poster child of infidelity toward leadership. He had lost total respect for an authority figure and passed it on to his grandson, Mizraim, the father of the Egyptians.

How do we know this?

> And it shall come to pass, when Pharaoh shall call you, and shall say, what is your occupation? That ye shall say, Thy servants' trade hath been about cattle from our youth even until now, both we, and also our fathers: that ye may dwell in the land of Goshen; for every shepherd is an abomination unto the Egyptians. (Gen. 46:33–34)

The spirit of Egypt is the spirit or attitude that considers true shepherds and servants of God an abomination. In the Hebrew language, the word *pastor* is synonymous with the shepherd of a flock. In the New Testament, the word *pastor* refers to the spiritual shepherd or overseer of spiritual sheep, fellowship, ministry, group, or local church. The word *abomination* in the Hebrew means "disgusting." Biblically, the Old Testament shepherd is a shadow of the New Testament pastor. Egyptians had a condescending attitude toward the true shepherds, such that they despised them.

A group that despises its leader will have trouble holding together for a move of God. The responsibility for this lies with the spirit of Egypt.

This is contrary to the spirit of love that resided within Shem and Japheth and their descendants which "covers a multitude of sins." When Noah was caught in a compromising position, it took the love-driven fidelity of his sons Shem and Japheth to cover his nakedness.

The spirit of Egypt seeks these opportunities to terminate revivals through the mistrust of ministry leaders. I'm by no means implying that shepherds or leaders should deliberately fail their fidelity tests, hoping to be covered. That would be foolhardy.

The fidelity of the group is tested whenever its "man of God" is caught with his "pants down." Should the group not resist the efforts made by the spirit of Egypt to get its faithful ones to sing along with the secular voices, the revival will be upended. Without the discernment of the spirit of Egypt, *the more the "nakedness" of group leaders and shepherds become commonplace, the more we will see infidelity being demonstrated by followers of fellowships, ministries, local churches, and groups.*

This is how an array of revival movements had been destroyed. Discernment is critical in averting this.

Fidelity without faith is a fallacy. You would have to have some degree of faith or trust in a person in order to exercise fidelity toward them.

> Believe in the Lord your God, so shall ye be established; *believe* his prophets, so shall ye *prosper*. (2 Chron. 20:20, emphasis added)

Love-driven fidelity protects this trust while the inebriated leader recovers from his drunken stupor. When it's all said and done, the revival group, fellowship, ministry, or local church must prosper.

The spirit of Egypt is the spirit of infidelity. It cannot abide in faithfulness. Whenever faith in a leader breaks down, a spiritual breach develops in the relationship between the group or flock and him. Due to this breach, the flow of spiritual revelation and anointing from leaders, mentors, or spiritual fathers to their sons is impeded. In this way, the wealth of spiritual truths, wisdom, and unction contained within them goes untapped—then the next generations of leaders become spiritually impoverished and backslide. We'll deal with the healing of the breach at Step 3 of Milestone 8.

*Action:* Your group must review their attitudes towards their leader to discern the machinations of the spirit of Egypt among them.

## Step 2: Discern another spirit

A young man had come to live with us while still at school in a polytechnic institute. We had hit it off earlier when he had been living in a downtown apartment. There, he'd been eking out an existence with one stoutly built technician, who had an unpredictable unruliness to his personality. But thanks to his darling heart, he had been generous enough to share his living space with Johnny and his sister. However, some bloody fisticuffs between himself and his host unfortunately occurred, making his departure imperative.

Now, having him within close proximity, we could chat all we cared, sometimes late into the night. These occasions sometimes drew the ire of my wife.

"Honey, why stay up so late? Come over and get some sleep," she said.

Strangely, these were the occasions when we developed the vital synergy that had welded our loyalties. Frankly, he was a lot of work and fun at the same time. Needless to say, he matured some.

Then, out of the pure blue—I don't quite remember when—he spontaneously made a comment as we strolled. He divulged a truism, but what caught me off guard was how fundamentally it communicated the message I had been called to proclaim—the word of faith.

"You've caught it! You've caught it!" I asserted. It was a classic case showing that some things aren't taught but rather caught. He had keenly followed my spirit and had gotten this revelation intertwined with his inner sensibilities.

It therefore came as little surprise when he began exhibiting a similar anointing in ministry as I'd experienced, especially when he courageously led the birthing of a revival in an Islamic nation. As a matter of fact, he exceeded my expectations. Many spiritual sons come and go, but a very few do turn out to be true friends. He has attained that, as you'll later find out. Even in his boisterousness, his fidelity cannot be questioned. His heart is in the right place. In comparison to many, and I mean many, I've discerned in him "another spirit."

> But my servant Caleb, because he had another spirit with him, and hath followed me fully, him will I bring into the land whereinto he went; and his seed shall possess it. (Num. 14:24)

The journey of every person in this world is to walk into the place of his or her dream and destiny. Every new day, men and women band together to receive visions or dreams from God. They also make a collective determination to pursue them to their ultimate fulfillment.

The purpose of the new birth is to bring every person into the possession of his or her divine dream and destiny. Churches, fellowships, ministries and teams also have visions and dreams that require a birthing into the natural realm. They're the encapsulation of a corporate calling.

However, the evidence of history has proved that these dreams are not always realized. Many people are very good beginners but not good finishers. Not all who begin well finish well. This world is full of men and women who are frustrated about not being able to attain what they envisioned. Their visions were divine, but their attitudes let them down. They failed to maximize on their moments when opportunity came knocking at their doors.

Moses, a man of God, received a vision for the Hebrew slaves in Egypt about their prophetic destiny. It was to possess a land flowing with milk and honey. With one accord, they believed this glorious prophetic vision. According to Exodus 12:37, six hundred thousand men, alongside their women and children, began the journey from Egypt to become ultimate possessors of the corporate vision called "the land flowing with milk and honey." Every group can begin something. It is easy to begin anything, hence the majority of the human population is made up of great beginners, and so were the Hebrews. We're all wonderful at starting things.

> And were all baptized unto Moses in the cloud and in the sea; ... And did all drink the same spiritual drink: for they

drank of that spiritual Rock that followed them: and that Rock was Christ. (1 Corin. 10:2, 4)

The beginning was wonderful for they were all baptized in the Red Sea unto Moses. In other words, they all experienced salvation through water baptism. They were also baptized in the cloud of God's glory, which refers to baptism in the Holy Spirit, for the cloud represents *the Spirit of God on the move or the anointing* (1 Corin. 10:2). They were all Spirit-led people, for they followed the pillar of fire and cloud.

Ultimately, God led them to the edge of the promised land. At this point, Moses sent twelve spies to survey the land for its possession.

> And they brought up an evil report of the land which they had searched unto the children of Israel, saying, The land, through which we have gone to search it, is a land that eateth up the inhabitants thereof; and all the people that we saw in it are men of a great stature. (Num. 13:32)

The day of opportunity was upon them, yet ten of the spies melted the hearts of the Hebrew people with an evil report of unbelief and fear, and they failed to possess the land of milk and honey. Therefore, they could not follow God fully from vision to possession. This set them back forty more years, and finally, only two of those who originally began the journey from Egypt succeeded in possessing the land. The rest died in the wilderness.

What was it that caused this massive failure and setback? The journey from vision to possession is fraught with several challenges. It does not matter how saved or anointed you are, these challenges have the capability of stealing your destiny from you and blocking your dreams or visions. The first challenge was the sight of the giants.

> And they told him, and said, We came unto the land whither thou sentest us, and surely it floweth with milk and honey; and this is the fruit of it. Nevertheless the people be strong that dwell in the land, and the cities are walled, and very great: and moreover we saw the children of Anak there. (Num. 13:27–28)

First, many fail to walk in their prophetic destiny because they encounter giants on their promised land. The question they ask is, How can God give me such a glorious vision while I find myself facing such gigantic odds? These impossible odds are the giants that roam our promised land. Every dreamer of destiny will have to deal with "the children of Anak" that roam his or her promised land.

Second, many fail to walk in their prophetic word or their land flowing with milk and honey because they see themselves as grasshoppers.

> And they brought up an evil report of the land which they had searched unto the children of Israel, saying, The land, through which we have gone to search it, is a land that eateth up the inhabitants thereof; and all the people that we saw in it are men of a great stature. And there we saw the giants, the sons of Anak, which come of the giants: and we were in our own sight as grasshoppers, and so we were in their sight. (Num. 13:32–33)

Grasshoppers cannot face giants because they are inferior to them. It takes a giant to overpower and kill another giant. The grasshopper sees its vision or dreams in two ways—externally and internally. Externally, the grasshopper sees giants, and internally, the grasshopper sees a grasshopper. The outer vision of the grasshopper makes every problem seem superior to the prophetic word, while the inner vision makes its potential look inferior to the prophetic word. The Hebrew people were divided into two groups: the giants and grasshoppers. Christians today are also in the same two groups.

The giants said they were able to possess the land, and the grasshoppers said they were not able to. The giants had faith to conquer the children of Anak, but the grasshoppers feared them. The giants were ready to drink and eat of the milk, honey and grapes of the promised land, but the grasshoppers were not ready to enter, eat and drink.

The problem of the Hebrews did not occur at the middle of their journey; it began before it. They had their grasshopper vision due to the years of abuse, depravation and molestation. Slavery had made them see themselves as no good. Every vision comes from a specific spirit (Joel 2:28).

One problem with tragedy and oppression is how they plant the spirit of fear and inferiority into their victims. The problem God had with the Hebrews was how to deliver them from what years of slavery had done to them. The grasshopper spirit they had, made them inferior to the giants of the promised land.

> And Caleb stilled the people before Moses, and said, Let us go up at once, and possess it; for we are well able to overcome it. But the men that went up with him said, We be not able to go up against the people; for they are stronger than we. (Num. 13:30–31)

What made Joshua and Caleb different from the rest of the Hebrew population? The Bible says they had "another spirit." What spirit did they have? Whereas the spirit of ten of the twelve spies said, "We be not able to go up against the people; for they are stronger than we," the spirit of Caleb said, "Let us go up at once, and possess it; for we are well able to overcome it."

When Caleb spoke that day, it was the spirit in him that did the speaking.

> We having the same spirit of faith, according as it is written, I believed, and therefore have I spoken; we also believe, and therefore speak. (2 Corin. 4:13)

They had acquired the spirit of a giant—the spirit of faith, through baptism in the Holy Spirit and believing the prophetic word

> "All were baptized into Moses in the cloud and in the sea, all ate the same spiritual food, and all drank the same spiritual drink" (1 Corin. 10: 2-4).

When the other ten spies spoke, it was the spirit in them that did the speaking. The spirit said, "We be not able to go up against the people; for they are stronger than we."

Jesus put it this way:

> O generation of vipers, how can ye, being evil, speak good
> things? for out of the abundance of the heart the mouth
> speaketh. (Matt. 12:34)

An evil spirit was speaking through these ten spies to the children of
Israel, and its negative effect was instantaneous.

> And all the congregation lifted up their voice, and cried;
> and the people wept that night. (Num. 14:1)

Joshua and Caleb identified this evil spirit and said,

> If the Lord delight in us, then he will bring us into this
> land, and give it us; a land which floweth with milk and
> honey. Only rebel not ye against the Lord, neither fear
> ye the people of the land; for they are bread for us: their
> defence is departed from them, and the Lord is with us:
> fear them not. (Num. 14:8–9)

The evil spirit speaking through the ten other spies was the spirit of
fear. Paul, in 2 Timothy 1:7, confirms that fear is an evil spirit.

The Spirit of God and His word delivered Caleb from the spirit of a
grasshopper—the spirit of fear. Now let us see the evil effect of the spirit
of fear on their journey.

> And all the children of Israel murmured against Moses
> and against Aaron: and the whole congregation said
> unto them, Would God that we had died in the land of
> Egypt! or would God we had died in this wilderness! And
> wherefore hath the Lord brought us unto this land, to fall
> by the sword, that our wives and our children should be a
> prey? were it not better for us to return into Egypt? And
> they said one to another, Let us make a captain, and let
> us return into Egypt. (Num. 14:2–4)

At this point, the evil spirit of fear had instigated an abortion of Moses's vision, and by saying "Let us make a captain," they were no longer faithful to their leader. They were asking for a new leader or captain.

> But my servant Caleb, because he had another spirit with
> him, and hath followed me fully, him will I bring into the
> land. (Num. 14:24)

A spirit like Caleb's is one that makes you follow God and pursue your divine dreams fully, not partially. To possess your promised land, you need to possess "another spirit."

You need to be delivered from the spirit of fear and possess the spirit of faith. You need to be delivered from the spirit of defeat and possess the spirit of dominion. God had taken the Hebrews out of Egypt but the effects of the oppression of Egypt remained.

The spirit of Egypt orchestrated an oppressive system that injected into these Hebrews the evil spirit of fear. When the sight of the giants stirred the spirit of fear in them, they immediately gravitated toward Egypt. Why? This is because the spirit of fear is associated with the spirit of Egypt. This is really strange, you might say, considering the centuries of oppression they suffered under the Egyptians. But have you ever wondered how people who were once delivered from alcohol and drugs find their way back to these instruments of bondage? It is for very much the same reason. The spirit of fear makes retreating to familiar, oppressive territory seem easier than advancing into an unknown future of liberty. The spirit of fear is skilled at making a great future look bad and an oppressive past look good.

You need another spirit to remain loyal, finish whatever vision or dream you began and realize your destiny. To overcome the giants sitting on your destiny and the grasshoppers living in your mind, you need to be delivered from the spirit of fear and infidelity and possess the spirit of a giant, the spirit of faith and the spirit of dominion.

In helping pioneer certain ministries, I found out that much cannot be achieved by men and women who haven't known deliverance from the spirit of fear, for somewhere down the line they will say words that will cause the hearts of their colleagues to weaken.

> Nevertheless my brethren that went up with me made the
> heart of the people melt: but I wholly followed the Lord
> my God. (Joshua 14:8)

The spirit of fear does not foster group fidelity; neither does the spirit of faith tolerate infidelity. This is why the same man who stilled the voice of fear in the Hebrew camp became the one who "wholly followed the Lord." He *followed* till their corporate vision was accomplished.

*Action:* Your group must clearly identify those they have discerned as permanently hooked to its vision. These individuals must be openly applauded.

## Step 3: Discern the porter

"No, not four months but three," said Nelson. He and I had been debating on how long it took for the revival group to grow from a small bunch of dedicated folk to a couple of hundred.

The fidelity of team members with a heart for evangelism had done the remarkable. They had met every single day, reaching out to the community and sharing a living Christ.

The growth of a revival group depends much on the people they impact daily with a revelation of Jesus. And this demands an unflinching fidelity to soul winning.

> And daily in the temple, and in every house, they ceased
> not to teach and preach Jesus Christ. (Acts 5:42)

My experience has shown that whenever a group, fellowship, ministry, worship band or local church becomes a channel for a move of God to reach the hurting world, its revival endures. God wouldn't trust a selfish fraternity with His glory, for He loves the unsaved world (John 3:16).

> Verily, verily, I say unto you, He that entereth not by the
> door into the sheepfold, but climbeth up some other way,
> the same is a thief and a robber. But he that entereth in by
> the door is the shepherd of the sheep. To him the porter

> openeth; and the sheep hear his voice: and he calleth his
> own sheep by name, and leadeth them out. And when he
> putteth forth his own sheep, he goeth before them, and
> the sheep follow him: for they know his voice ... I am the
> door: by me if any man enter in, he shall be saved, and
> shall go in and out, and find pasture. (John 10:1–4, 9)

In this passage, Jesus refers to Himself as both the shepherd and the door. As the shepherd, He calls His own sheep by name and leads them out. There are two specific things associated with the shepherd—Jesus, He calls and leads the sheep. Thus, we have the call of the Lord and the leadership of the Lord. For your information, the call of the Lord is not only associated with the five-fold minister or leader—that is, the apostle, prophet, evangelist, pastor, and teacher. The call of the Lord is rather associated with every sheep in the fold. For true fidelity to be established in the local church or the sheepfold, it is of utmost importance that every sheep knows that he or she has been called of the Lord. All sheep in the fold have been called by the Lord to be led by Him.

To be led by the Lord, the shepherd (Ps. 23:1), an individual must first enter the sheepfold and become one of His sheep. The entrance is by the door of the sheepfold. Through John 10:9, we know the Lord is the door of the sheepfold. The Lord is the only one who gives a person access to membership in the fold. He said, "I am the way, the truth, and the life: no man cometh unto the Father, but by me" (John 14:6).

Who then is the porter or the doorkeeper of the sheepfold? According to John 10:9, "the door" is the way to salvation. Since the Lord is "the door" or "the way," He is also our Savior. Jesus, or Yeshua, is His name, and it means *the Lord is Salvation*. The porter or the doorkeeper is the one who opens the door for "any man" to "enter in" to be saved. The porter is a leader who leads people to salvation. And his job is specific: He opens the door of salvation—Jesus Christ our Savior—to "any man."

*The porter is the evangelist*. The evangelistic minister is the soul winner of the group, an exemplary and followable leader. He reveals Jesus continually to the unsaved. This is the primary purpose of every move of God. There is no need to seek God for heaven's fire to fall if we intend to keep it from the world.

Without the porter's leadership, no person becomes a trustworthy member of a revival group. We all at some point have to follow the leadership of the porter to become loyal participants of the fold; fellowship, ministry or local church. His fidelity is a key to the group's survival. Each fellowship, ministry or local church hungry for a move of God needs to discern the fidelity of the porter among them.

*Action:* Your group should take an inventory of the evangelists they have discerned among them. The continuous fruit of the porter's labor should be a key to their discernment.

## Step 4: Discern the good shepherd

"Can I be of any assistance to you?" the man said with much composure. He had come to my aid upon hearing the tragic news; a family member had suddenly passed. It was a tumultuous moment, and the gnawing pain of grief was, as it were, eating up my bowels. Some malevolent forces had struck; their salvo had hit my home.

I had fortuitously been brought into a spiritual grazing pasture among the brethren. Metaphorically, its grass was a lush green, and I loved it. My seeking soul seemed to have found a resting place. But in that sheepfold, I had run into diverse shades of leaders. Ultimately, I had been led to abide under the ambit of one shepherding minister, his shepherding sacrifices, and his care. This was needful, for the apostolic father of our beloved movement had moved on to greener pastures.

It had been decades since we parted ways. Now there he sat, his presence unsolicited for and spontaneous. He was ready to hold my hand through "the valley of the shadow of death." What can I say? I had shepherded others, and now I was in need of it—a good bit of it. Discerning it wasn't difficult; he was right there before me. His fidelity had held till this day.

> I am the good shepherd: the good shepherd giveth his life
> for the sheep ... I am the good shepherd, and know my
> sheep, and am known of mine ... and I lay down my life
> for the sheep. (John 10:11, 14–15)

Having entered "the door" into the sheepfold through the ministry of the doorkeeper, a person becomes saved and then joins the membership of the sheepfold. The leadership of the evangelist, as strategic as it might seem, only introduces people to the Savior Jesus Christ. At this point, Jesus Christ becomes their good shepherd, for He said, "I am the good shepherd." In the local sheepfold, though, we're made subject to another leadership, that of the pastor, or His under-shepherd.

> The elders which are among you I exhort, who am also an
> elder, and a witness of the sufferings of Christ, and also a
> partaker of the glory that shall be revealed: Feed the flock
> of God which is among you, taking the oversight thereof,
> not by constraint, but willingly; not for filthy lucre, but of
> a ready mind; Neither as being lords over God's heritage,
> but being ensamples to the flock. (1 Peter 5:1–3)

In these verses, the apostle Peter writes to the elders, admonishing them about their role in the local church, fellowship, ministry, group or fold. He tells them to "feed the flock of God." These elders are spiritually mature men or women who offer leadership to the sheep in the fold by "being examples." As men and women who "feed the flock of God," they're actually shepherds. The apostle Peter is here instructing them to be good shepherds of the flock. He then adds, "And when the chief Shepherd shall appear, ye shall receive a crown of glory that fadeth not away" (1 Peter 5:4).

Being a good shepherd is necessary because, there is an eternal reward for being the kind of exemplary leader that feeds the flock of God. Peter refers to the Lord as the chief Shepherd who rewards. These shepherds of the local church, fellowship, ministry or fold of sheep only become good because they demonstrate the traits of the chief Shepherd of the universal sheepfold, for He said, "I am the good shepherd."

The good shepherd should necessarily have the heart of the chief Shepherd—Jesus Christ. The heart of Jesus is a good heart, for He calls Himself the good shepherd. In other words, the good shepherd is Christlike in all that he or she does. The good shepherd should have the good heart of a good leader or local church pastor. This good heart causes the leader to lay his or her life down for the sheep. The good shepherd feeds the sheep with the life of God, and he or she does this through imparting God's revealed word.

> And I will give you pastors according to mine heart, which shall feed you with knowledge and understanding. (Jer. 3:15)

Good shepherds feed the sheep with knowledge and understanding. They lay their lives down for their flock, and thus are always the first to arrive and the last to leave "the pasture." They are the first to be there to ensure that there are no wolves, bears or lions lurking in the woods. The pasture is the feeding area of the flock, the place where they chew on knowledge and understanding—their doctrine. Should any devourers be present, the good shepherd will take on the attitude of David, lay his or her life down, and fight them off. I have on many occasions seen good shepherds take on the attitude of David and fight off with vehemence the destructive machinations of the wolves, lions and bears that appear on the horizon of the pasture.

Good shepherds are also the last to leave to ensure that none of the sheep have followed the stranger or gone astray or missing as they grazed the pasture. They check out the messages shared during the house fellowship meetings in their neighborhood. Like David, they stay, weep, and cry with the sheep in their desperate moments.

> He chose David also his servant, and took him from the sheepfolds: From following the ewes great with young ... (Ps. 78:70–71)

In a nutshell, all good shepherds are marked by their unflinching fidelity to the flock of God.

Through the years, I have come to the definite conclusion that the true desire of all sincere sheep is to follow the ministry of a good shepherd. For the most part, they seek till they find these good shepherds. They do so by being led by the chief Shepherd to lie down in the green pasture of a specific fellowship, ministry, group or local church, *becoming faithful till the end.*

He maketh me to lie down in green pastures: he leadeth
me beside the still waters. He restoreth my soul: he leadeth
me in the paths of righteousness for his name's sake. (Ps.
23:2–3)

By following the righteous guidance of the chief Shepherd, Jesus
Christ, each sheep will discern his or her good shepherd and join his or
her appointed sheepfold.

*Action:* The people within your group must discern the good heart
of their shepherd and settle in their sheepfold with unflinching fidelity.
Should any discern otherwise, it would be prudent to encourage him or
her to move on to another group of his or her own choice.

## Step 5: Discern the stranger

I sat stunned as Mr. A narrated his dream, a strange dream. "I can tell
you this—this is a direct sign of witchcraft," he said pensively.

He had divorced his wife for another lady who had recently joined the
assembly—a novice. "And you know what? One of the proofs I have is she
was trying to hide some stuff from me in the wardrobe," he said.

"But that's not enough evidence of witchcraft?" I probed calmly.

He quickly quoted a string of Bible verses to support his queer choices.

Earlier, I had warned this gentleman of an impending assault on his
marriage. I had told him that this setup was demonically orchestrated. It
had been many months at this point since the Holy Spirit revealed in a
dream this nefarious plot against his home. They were a nice couple with
well-raised kids. But it had all tragically played out, and I felt sad that he
hadn't heeded the warning of the dream.

The strange part of this saga was that he had received counsel from
some pastors, but it had only emboldened him. He felt justified in his
actions. It runs contrary to sound doctrine and basic sense.

These pastors are strange shepherds with strange views. They cannot
be good shepherds. They are un-followable leaders.

For the time will come when they will not endure sound
doctrine; but after their own lusts shall they heap to

themselves teachers, having itching ears; And they shall turn away their ears from the truth, and shall be turned unto fables. (2 Tim. 4:3–4)

Through my years of pastoral ministry, I have found out that most believers cannot tell the voice of the devil from the voice of the Lord. Some of the flock have followed strange shepherds who have led them to make strange choices, sometimes choices of infidelity that have produced broken marriages, homes, relationships, fellowships and churches.

I was prompt this day, arriving at the usual 2:00 p.m. to pick up my kids from the community school. Across the yard, my eyes located a lady who had just strolled her way to the foyer. Efficiently, my memory served me well, and immediately—I realized, I knew her from way back. She was a young lady who had been saved in an earlier revival and turned out to be the very spiritual type.

"Hi! How are you doing?" I asked, and she turned. Her eyes lit up when she saw me, and she ambled in my direction. She had actually left her home city to be with her husband in the port city, where I had been stationed for a while shepherding a new revival group.

"Hi!" she said affectionately. She wore a sleeveless white blouse over slacks of the same color; perhaps this was what drew the attention of my impatiently darting eyes. I had been waiting for the kids to exit their classrooms.

"How's your husband?" I asked.

I had met her with her family years back. Her kids were quite small then, which informed me that, as a couple, they had just begun raising a family.

"My husband?" she replied. "We're no longer together."

"Why? What happened?" I prodded.

"He's not my real husband," she said.

I felt stung by her words, yet my interest was stirred. "Who's your real husband then?"

"Oh, he's in another country."

"Which country, if I may ask?"

"Do you have the time? It's a long story," she replied, gazing into my eyes with a seeming dilemma, perhaps wondering whether to trust me or not.

She chose to continue. "Well, I met him in the spirit world while engaging in spiritual warfare. Through this, my spirit relocated to another country," she told me.

I felt bizarrely surprised, wondering what might have happened since we last met.

"Have you met him face to face before?" I inquired.

"No, not at all," she replied. "But we will someday."

The sudden sound of kids invading the foyer grabbed our attention.

"We'll have to continue this conversation some time," I said.

"Yes, yes," she responded, grabbing her daughter, who had clutched at her cotton pants. I turned with my mind completely blown, like I had just seen a paranormal thriller.

At the time of this conversation, contrary to the significant spiritual counseling she had received, she divorced her husband to be with this imaginary one. She claimed that she was still a believer, but it was obvious that she had been following strange voices—voices that had ruined her marriage and her home. Many have become heretics simply by following strange voices, and then they wrest or twist the scriptures to fit their mental delusions.

> And when he putteth forth his own sheep, he goeth before them, and the sheep follow him: for they know his voice. And a stranger will they not follow, but will flee from him: for they know not the voice of strangers. (John 10:4–5)

Here, the Lord speaks about His sheep saying, "And a stranger will they not follow, but will flee from him: for they know not the voice of strangers." The *stranger* here refers to someone other than the good shepherd, someone with an attitude that is totally foreign to what the sheep are used to. What does the stranger have that causes the sheep to shun his leadership? The stranger has a strange voice, a voice unlike the voice of the good shepherd. Jesus referred to Himself as the good shepherd. Hence, the voice of the stranger can be correctly described as one that speaks contrary to the voice of the Lord. The voice of the Lord is in perfect agreement with His word. In John 1:14, Jesus is the word of God that became flesh. It is therefore reasonable to say that the voice of the good shepherd is the voice of the word of the Lord. On the other hand, the voice of the stranger is a voice that speaks contrary to the word of the Lord. Any voice that speaks in opposition to the word of the Lord is a strange voice.

In Titus 3:10, Paul admonishes, "A man that is an heretick after the first and second admonition reject."

The word *heresy* is translated from the Greek word *hairetikos*, which means "one who stirs up division or creates and fosters factions." The strange shepherd's voice creates heresy. It creates a faction who will "heap to themselves" seductive teachers, a totally different group from the true sheep. The true sheep "will flee from him," the stranger.

Now, we know from the narrative that certain sheep have followed heresies or strange voices. A true shepherd will lead the true sheep in his footsteps toward true fidelity, and a strange shepherd will lead the false sheep in his footsteps toward false fidelity. False fidelity creates factions within revival groups.

The brethren also had brief interactions with strange voices. It's hard to determine whether this served primarily as the catalyst for the ultimate fragmentation of that revival ministry.

"It's the missing link," said one brother.

The debate about the seeming decline of discipleship had escalated. But that which began as a simple discussion had snowballed into full-fledged factionalism. Heresy was in the making.

A suburban fellowship of the group had soon begun to entertain revelations and visions that were averse to those seen by the brethren at Caprice. As the saying goes, "there's no smoke without fire." You cannot have heresy without the activity of a heretic. Somehow, the dissent was resolved. I'll leave it at that.

> Now the Spirit speaketh expressly, that in the latter times
> some shall depart from the faith, giving heed to seducing
> spirits, and doctrines of devils. (1 Tim. 4:1)

Those who depart from the faith and give heed to the strange voices of strangers have yielded unconsciously to seducing spirits: these are false sheep. With the true sheep, "a stranger will they not follow, but will flee from him."

You would often hear about major revival movements being fragmented and their participants scattering due to heretical teaching. It's very easy for folks given to "deep spirituality" to also go on to the "deep end." They had proffered some "deep" teaching that wasn't really deep; they were strange voices leading men into seduction. It's a fact that you can't substitute sound doctrine with paranormal experiences. It will open the door to seducing spirits.

The stranger's voice will produce false fidelity to fellowships, ministries, groups and local churches, for sooner or later these false sheep will depart from the faith. They would rather follow the strange voice than their shepherd's. It will sadly take the production of bad results to figure out the falsehood. On many occasions, this comes a little too late for the victims.

The members of the Peoples Temple of the Disciples of Christ, led by Jim Jones, found this out in the wooded hinterland of Guyana. Lured into mass suicide as the pathway to heaven, hundreds died needlessly. They were a group that, in its origins, dissented from the Somerset Methodist Church (Jim Jones 2016). *Following what you need to flee from will surely lead you into seduction and destruction.* "And a stranger will they not follow, but will flee from him: for they know not the voice of strangers."

*Action:* Your group members must carefully judge their teaching and prophecies regardless of how anointed their meetings are. This is to help discern the presence of strangers among them.

## Step 6: Discern the hireling

The ministry was in dire need of a keyboardist, and a good friend of mine had suggested one. He felt he knew this bloke quite well, so with glowing words he lauded his skillfulness. In addition, some keyboard tuition was to be offered for a fee.

His work began in earnest, and I'll say, it went quite well—until his tendency for tardiness began to show. I had overly relied on the opinion of a trusted lieutenant. This can sometimes prove very precarious to the flock we oversee.

I withheld a few payments for some absenteeism, because I felt he was in breach of his contract. He vehemently disagreed. In his view, payment was mandatory in spite of the reneged duties.

*Isn't he amazing?* I thought.

However, his murmuring wouldn't have come to my attention save for the habitual complaining on his part. How did I know? The person who recommended him alerted me. I felt stabbed in the back that day. The church terminated the agreement and paid him the difference "owed" him. And that was it.

This chap obviously was in it for the money and nothing else. That bothered me greatly. We had discerned wrongly.

He cared little for the flock "because he is an hireling, and careth not for the sheep" (John 10:13).

> But he that is an hireling, and not the shepherd, whose own the sheep are not, seeth the wolf coming, and leaveth the sheep, and fleeth: and the wolf catcheth them, and scattereth the sheep. The hireling fleeth, because he is an hireling, and careth not for the sheep. (John 10:12–13)

A hireling is somebody who works *only* for money, a wage or salaried worker. This is the spirit of a mercenary who merchandises his or her gifting for a fee. The hireling's "god" is his or her belly. In our case, the honorarium mattered more than his passion for nourishing the flock. In a heartbeat, hirelings will take advantage of the sheepfolds: fellowships, ministries and local churches in desperate need of gifted sheep or shepherds.

In the apostle Jude's day, there was a group who practiced the doctrine of Balaam, and some of their activities influenced the church of Pergamos (Rev. 2:2, 8).

> Woe unto them! for they have gone in the way of Cain, and ran greedily after the error of Balaam for reward, and perished in the gainsaying of Core. (Jude 1:11)

The apostle Peter also describes this group.

> Having eyes full of adultery, and that cannot cease from sin; beguiling unstable souls: an heart they have exercised with covetous practices; cursed children: Which have forsaken the right way, and are gone astray, following the way of Balaam the son of Bosor, who loved the wages of unrighteousness. (2 Peter 2:14–15)

Who was Balaam? He was a prophet who preceded Christ but gave several authentic prophecies with a financial motive because he "loved the wages of unrighteousness." Balaam's doctrine was built on the character of a false prophet. It is the teaching that justifies the lifestyle of a hireling.

The name *Balaam* in the Hebrew language means "a devouring glutton." He was also called the son of Bosor or Beor, which some translators believe is a derivative of the word *Basar,* meaning flesh. As a result, the term *son of Bosor* is translated by some as "the son of carnality." A hireling acts the way he or she does because he or she is covetous, a devouring glutton, the product of a carnal upbringing.

Although hirelings are everywhere within fellowships, ministries, local churches and groups, they particularly abound within the church's music industry. Most of them fail the money and the motive tests in fidelity. They don't have any sense of fidelity toward the flock.

Even within the headship ministries of the apostle, prophet, evangelist, pastor, and teacher, "the way of Balaam" isn't avoidable. Although "the scripture saith, Thou shalt not muzzle the ox that treadeth out the corn. And, the labourer is worthy of his reward" (1 Tim. 5:18), it's the recipient of ministry who is being addressed and not the minister—"the ox" or "the labourer."

The minister's motive for ministry must be based purely on the grounds of love for the hurting. He or she would do well to leave the benefactors to obey the scriptures by themselves.

And Jesus went throughout all the cities and villages, teaching in their synagogues and proclaiming the gospel of the kingdom and healing every disease and every affliction. When he saw the crowds, he had compassion for them, because they were harassed and helpless, like sheep without a shepherd (Matt. 9:35–36).

When the Lord saw the multitude, He didn't see a large honorarium at the end, but rather a people that "were harassed and helpless, like sheep without a shepherd."

This was the motive that drove Him to go "throughout all the cities and villages, teaching in their synagogues and proclaiming the gospel of the kingdom and healing every disease and every affliction."

But who is it that would financially bless the compassionate minister? It is not the audience but the Lord. For "the blessing of the Lord makes rich" (Prov. 10:22).

The good shepherd does none of these; rather he or she lays his or her life down as a sacrifice for the flock. Good shepherds are the members of the sheepfold who are the true disciples of the chief Shepherd—Jesus Christ; through a genuine relationship, they have imbibed the good spirit of the Lord. This is a faithful spirit. Epaphras is one such sterling example.

> Epaphras, who is one of you, a servant of Christ, saluteth you, always labouring fervently for you in prayers that ye may stand perfect and complete in all the will of God. For I bear him record, that he hath a great zeal for you, and them that are in Laodicea, and them in Hierapolis. (Col. 4:12–13)

He labored fervently so that the members of the local church would do well, not so they would buy him the latest model of a car. His fidelity was drawn from a pure motive. At the end of our earthly ministry, our testimony should reflect that of the apostle Paul, Epaphras's mentor.

> I have coveted no man's silver, or gold, or apparel. (Acts 20:33)

> But he that is an hireling, and not the shepherd, whose own the sheep are not, seeth the wolf coming, and leaveth the sheep, and fleeth: and the wolf catcheth them, and scattereth the sheep. (John 10:12–13)

Since the hireling cares only for financial rewards and not the sheep, should the flock be threatened by any challenge, he is likely to hit the road unless offered a pay raise. The hireling demonstrates a false kind of fidelity that does not survive a pay cut or the absence of finances. In the absence of cash, they start out murmuring and complaining and then disappear at the tail end of their impatience.

I had visited a church planted by a friend of mine. They'd been experiencing some difficulties and had had to worship in a classroom. Nevertheless, a spiritual revival had accompanied their pioneering effort. I preached for him on one occasion and had a great time.

"I'm being affected. I'm touched!" hollered one gentleman seated right in front of me. These interjections went on throughout my message. I assumed he was the most blessed that night. I asked the minister after the service, "Who's that excited fellow who's been hollering?"

"He's a new pastor we just employed," he said.

"Oh, great," I said.

A while passed, and I preached for the church again. No hollering occurred, and the shouter wasn't visible. After the service, I asked, "Where's my good friend, the young hollering pastor?"

"He left the church," the minister said.

"Oh? What happened?" I asked.

"He told us his salary wasn't enough."

I was frankly surprised. Had all the hollering been a fluke? It goes without saying that the yeller had failed the money test. He was a hireling. Revival groups should peer through all the hypocrisy and discern the hirelings among them.

*Action:* Your group must look out for those who fail the money test. These members will end up as hirelings. They should be discouraged and the selfless members encouraged.

## Step 7: Discern the thief

Standing within the shadows of a dimly lit front yard; this gentleman and I had been trying to develop some mutual understanding. The wooden gate hid our silhouetted frames.

"I—I'm a wizard," he stammered. I felt my visage change, and I drew a deep breath. I gazed silently into his handsome face overshadowed by the darkened façade.

I had known him at home for a while. He was an articulate fellow who had enjoyed a prestigious education. Our paths had crossed again in college, where he had exhibited some queer attitudes.

*Some exorcism for his tortured soul wouldn't hurt, would it?*

Now, for some bizarre reason, he had found the effrontery to make a confession.

*Why now?* I nervously thought.

"I'm a unicorn and have a horn. Just by bowing before a pregnant woman, I can terminate her pregnancy," he said.

The surreal nature of the confession was enhanced by how long he had participated in our revival meetings. Being recently under the weather, I had just fought my way through to recovery since the end of my final semester. It had been six months.

"I'm part of a coven, and I've been assigned to kill you. But I failed; now I'm burning all over. I felt if I could confess my diabolic operations, it might stop," he said. I was overwhelmed with bemusement.

"Look, I'm here to counsel a couple who have been waiting. Why not come over to my home tomorrow?" I hastily interjected.

"Oh—oh, okay," he muttered. And so we went our separate ways till the next day, when he fed me an earful of his evil machinations.

Homes, businesses, pregnancies, lives, and ministries—his witchcraft power had destroyed them all. And his numerous victims had been robbed of peace, happiness, prosperity—the list goes on and on. The majority of them were fellow worshippers of charismatic renewal centers.

*But I thought this guy was a believer?* My mind whirled.

That morning, in the living room, my worldview underwent a radical overhaul.

> Verily, verily, I say unto you, He that entereth not by the
> door into the sheepfold, but climbeth up some other way,
> the same is a thief and a robber ... The thief cometh not,
> but for to steal, and to kill, and to destroy: I am come that

they might have life, and that they might have it more abundantly. (John 10:1, 10)

The Greek word used in these passages for *thief* means "impostor," "bandit," "highway man," "insurrectionist," and "plunderer."

I have heard many Pentecostal ministers on multiple occasions interpret the thief in John 10:10 as being Satan. However, upon a careful examination of the text, I have been led to a different conclusion. This text has nothing more to do with Satan than a monkey has to do with being an IT expert. You'll have to view the preceding chapter to properly understand the context. In verse 40 of John 9, Jesus is talking to the Pharisees about spiritual blindness. When He said in John 10:1, "Verily, verily, I say unto you," He was referring to the same group of people, the Pharisees. The context doesn't change just because a new chapter begins. Jesus was answering a question that the Pharisees posed in John 9, *in* John 10. According to John 10:1, the thief or a robber refers to those who have made an illegal entry into the membership of the sheepfold. The legal entry into the sheepfold is by the door. Without entering through the door, a person becomes a thief or a robber. Now, why did He tell the Pharisees about an illegal entry into the sheepfold?

Then said Jesus unto them [the Pharisees] again, Verily, verily, I say unto you, I am the door of the sheep. (John 10:7, brackets added)

This is because the Pharisees sought to avoid Jesus in order to join the sheepfold of God the Father. But "Jesus saith ..., I am the way, the truth, and the life: no man cometh unto the Father, but by me" (John 14:6). Jesus said He was the way and door to God the Father, but the Pharisees thought He could be ignored on their way to His Father. This He said, made them thieves and robbers for they didn't use the approved entrance into the sheepfold.

Yes, the Pharisees were children of the Devil, for He said to them in John 8:44, "Ye are of your father the devil, and the lusts of your father ye will do. He was a murderer from the beginning."

But Satan is not a Pharisee, is he? However, I would agree that he did use the Pharisees mightily.

The thief or robber enters the sheepfold—the local church, fellowship, ministry, or group, which in the days of Jesus's ministry was the synagogue—but not through an encounter with the door or way, which is Jesus Christ. Why would anyone go through the door?

> I am the door: by me if any man enter in, he shall be saved,
> and shall go in and out, and find pasture. (John 10:9)

The purpose for entering through the door is to be saved and to become a viable member of the sheepfold—the local church or synagogue. For the thief to avoid going through the door, he or she really avoids an encounter with Jesus and his or her personal salvation. The thief or robber isn't saved and doesn't know Jesus, but operates very much within the sheepfold—the synagogue. But why does the thief avoid going through the door? To get saved? No.

> The thief cometh not, but for to steal, and to kill, and to
> destroy. (John 10:10)

Thieves have a diabolical agenda "to steal, and to kill, and to destroy," said Jesus. They're in the local church or synagogue not to get people saved but to fulfill the lusts of their father—Satan. Jesus said the lust of Satan was to murder (John 8:44).

What the Pharisees did in the synagogue during Jesus's day was equal to robbery, murder, and destruction. They used their diabolical doctrine—the pharisaic leaven—to rob the Jews of their faith in Jesus as their Messiah, and when they made converts, they injected them with their venom of spiritual death.

> Woe unto you, scribes and Pharisees, hypocrites! for ye
> compass sea and land to make one proselyte, and when
> he is made, ye make him twofold more the child of hell
> than yourselves. (Matt. 23:15)

Jesus was saying that the Pharisees weren't saved and that when they had made a proselyte or convert, he or she became worse than themselves—"the child of hell." The Pharisees were murderers because they set unsuspecting people on their way to eternal damnation. Moreover, should those with true faith oppose their doctrine, they would be physically murdered. The apostle Paul, as you know, was once a Pharisee, and this was his confession: "Men and brethren, I am a Pharisee, the son of a Pharisee" (Acts 23:6).

> For you have heard of my former life in Judaism, how I persecuted the church of God violently and tried to destroy it. (Gal. 1:13 ESV)

It was Paul, then Saul, who instigated the murder of Stephen, the first martyr of the church. And they "cast him [Stephen] out of the city, and stoned him: and the witnesses laid down their clothes at a young man's feet, whose name was Saul" (Acts 7:58, brackets added).

Yes, the Pharisees were robbers and murderers and were very destructive. They did this in such a hypocritical way that it was even hard for some discerning minds to see (Matt. 23:15).

Hypocrisy is a symptom of false fidelity. The question though is, are there these kinds of thieves or robbers in the church today? Surely there are, for the apostle Jude made this observation.

> For there are certain men crept in unawares, who were before of old ordained to this condemnation, ungodly men, turning the grace of our God into lasciviousness, and denying the only Lord God, and our Lord Jesus Christ. (Jude 1:4)

Notice that Jude said that these men deny "the only Lord God, and our Lord Jesus Christ." They avoided "the door"—Jesus Christ. They are "ungodly men" and therefore have never been saved from sin. Now look at how they entered in; they "crept in unawares." The picture you get is that of a thief who stealthily enters a given space. The Amplified Bible puts it this way: "For certain men have crept in stealthily [gaining entrance secretly by a side door]."

So how did certain evangelical churches end up having occultists serving in the upper echelons of their ministry? They did so by "gaining entrance secretly by a side door." I remember some evangelical folks calling these groups "secret societies." Within these fraternities, unsaved men gathered secretly behind closed doors to dabble in the occult.

Secretly, these men and women opposed the genuine move of God within their local churches. Through their false doctrine, they robbed many of their authentic faith in Jesus Christ. Like the Pharisees, they did their sneaky work camouflaged as religious groups. Jude goes on describing these men as those who "despise dominion, and speak evil of dignities" (Jude 1:8 AMP).

Here, the word *dominion* in the Greek is *kyriotes,* which means "constituted authority" or "lordships." This means that these men openly despised leadership. These thieves exalted themselves above the decisions of divinely established authority figures in their local churches; they always liked to "climb up some other way."

A newspaper article carried the news of a minister who had shepherded a local church in a southern Ghanaian port city. I was intrigued because it was the city in which I had earlier led a revival group.

He had somehow convinced one of his church members, a dad, to permit his teenage son to lodge at his home. Later, after the lad had lived there for a while, he was found to be ill with a disease with strange symptoms.

The medical diagnosis revealed that the boy had been infected with HIV. Police detective work revealed that the child had contracted it from his host (Abotsi 2013). It goes without saying that some sexual liaison had occurred between the two.

The infidelity of this pastor had caused great damage to the spiritual faith of the victim and his family, I can guarantee you that. He had stolen their faith and this boy's innocence.

Remember Sasha? How did she get in among the brethren and gain their respect? She got in *some other way.*

Folks like her and this port city pastor hadn't had a life-changing encounter with Jesus Christ. They weren't saved; they were thieves and robbers.

They had no true fidelity toward the Lord, and they undermined divine authority. The Greek word for *dignities* here is *doxa,* which means "glory" or "the glory of God." They speak evil of the manifestations of the glory of God in the church and contravene the move of God there.

> All that ever came before me are thieves and robbers: but
> the sheep did not hear them. (John 10:8)

Jesus was making a categorical statement against the Pharisees who preceded Him in history and claimed to be a part of the sheepfold, yet chose their own "path" to God, believing in a resurrection but not in Christ Jesus (Acts 23:6–8). The resurrection doctrine was their *other way* into the sheepfold.

Today, the half-truth doctrines of certain impostors have misled many and robbed them of their salvation. These are thieves and robbers or highway men; they hijack the faith of those on their way to finding the reality of God. Their half-truths have misled the faith of many. The doctrine of *the infidel* is knocking at the hearts of the faithful. How did these thieves fill these positions? They crept or climbed in some *other way* or by a side door.

Some thieves in a major worldwide denomination have raped children and stolen their innocence. I once watched a documentary aired by PBS about the story. I listened as adults who had had their chastity ripped from them while children wept their eyes out. They painfully narrated the ordeals they had suffered at the hands of trusted church leaders (Thomas 2014).

The greater reality is that these robbers have robbed the faith of these victims and their families.

*Action:* Your group should pay attention to the morality of its members and conduct deliverance ministration from time to time. This is to aid in discerning the presence of the thieves and robbers who had crept in without a genuine encounter with Jesus Christ.

## Step 8: Discern the sheep

"I'm the Lord." These words ended the speaker's fervent rendition of what I thought was a strange poem. I was thrown completely off guard. *If she's actually referring to her good self, then she's lost her marbles,* I thought. It all sounded narcissistic to me.

"Please don't bring me here again," I told Martin. He had brought me to the afternoon Bible study with a campus charismatic group, my first. This was approximately twelve hours before my dawn spiritual "revolution" among these people.

"Oh? Why?" he responded.

"I guess you heard what she said, didn't you?" I voiced my agitation. I was pointing toward the speaker of the funny poetry I'd just heard.

"What did she say?"

"She said, 'I'm the Lord,'" I replied.

After letting out a laugh, as though he was fancifully tickled, he replied, "Oh, oh, it's called *prophecy.*"

I was illiterate in these matters, and it showed. Martin undertook this mentorship with glee, quoting a few scriptures to buttress his point. I believed him, and it was a good thing that I did. Hearing the voice of Jesus, the good shepherd, became my preserve as well.

> And I fell at his feet to worship him. And he said unto me, See thou do it not: I am thy fellowservant, and of thy brethren that have the testimony of Jesus: worship God: for the testimony of Jesus is the spirit of prophecy. (Rev. 19:10)

"The testimony of Jesus is the spirit of prophecy." This was crucial in giving me the needed prophetic connection that fueled my fidelity. Through it, I clearly heard my call to serve among the brethren.

> But he that entereth in by the door is the shepherd of the sheep. To him the porter openeth; and the sheep hear his voice: and he calleth his own sheep by name, and leadeth them out. And when he putteth forth his own sheep, he goeth before them, and the sheep follow him: for they know his voice. (John 10:2–4)

There are three critical signs that the Lord gave about the true sheep in the sheepfold. These are that "the sheep hear" the voice of the shepherd, the sheep are "called," and "the sheep follow" the leadership of the shepherd. The sheep demonstrate their fidelity to the shepherd by following his or her leadership, but this is firmly rooted in their capacity to "hear" the shepherd's voice and obey his or her "call."

It's obvious from what the Lord is saying that all true sheep should have discernment for His voice and thus can hear when He calls. This in my opinion is the root of their fidelity, for as the sheep obey the call, they can then demonstrate faithfulness to Him. You must be faithful to the Lord if you have to be faithful to His church.

> And a certain woman named Lydia, a seller of purple, of the city of Thyatira, which worshipped God, heard us: whose heart the Lord opened, that she attended unto the things which were spoken of Paul. And when she was baptized, and her household, she besought us, saying, If ye have judged me to be faithful to the Lord, come into my house, and abide there. And she constrained us. (Acts 16:14)

Through hearing the Lord's voice they're able to intimately know Him. The sheep knows the shepherd through knowing His voice. This is the basis for the sheep's fidelity to the shepherd's flock.

> I am the good shepherd, and know my sheep, and am known of mine. (John 10:14)

The true sheep knows the chief Shepherd—Jesus Christ. The Greek word translated as *known* in this verse is *ginosko* which means "to acknowledge or understand." As the sheep hear the shepherd's voice daily, they come to acknowledge and understand Him. This is what makes it easy for them to be led by Him and hence facilitate their following. The quality of their following will determine the quality of their fidelity. The beginning of this sheep–shepherd rendezvous occurs through "the door" of the sheepfold. Jesus said that He's not only the shepherd but also "the door" of the sheepfold.

> I am the door: by me if any man enter in, he shall be saved,
> and shall go in and out, and find pasture. (John 10:9)

All true sheep have had an encounter with "the door"—Jesus Christ—and have experienced His salvation. A genuine salvation experience will ultimately lead to hearing the Lord's voice and getting to know Him through fellowship so we can hear His call and obey it.

On the road to Damascus, Paul entered "the door" by a glorious light and became saved through this dramatic encounter. In the same experience, he heard the voice of the chief Shepherd calling him into the ministry (Acts 26:12–20). In Damascus, Paul joined the sheepfold and began to obey the call upon his life (Acts 9:17–21). His fidelity to God's call is what led to him being promoted in Antioch by the chief Shepherd to the apostolic ministry (Acts 13:2–4). We know this from what he wrote to Timothy.

> And I thank Christ Jesus our Lord, who hath enabled
> me, for that he counted me faithful, putting me into the
> ministry. (1 Tim. 1:12)

I'll say this—without a genuine salvation experience followed by the three critical signs mentioned by the Lord, the sheep will most likely go astray and into false fidelity. "All we like sheep have gone astray; we have turned everyone to his own way" (Isa. 53:6).

They don't try to follow the Lord by turning "every one to his own way," their own way of worship and doing ministry. Because they don't have the three essentials in their lives, they end up following the voice of the strange leader.

I heard of a case in South Africa in which the followers of a particular ministry munch green grass like sheep to obtain miracles (Blair 2014). This is a form of false fidelity, for the "pasture" written about in scripture isn't natural grass since the "sheep" aren't natural sheep (John 10:9). The motive behind this action didn't come through hearing the voice of Jesus but of a false shepherd. Jesus Christ never encouraged the chewing of grass as a method for healing the sick or working miracles. It's only by fidelity based on hearing the voice of the chief Shepherd through a true Spirit-led leader that eternal life and security will continually be found.

> My sheep hear my voice, and I know them, and they follow me: And I give unto them eternal life; and they shall never perish, neither shall any man pluck them out of my hand. (John 10:27–28)

*Action:* Your group must yield to the Lord in seeking His face, till one by one each hears His voice. This will open the door for the spirit of prophecy to work among them.

## Step 9: Discern the wolf

I looked searchingly into the woman's eyes. But she turned away as if to hide from my perceiving gaze. The sounds of her sobs gnawed at my bowels.

What in the world would drive this pretty lady into such isolation? She wearily slumped her shivering frame against a wooden pole right behind the assembly hall. It was dark, and the awkwardness of her demeanor had drawn a few concerned stares from passers-by.

"What's the problem?" I pressed.

We had been lodging on the campus for a few days. Our annual convention was in session. The church had found it apropos to rent the high school facility as it was the most frugal thing to do. I skimmed over the environs, at the back-and-forth scurrying of those leaving for the dorms.

Her sobs continued, a decibel higher.

"You can share your issues with me," I said. She stole a quick glance at me; her eyes conveyed an uncertainty of trust.

"You can trust me. Please tell me," I softly implored.

She got a little quieter. Then, as if cautiously unbinding bandages, she bared her wounded soul.

Through the years, I've dealt with young ladies who had been manipulated into having liaisons with "spiritual" leaders. Hers was a classic case. In the process, she had become pregnant and was being pressured to have an abortion. The emotional and spiritual toll was immense. With some others, it had left them damaged and even demonized. This isn't fidelity to the flock, not by a long shot.

> But he that is an hireling, and not the shepherd, whose own the sheep are not, seeth the wolf coming, and leaveth the sheep, and fleeth: and the wolf catcheth them, and scattereth the sheep. (John 10:12)

The wolf is a ravenous beast that devours its prey; he sees the flock as his spoil, a people to be taken advantage of. They're takers or devourers, coming with the objective of destroying, dividing, and scattering the flock and then vanishing into the wild.

> For I know this, that after my departing shall grievous wolves enter in among you, not sparing the flock. (Acts 20:29)

The Greek word translated as *sparing* is *pheidomai,* and it means "being tender." The wolf is not tender with the flock; he is very harsh with them. The apostle Paul points directly to the cause of the wolf's ravenous nature; the word he uses is *grievous,* meaning "severe or violent." The wolf does not have the tender or compassionate nature of the good shepherd. His nature runs counter to the nature of Jesus, the chief Shepherd. Jesus has compassion on the scattering sheep, but the wolf instigates the scattering.

> But when he saw the multitudes, he was moved with compassion on them, because they fainted, and were scattered abroad, as sheep having no shepherd. (Matt. 9:36)

Another translation puts it this way:

> I am conscious that after I am gone, evil wolves will come in among you, doing damage to the flock. (Acts 20:29 BBE)

The harsh and abrasive behavior of the wolf ultimately does damage to the flock. The wolf is an overbearing and abusive person. But many don't know how easy it is to spiritually degenerate to the level of a wolf. At the end of the day, none of us can give others what we don't have, so hurting people hurt others; wounded people wound others; and victims of abuse victimize others with abusive words or behaviors, sometimes unknowingly. Backslidden ministers and church folk can lose the nature of the sheep and take on the nature of a wolf.

The wolf sees the young ladies or "big" men of the sheepfold as objects of their sexual and financial fantasies. He pursues them as his prey.

Since God describes His people as the sheep of His pasture, it is appropriate to say that the wolf can never be a true child of God.

> Behold, I send you forth as sheep in the midst of wolves:
> be ye therefore wise as serpents, and harmless as doves.
> (Matt. 10:16)

The wolves in this scripture refer directly to the unsaved crowd that Jesus's disciples had to deal with in His day. Jesus never considered these men as being children of God; He rather considered them as children of the devil (John 8:44).

The wolf can wear the camouflage of a child of God to hide his real identity. Jesus explains in John 10:12 that the wolf has a demeanor underneath that scatters the flock of the sheepfold.

> He that is not with me is against me: and he that gathereth
> not with me scattereth. (Luke 11:23)

From this comment, we know that the wolf scatters because he isn't with the Lord and does not gather the flock with Him. The wolf scatters the flock of the ministry, fellowship, group or local church because he is actually against the Lord's vision of one sheepfold–one shepherd (John 10:16).

No one can be a true child of God and still exhibit infidelity "against" the Lord's vision. I made it a part of my determination many years ago never to leave any gathering unto the Lord worse off than I joined them. I'd rather leave that community of believers a better group than I met them. Contrary to popular opinion, splitting a sheepfold or a local church to form a new one isn't the sign of a good shepherd; for a leader who's with the Lord "gathereth" with Him; this is genuine fidelity.

> Beware of false prophets, which come to you in sheep's clothing, but inwardly they are ravening wolves. (Matt. 7:15)

Thus, these wolves have a dual personality; the camouflage is outward, and their true, ravenous nature is inward. It is the dual personality of a wolf and sheep. He is unsaved but puts on the religious attitude of a Christian. The wolf calls himself a Christian, yet when challenged, his violent, devouring nature shows up. The wolf cannot bear the fruit of the Spirit. He or she isn't a peaceful man or woman at heart. He only acts peacefully till someone crosses him, and then the wolfish nature manifests forth. Some of these wolves serve in the highest level of ministry; this is why Jesus remarked that we should beware of false prophets who are cast in their mold.

The wolf, by its very devouring, brash, and hypocritical demeanor, cannot woo the fidelity of the flock and hence will scatter them. The wolf needs a radical change of nature if it is to succeed in shepherding the flock; the wolf must repent. As leaders, we must make it easy for our followers to crown us as kings.

> All these men of war, that could keep rank, came with a perfect heart to Hebron, to make David king over all Israel: and all the rest also of Israel were of one heart to make David king. (1 Chron. 12:38)

*Action:* Your group should be vigilant in observing all attitudes that have the potential of scattering its membership. All overbearingly harsh and abrasive behavior must be discerned and discouraged.

## Step 10: Discern your spiritual father

In the upper room, the incubation of the brethren occurred. The campus leader did more than point to the locale of the revival group; he repeatedly drew our attention to their endearing leader. I nursed a sudden urge to meet this fellow.

We'd been loitering about all afternoon soul-winning. A taxi parked by the curb, a door swung open, and its passenger stepped out. We had first ignored its approach, but now, the creaking sound of hinges drew our attention. We turned and saw a gentleman.

"Captain!" the campus leader yelled as he raced for his luggage. He had obviously been agog about his return for a while. I was clueless.

With gaiety, he hoisted his baggage onto his head and carried it away. I gaped at the load-carrying action. The affinity was obvious.

*Who might this be?* My mental recall went into overdrive. And then came my aha moment. I just hoped I was accurate somehow.

*Doesn't the name* Captain *ring a bell? Could that be the leader he raved about?* I wondered.

In the coming months, I watched from afar, learning a whole lot from where I metaphorically stood. I finally concluded that *Captain* wasn't a nickname. Its coinage, I believe, came out of an effort to discern an appropriate fatherly title. He was the protagonist among the brethren, an apostolic voice, our movement's father.

> For though ye have ten thousand instructors in Christ, yet have ye not many fathers: for in Christ Jesus I have begotten you through the gospel. (1 Corin. 4:15)

The Old Testament began with the writing of the prophet Moses and ended with the writing of the prophet Malachi. The New Testament began with the writing of the apostle Matthew and ended with the writing of the apostle John. Thus, the apostle and the prophet are biblically the two pioneering or foundational ministries.

> And are built upon the foundation of the apostles and prophets, Jesus Christ himself being the chief corner stone. (Eph. 2:20)

Fire is symbolically linked with the apostolic and prophetic ministries. Moses's prophetic ministry was associated with fire (Heb. 12:18, 21), as was Elijah's (1 Kings 18:24, 38). Peter's apostolic ministry was launched by fire on the day of Pentecost (Acts 2:1–4, 14).

Elijah's Old Testament prophetic ministry and the New Testament ministries of Jesus's apostles have both produced spiritual revival.

Fire in this way represents the Holy Spirit's revival work. The apostles and prophets through their unique roles produce revival movements. It's their calling.

The apostle and the prophet are both fathering ministries. They father revival movements by birthing spiritual sons.

The apostle Paul called Timothy a son (Phil. 2:22), and the prophet Elisha called Elijah a father (2 Kings 2:12). Thus, it takes a fathering spirit to birth a revival and lay a spiritual foundation. As we carefully investigate scripture, it is easy to see one common characteristic of these revival and foundational ministries: they cannot tolerate false sons. Samuel, under the spirit of prophecy, couldn't tolerate the false sonship of Saul. David, under the prophetic anointing, could not tolerate the false sonship of Absalom. And Elisha couldn't tolerate the false sonship of Gehazi.

Jesus Christ, under the apostolic anointing, couldn't tolerate the false sonship of Judas Iscariot, and the apostle Paul couldn't tolerate the false sonship of John Mark (Acts 15:36–40).

Now, let's recap. First, the apostle and prophet are pioneering or foundational ministries. Second, the apostle and prophet through their unique roles produce revival movements. Third, the apostle and prophet are fathering ministries.

> And it came to pass, when they were gone over, that Elijah said unto Elisha, Ask what I shall do for thee, before I be taken away from thee. And Elisha said, I pray thee, let a double portion of thy spirit be upon me. And he said, Thou hast asked a hard thing: nevertheless, if thou see me when I am taken from thee, it shall be so unto thee; but if not, it shall not be so … And Elisha saw it, and he cried, My father, my father, the chariot of Israel, and the horsemen thereof. And he saw him no more: and he took hold of his own clothes, and rent them in two pieces. He took up also the mantle of Elijah that fell from him, and

went back, and stood by the bank of Jordan. (2 Kings
2:9–10, 12–13)

At the end of their journey, Elisha cried, "My father, my father" to
Elijah. Ultimately, it's only true sons who inherit the legacies of their
fathers. As a result of this, it's only true sons who see themselves at the end
of their fathers' season in ministry, for legacies are only inherited at the
end, not at the beginning. The spirit and the mantles of the fathers are only
passed on to the sons at the end. It is inappropriate to invest yourself in
the life of someone who does not see himself or herself at the end of your
journey. As a result of this, long-term fidelity is the hallmark of every true
son. Visions by nature never speak of the beginning or of the middle of
your season but of the end (Hab. 2:3). Visions tarry for very long periods;
hence, it's only those who see themselves at the end who stay the course.
Fidelity is not an event but a journey. The cry of a true son can be accepted
only by the father at the end. We have sometimes invested ourselves in
the lives of men and women who didn't see themselves at the end—the
moment they'll see you *go*.

How does a revival group, fellowship, local church or ministry discern
its spiritual father? Son-ship in the new covenant is gender neutral. "There
is … neither male nor female: for ye are all one in Christ Jesus" (Gal. 3:28).

In this sense, spiritual fatherhood is not based on the natural capacity to
bear seed but rather the spiritual capacity to do so. In the New Testament,
a female can spiritually father another person in the Lord by becoming a
spiritual seed-bearer. The spiritual seed is the word of God.

Being born again, not of corruptible seed, but of
incorruptible, by the word of God, which liveth and
abideth forever. (1 Peter 1:23)

The sower soweth the word. (Mark 4:14)

The one who carries the spiritual seed of the word then automatically
becomes the spiritual father. Out of this seed, a new generation of spiritual
sons will be reproduced. Regardless of gender, should a person sow the seed
of the word into the heart of another person, the born-again experience will

make him or her a spiritual father. A female in this way can also say, "But ye know the proof of him, that, as a son with the father, he hath served with me in the gospel" (Phil. 2:22). The apostle Paul called his spiritual seed "my gospel," and by it all his spiritual sons were reproduced (Rom. 16:25).

Spiritual sons are not only the product of the spiritual seed carried by their spiritual fathers but are also nourished by the same person into spiritual manhood.

> My little children, of whom I travail in birth again until
> Christ be formed in you. (Gal. 4:19)

All fathers have the responsibility to sow the seed or sperm that produces a child and then raise that child into an adult. Paul uses the word *again* to indicate a second effort. The first effort produces a spiritual baby, but the second effort produces a mature believer. There is travail involved in this as well.

> And he gave some, apostles; and some, prophets; and
> some, evangelists; and some, pastors and teachers; For the
> perfecting of the saints, for the work of the ministry, for
> the edifying of the body of Christ. (Eph. 4:11–12)

Despite the fact that the apostle and prophet have unique roles in fathering revival movements, generic spiritual fatherhood isn't exclusive to them. Evangelists, pastors, and teachers can also father other believers through the preaching of the gospel and the teaching of God's word. This is called discipleship: "the equipping of the saints, for the work of the ministry."

*Action:* Your group must discern its anointed pioneering figure—its father. An individual member defers to the group's father for ultimate spiritual instruction and nurturing. The titles used for them will differ for each ministry. Your group would be no exception.

## Step 11: Discern the cause of spiritual infidelity

I often heard growing up that honesty is the best policy. Hence, I wouldn't attempt to pose as a fellow wholly untainted by spiritual infidelity. I was and will *always* be a work in progress.

"What are we going to do?" I asked, skimming over the faces of my colleagues. The response I received indicated that they were as much at sea as I was. We'd been concerned recently about the state of the ministry, that it seemed we'd been going around in circles.

"We need a clear-cut vision," someone said. It was obvious that the others had been engaging one another on the subject. We had intimated much since our days among the brethren. The statement amazed me because I had suggested the same thing several years back. Now we were having a déjà vu moment. Like it's said, what goes around comes around.

I felt pissed.

"So what are we going to do?" I chimed in again. Some visiting American ministers had made some suggestions. They had felt that, praying for the demise of the senior pastor was the solution. Ouch!

*Now why in the world would they suggest that?* I thought. I had a repulsive feeling in my gut. Though I wasn't the leader's spiritual son, I frankly thought this was overkill.

Long story short, the following months took the ministry through some stormy weather. The dissent reached a crescendo.

I therefore sought God for months about the infidelity I had witnessed within the revival group. At the tail end, I personally took my part of the blame and asked to be "honorably discharged" from my duties. I was released with the group's blessing. I learned later that others followed. Sadly, this shouldn't have happened, and it left a sour taste in my mouth for years. I nevertheless left the situation with an object lesson: infidelity is caused by both internal and external influences.

> Behold, I will send you Elijah the prophet before the coming of the great and dreadful day of the Lord: And he shall turn the heart of the fathers to the children, and the heart of the children to their fathers, lest I come and smite the earth with a curse. (Mal. 4:5–6)

The hearts of the sons have for some reason been turned from their fathers (Mal. 4:5). This is because there is a cursed agenda on the part of the forces of darkness to sever the relationship between the fathers and their sons. I once heard a servant of God express that, once Satan finds out that a specific relationship is key to a person's destiny, he'll seek to sever it by any means necessary. It was the Devil who sought to sever the covenant between Judas Iscariot and Jesus Christ, his mentor, so that a curse could be released on the earth. He tried the same strategy with Peter. Do you remember Peter's denial of the Lord? (Mark 14:66–72).

> And the Lord said, Simon, Simon, behold, Satan hath desired to have you, that he may sift you as wheat: But I have prayed for thee, that thy faith fail not: and when thou art converted, strengthen thy brethren. And he said unto him, Lord, I am ready to go with thee, both into prison, and to death. And he said, I tell thee, Peter, the cock shall not crow this day, before that thou shalt thrice deny that thou knowest me. (Luke 22:31–34)

Why will the Devil seek to destroy the covenant between a pastor and his flock, a leader and his followers, a spiritual father and his sons? It is simply because spiritual fatherhood is a very grave issue. Jesus explained it by quoting Zechariah the prophet.

> And Jesus saith unto them, All ye shall be offended because of me this night: for it is written, I will smite the shepherd, and the sheep shall be scattered ... But Peter said unto him, Although all shall be offended, yet will not I. And Jesus saith unto him, Verily I say unto thee, That this day, even in this night, before the cock crow twice, thou shalt deny me thrice. (Mark 14:27, 29–30)

Please notice that Zechariah's prophecy and Satan's attempt to "sift as wheat" are both tied to Peter's denial of the Lord. The Devil's goal was to cause Peter to deny his leader so he could "smite the shepherd" and scatter the sheep away from him. Satan's desire was to break the fidelity between Peter and his mentor, Jesus, so he could scatter and curse the Lord's ministry.

How would the forces of darkness achieve this? It's a combination of two things.

*Internal Influences*

> "And Jesus saith unto them, All ye shall be offended because of me this night."

On this occasion, Jesus was addressing His disciples about their offenses.

In my narrative, we had been made to trudge on without a clear-cut vision; you'd see that these internal influences came from our angst with leadership choices. We became offended.

*External Influences*

> Then assembled together the chief priests, and the scribes, and the elders of the people, unto the palace of the high priest, who was called Caiaphas, And consulted that they might take Jesus by subtilty, and kill him ... Then one of the twelve, called Judas Iscariot, went unto the chief priests, And said unto them, What will ye give me, and I will deliver him unto you? And they covenanted with him for thirty pieces of silver. And from that time he sought opportunity to betray him. (Matt. 26:3–4, 14–16)

Prior to betraying Jesus, Judas Iscariot consulted and covenanted with the Sanhedrin. In a similar vein, the infidelity that rocked the revival ministry was also externally influenced by our consultation with the American ministers.

At this stage, we'll examine the influences behind the infidelity of Absalom, David's son.

> David's son Amnon was in love with her [Tamar]. And he was so deeply in love that he became ill because of his sister Tamar; for she was a virgin, and so it seemed hard

to Amnon to do anything to her. (2 Sam. 13:1–3, brackets added)

Something dangerous was obviously brewing in David's home. Amnon, the most senior among the princes, had developed a sexual affinity for his younger sister, Tamar. Her stunning beauty had stirred such fantasies of perversion that his raging hormones had driven him to illness. He called it love, the head-over-heels kind. And he was losing his mind.

As Amnon's plight worsened, he began to lose significant weight. His friend and cousin Jonadab noticed the sudden change in his health, so he quizzed him.

And he said to him, O son of the king, why are you getting thinner day by day? will you not say what your trouble is? And Amnon said to him, I am in love with Tamar, my brother Absalom's sister. (2 Samuel 13:4 BBE)

After revealing his desires to Jonadab, the two undertook to orchestrate an incestuous rape scene. This is the kind of counsel you get when you keep bad company, and Jonadab was a very bad friend. These two sinister minds developed a believable plan that even hoodwinked King David. Amnon therefore manipulated the king to naively permit the hatching of their evil machination (2 Sam. 13:5–10). The opportune time arrived, and Amnon was found alone with Tamar in his bedroom.

And ... he [Amnon] took hold of her [Tamar], and said unto her, Come lie with me, my sister. And she answered him, Nay, my brother, do not force me; for no such thing ought to be done in Israel: do not thou this folly. And I, whither shall I cause my shame to go? and as for thee, thou shalt be as one of the fools in Israel. Now therefore, I pray thee, speak unto the king; for he will not withhold me from thee. Howbeit he would not hearken unto her voice: but, being stronger than she, forced her, and lay with her. (2 Sam. 13:11–14, brackets added)

The rape of Tamar, like all such dastardly deeds, is one of the most sadistic acts of injustice to ever afflict anyone. Amnon had no mercy.

> Then Amnon hated her exceedingly; so that the hatred wherewith he hated her was greater than the love wherewith he had loved her. And Amnon said unto her, Arise, be gone. And she said unto him, There is no cause: this evil in sending me away is greater than the other that thou didst unto me. But he would not hearken unto her. (2 Sam. 13:15–16)

Amnon was the senior brother and ought to have rather protected his younger sister, but he did not. This was enough to evoke in anyone a righteous sense of injustice. With her virginity broken in such a cruel way, "Tamar put ashes on her head, and rent her garment of divers colours that was on her, and laid her hand on her head, and went on crying" (2 Sam. 13:19).

Absalom found out about the raping of Tamar.

> And Absalom spake unto his brother Amnon neither good nor bad: for Absalom hated Amnon, because he had forced his sister Tamar. (2 Sam. 13:22)

At this point, Absalom was rankled by a reasonable sense of injustice. With this set in his mind, the conditions were ripe for hate and bitterness to develop.

When people feel hard-done by a leader's actions, and in this case David's permissiveness, their minds become a breeding ground for infidelity. Absalom acted out his feeling of injustice by assassinating Amnon, the rapist. He took matters into his own hands.

> Now Absalom had commanded his servants, saying, Mark ye now when Amnon's heart is merry with wine, and when I say unto you, Smite Amnon; then kill him, fear not: have not I commanded you? be courageous, and be valiant ... And Jonadab, the son of Shimeah David's brother, answered and said, Let not my lord suppose that

they have slain all the young men the king's sons; for
Amnon only is dead: for by the appointment of Absalom
this hath been determined from the day that he forced his
sister Tamar. (2 Sam. 13:28, 32)

He then undertook to inflict injury on his father's political career.

But Absalom sent spies throughout all the tribes of Israel,
saying, As soon as ye hear the sound of the trumpet, then
ye shall say, Absalom reigneth in Hebron ... And there
came a messenger to David, saying, The hearts of the
men of Israel are after Absalom. And David said unto all
his servants that were with him at Jerusalem, Arise, and
let us flee; for we shall not else escape from Absalom:
make speed to depart, lest he overtake us suddenly, and
bring evil upon us, and smite the city with the edge of the
sword. (2 Sam. 15:10, 13–14)

This was for being complicit in the rape of Tamar.

Then David sent home to Tamar, saying, Go now to thy
brother Amnon's house, and dress him meat. (2 Sam. 13:7)

Absalom's infidelity deepened when he staged a public sexual orgy
with his father's concubines (girlfriends), King David's harem.

And Ahithophel said unto Absalom, Go in unto thy
father's concubines, which he hath left to keep the house;
and all Israel shall hear that thou art abhorred of thy
father: then shall the hands of all that are with thee be
strong. So they spread Absalom a tent upon the top of the
house; and Absalom went in unto his father's concubines
in the sight of all Israel. (2 Sam. 16:21–22)

*The Internal Influence*

And Absalom spake unto his brother Amnon neither good
nor bad: for Absalom hated Amnon, because he had forced
his sister Tamar. (2 Sam. 13:22)

*The External Influence*

But Amnon had a friend, whose name was Jonadab, the
son of Shimeah David's brother: and Jonadab was a very
subtil man. (2 Sam. 13:3)

The wrong external influence of Jonadab, a bad friend, and the
offensive internal influence of Tamar's rape, dovetailing into her unjust
treatment, were the catalysts for Absalom's infidelity.

***Action:*** Your group should constantly monitor their external
influencers and the psyches of offended members. Both internal and
external influences must be discerned and addressed forthrightly.

## Step 12: Discern the sons of the prophets

I write not these things to shame you, but as my beloved
sons I warn you. For though ye have ten thousand
instructors in Christ, yet have ye not many fathers: for in
Christ Jesus I have begotten you through the gospel. (1
Corin. 4:14–15)

It's been a while now since the brethren got fragmented at the lido
downtown. The fallout of the dissolution led us on a path of seeking other
voices in our lives.

"I want you to father me again," the young man said.

I had not particularly considered myself in that role till he brought it
up. Honestly I felt humbled. Gazing into his sincere eyes, I gave him my
assurances. In a white short-sleeved shirt with a nice necktie donned over
a pair of well-ironed pants, he had taken himself very seriously. And he
said he needed my mentoring.

When he left, I began to consider the responsibility he had just thrust on me. I took in a deep breath. I had a lot of sorting out to do in my own turf, much less bearing another's burden. *I'll do my best*, I thought after musing a while.

I had just arrived home after six months abroad and needed to see my way forward clearly. More so, my wife and I had just welcomed our baby girl. Yet I felt elated to be counted worthy of spiritual fatherhood.

Actually, he had gotten saved under my ministry some years back; that evening still runs in my memory. If that's what it takes to be a spiritual father, then I guess he's right.

Several years passed, and we had not met about mentorship. I still thought about him often, though. Then, a photo of his flashed across my view and startled me. I was riding through town, and I saw a church ad that bore his image. The ad was for what we'd call prophetic services.

My inability to honor my word wasn't deliberate. Moving into a new house and getting a new work started consumed much of my focus. That being said, I set the ball rolling to invite Brother S over. Perhaps a ministry session with our revival group would be a great opportunity to reconnect. He was well received at our ministry center that day.

"I planted a seed into the ministry of my spiritual father," he said. I knew he wasn't referring to me, for no "seed" had yet come down the pike from him, at least not that I knew of. As the message unraveled, it became clear that it was another, a prominent prophet. He evidently had more than one spiritual father. Did I feel replaced? No. He needed an accurate discernment of the difference between an instructor and a father.

> And the sons of the prophets that were at Jericho came to
> Elisha, and said unto him, Knowest thou that the LORD
> will take away thy master from thy head to day? And he
> answered, Yea, I know it; hold ye your peace ... And fifty
> men of the sons of the prophets went, and stood to view
> afar off: and they two stood by Jordan. (2 Kings 2:5, 7)

The "sons of the prophets" didn't see the prophet Elijah as their "master" but Elisha's. It was obvious that they hadn't served the man of God. They weren't his servants but viewed him from "afar off."

Who is your spiritual father? Whose mantle do you want to carry? Whose spirit have you imbibed? Who fathered you? Whose unction do you possess? There is good spiritual DNA and defective spiritual DNA that is transferable through spiritual fatherhood. If you've inherited a good spiritual pedigree from a great spiritual father, then be careful that nothing terminates the fidelity between you two. Find a way to be his servant.

You cannot be the son of several fathers. You can be the son of only one father. There is nothing like the "sons of the prophets" but rather the sons of *a* prophet. Under Elijah's prophetic fatherhood, there were these "sons of the prophets." They did not consider him as their sole spiritual father. They considered multiple prophets as their spiritual fathers. They were not totally faithful to Elijah, but Elisha was. There is no record of Elisha calling anyone else apart from his biological father as father save Elijah.

> And it came to pass, as they still went on, and talked, that, behold, there appeared a chariot of fire, and horses of fire, and parted them both asunder; and Elijah went up by a whirlwind into heaven. And Elisha saw it, and he cried, My father, my father, the chariot of Israel, and the horsemen thereof. And he saw him no more: and he took hold of his own clothes, and rent them in two pieces. (2 Kings 2:11–12)

Elijah was undisputedly the spiritual father of Elisha. The sons of the prophets were disqualified from inheriting the mantle of Elijah because they never served him, but watched him from afar. This didn't flesh out their fidelity.

All sons of the prophets are false sons and cannot inherit the mantles of their spiritual fathers. The spirit of Elijah didn't fall on the sons of the prophets but fell on the one who called him "my father."

> He took up also the mantle of Elijah that fell from him, and went back, and stood by the bank of Jordan; And he took the mantle of Elijah that fell from him, and smote the waters, and said, Where is the Lord God of Elijah? and when he also had smitten the waters, they parted hither

and thither: and Elisha went over. And when the sons of
the prophets which were to view at Jericho saw him, they
said, The spirit of Elijah doth rest on Elisha. And they
came to meet him, and bowed themselves to the ground
before him. (2 Kings 2:13–15)

Once the bond between you and your spiritual father is broken, you
become a false son wherever you go. Naturally, when those who share a
specific father gather, strangers find it awkward to hang with them. Why?
This is because they share common traits and a common history, and they
laugh at common stories. Outsiders never seem to fit in. All false sons tend
to be in one way or another vagabonds and hobos. Their fidelity belongs
elsewhere.

It's totally unrealistic for a person to be the son of several prophetic
fathers. This doesn't exist anywhere. You can be the son of only one father.
Spiritual vagabonds and hooligans are unstable souls who run from one
spiritual influence to another.

Today, our fellowships, ministries, local churches and groups are
infiltrated by false spiritual sons and daughters. There are multitudes of
men and women who do not carry the supernatural DNA, "mantles" of
the fathers under whom they serve. They exhibit foreign attitudes. The
lack of discernment of whose seed you are, produces sons of the prophets.

Mantles are the inheritance of sons, not vagabonds, bastards, and
hobos. A hobo doesn't belong to a specific home. Hobos move from place
to place. If you've been moving from one group to another, then you're a
spiritual hobo and cannot inherit the mantle of any spiritual father. The
sons of the prophets end up becoming the rolling stones that gather no
moss. This path is a labyrinth, I'm sad to say.

*Action:* Your group should identify its spiritual father and make
practical their fidelity to him or her. This could be done through daily
serving the man or woman.

## Step 13: Discern the sons of Belial

"I don't trust women!" the young man said with such forcefulness
that I was taken aback. *Now why in the world would he say that?* I thought.

We had just been through an embarrassing moment of disclosure. The service had concluded, and a spur-of-the-moment meeting was in session. A liaison with a lady within the choir had come to my attention. The irony is that, it had occurred in a tryst between this untrusting fellow and her.

*And he didn't trust her after all this?* I took a quick gaze at the floor, feeling sick to my stomach. Moreover, he was the son of a Pentecostal preacher and knew most things about the ministry, much of which many of the church folks did not know. In my opinion, this fornication was a no-no.

I sat back and took a deep breath. I recalled that he had once told me about an affair he'd had with an elderly woman. I did not believe him. First of all, it was too base for a decent conversation, and second, it sounded like a barefaced lie to me. However, it didn't take very long for his unruly ways to show, fomenting trouble within groups of the local church. Staring at the face of his latest victim, I felt sorry for her that afternoon. It was quite a price to pay for having a crush on the wrong church guy.

Later, he admitted that he had come out of a broken home and had been adversely affected by the dysfunction in the ministry of his dad. But much to my dismay, these pernicious ways had begun to spread distrust within our assembly, almost upending the revival we had experienced for months. He was a son of Belial.

> Now the sons of Eli were sons of Belial; they knew not the
> LORD. (1 Sam. 2:12)

The word *Belial* is also used for some of the men of David; they are called men of Belial in 1 Samuel 30:22. They are wicked, destructive and selfish men, because they "knew not the Lord." It is one of the names of Satan. Of such were the sons of Eli. They were sons of the priesthood ministry and yet demonstrated the sonship of Belial. *Belial* in the Hebrew means "destructive."

In the ministry of Eli, the sonship of Belial was unfaithful. Fidelity isn't the mindset of these sons of destruction. If the Levitical priesthood was such a holy priesthood, then how did the sons of Eli the high priest become the sons of Belial? This was because they "knew not the Lord" (1 Sam. 2:12).

In reference to 1 Samuel 2:12, the word *knew* in the Hebrew is *yada,* which is the same word used in the Bible for "sexual intimacy." Hophni and Phinehas became sons of Belial because they practiced religion without intimacy with God. One of the greatest tragedies of the ministry is the ability to professionally execute its daily assignments without consulting the mind of God. The sons of Belial have a spirit of independence— independence from the Spirit of God. The sons of Eli erred from a loyal relationship with God and His people because they had no intimacy with God. They knew the song of the Lord yet did not know the God of the song; they knew the word of God but did not know the God of the word.

The sons of Belial are products of ministerial destruction. The sons of Eli were born and raised in a period when their father's ministry was spiritually falling apart. The prophet Samuel was raised by God to fix a broken priesthood.

> And the word of the LORD was precious in those days; there was no open vision. (1 Sam. 3:1)

It's very difficult to know the Lord in a broken ministry. When fellowships, ministries, groups, and local churches fall apart, the spiritual sons who come out of such situations can be very selfish and destructive. This happens because they do not have an intimate relationship with God, which could forestall all the negative fallout of a broken ministry. They don't trust anyone because they do not trust the Lord; hence, they find it difficult to be loyal to leadership. Sons of Belial mostly come out of broken homes and churches.

> Now Eli was very old, and heard all that his sons did unto all Israel; and how they lay with the women that assembled at the door of the tabernacle of the congregation. And he said unto them, Why do ye such things? for I hear of your evil dealings by all this people. Nay, my sons; for it is no good report that I hear: ye make the LORD'S people to transgress. (1 Sam. 2:22–24)

Did they listen? No.

> Notwithstanding they hearkened not unto the voice of their father. (1 Sam. 2:25)

Eli's home had fallen apart; he could not father his sons effectively for they did what they liked. The sons of Eli were unfaithful in their marriages, for though married they slept with the women in the congregation.

Loyal characters can emerge only out of disciplined environments. God therefore spoke through a man of God, saying,

> And I will raise me up a faithful [loyal] priest, that shall do according to that which is in mine heart and in my mind: and I will build him a sure house; and he shall walk before mine anointed for ever. (1 Sam. 2:35, brackets added)

God wanted a loyal priest who will have a sure house rather than a broken home. The phrase *sure house* in the original Hebrew means "faithful family."

Sons of Belial are products of broken spiritual homes. Sons of Belial tend to repeat learned behavior. Because they come out of local churches, ministries, and fellowships that were split, they find nothing wrong with splitting other groups and churches. To begin with, bearing the brunt of their chaotic circumstances poisoned their minds about church leadership. They feel that sacrificing their efforts for a church group to be successful down the line is not worth it. The sons of Belial are broken people—people broken by church politics and bad examples at home. When churches are split, Satan turns his hands on the followers, especially "the little ones", for they do not yet know intimately the God whom they have believed.

… smite the shepherd [the Pastor], and the sheep [the congregation] shall be scattered: and I will turn mine hand upon the little ones [the immature]. (Zech. 13:7, brackets added)

Satan turns his hands on the immature to deceive, demobilize, and destroy them. Sons of Belial are the product of this satanic agenda. After the ministry is broken, the sons of Belial are abused by the enemy, broken by his oppression, and used by him to promote his goals. It always takes a sovereign act of God for a person from a broken home and local church to turn out right, and knowing the Lord intimately is a major key.

*Action:* Your group members must hold up and be loyal to the highest ethical standards that reveal the sons of Belial among them. This leaves them with no choice than to either get transformed in their attitudes or to exit the membership.

## Step 14: Discern the sons of Zeruiah

I've often heard that hurting people hurt people. Most folks can give only what they have, so if they have hurts, then they give hurt.

"You've betrayed the details of our conversation," the gentleman insisted. We had gone back and forth over what I sincerely felt was an unnecessary nitpicking. He had felt unfairly targeted by an analogy I used during my preaching.

"But the facts don't attest to that," I said.

It was a cry over supposedly spilt milk, and he wasn't ready to let go. I had earlier felt that I had done quite well with him, but that wasn't the case anymore.

Needless to say, he had dropped off a resignation letter and felt his obstinacy was justified. Was I surprised? I'll say maybe.

Prior to joining our group, he'd sat across from me with a coy demeanor. The narrative he'd given that afternoon had unearthed several injurious experiences at the hands of his former pastors and mentors. I had interacted with many such counselees through the years, and I always did my best to disabuse their minds of their "perpetrators." I had hoped to help him get over his hurts and move on.

His plight did touch my bowels of compassion, though. I figured some homely environ might be needed to placate his pain.

"Look, we'll be having a crusade in a few weeks. Why not come along?" I said.

"It'll be my pleasure," he answered, a sheepish smile flitting across his face.

The team did its utmost in the coming months to offer a cozy ambience for their wounded brother. But try as they might, they had been stung by his contrived accusation. They sat bemused.

The holy writ says, "A brother offended is harder to be won than a strong city: and their contentions are like the bars of a castle" (Prov. 18:19).

This particular man's unhealed wounds and unresolved offenses go way back. In the following weeks, I brushed off all reminiscence that could possibly set the team on a guilt trip because honestly, deep in my gut, I believed they had all given their best. Wounded people are hard to please.

> And I am this day weak, though anointed king; and these men the sons of Zeruiah be too hard for me: the LORD shall reward the doer of evil according to his wickedness. (2 Sam. 3:39)

The word *Zeruiah* in the Hebrew means "wounded." These are spiritual sons raised by spiritual parents with wounded spirits. There are wounds of the flesh and the spirit; we are dealing here with the wounds of the human spirit.

> The spirit of a man will sustain his infirmity; but a wounded spirit who can bear? (Prov. 18:14)

A spiritual parent with a wounded spirit cannot raise balanced children. These children know no mercy. They do not know there is a time to smite with deadly intent and a time to heal (Ecc. 3:3). One of the sons of Zeruiah was Joab who was unfaithful to David because he could easily spill blood in the time of peace (1 Kings 2:5). Joab could not tell the difference between the faithful wounds of a friend and the unfaithful wounds of an enemy. It was dangerous to cross Joab (2 Sam 2:23).

Children of the wounded are hard people because they are accustomed to abuse. Their parents were wounded and hurting; and wounded parents produce wounded children. Since people can only give what they have, these parents could only give hurt and pain to their children. Through their words and actions, they produced wounded children.

The name *Joab* in the Hebrew means "fathered of Jehovah." How could it be then, that a man fathered by a merciful God turn out to be so merciless? From where did Joab get his wounds?

In the book of Zechariah, we have an explanation.

> And one shall say unto him, What are these wounds in thine hands? Then he shall answer, Those with which I was wounded in the house of my friends. Awake, O sword, against my shepherd, and against the man that is

> my fellow, saith the LORD of hosts: smite the shepherd,
> and the sheep shall be scattered: and I will turn mine hand
> upon the little ones. (Zech. 13:6–7)

When asked where his wounds were received, the prophet answered "in the house of my friends." The Hebrew word *friend* here actually means "loved one" or "acquaintance." This means that most spiritual wounds incurred in a lifetime will be received in the spiritual house of our loved ones or close associates. In the seventh verse, we see which house it was— the house of his shepherd. The word *shepherd* is the same Hebrew word for *pastor*. This is the spiritual house of his pastor, the local church. In reality, God, our heavenly Father, fathers all of us; however, He does so through the local church, fellowship or ministry's pastor. In this case, the pastor, the delegated spiritual father over the believer, was smitten by an enemy's sword. Now the prophet has a wounded pastor and spiritual father to nurture him, and a hurting shepherd will hurt the sheep because that is all he or she has to offer.

Wounded sheep scatter with wounded hearts. How could one fathered by the Lord become the wounded child of the wounded? It could happen if the child was wounded in the local church of the pastor who himself was nursing a wound.

Bleeding leaders abound in the church of Jesus Christ. Pastors are prime targets of the enemy, for their wounds are transferable through their ministry.

A wounded person or pastor can be a very nice person—that is, until his or her wounds are touched by a misconstrued word or statement. Because most pastors hide their wounds and never talk about it, it's easy to touch these sensitive areas of their lives without knowing it. A wound in the spirit can easily be hidden from sight. A quick temper can be an easy pointer to a wounded spirit. Most resentful, hateful, bitter, angry, cynical, vindictive, vengeful people are wounded persons hiding their wounds behind their emotional dysfunction.

King Saul was such a leader who suffered from the wounds of satanic oppression. His wounds of rejection, personal pain, and insecurities made him a very hurtful man to David. But David, by the meaning of his name, was a lover, and the love of God protected him. However, most of those children who leave these ministries leave with wounds in their spirits. Certain common traits typify wounded children: they are rebellious to spiritual authority, resent spiritual authority, and cannot be faithful to spiritual authority or trust spiritual authority with their fidelity.

Wounded children haven't yet been healed from the abuse they endured from their wounded spiritual fathers. Wounded children run from spiritual authority. Spiritual children who do not forgive their spiritual fathers cannot trust and be faithful to their future leaders, for sooner or later their fallible traits will send them panicking and packing. The sons of Zeruiah are malicious and unstable sons.

*Action:* A culture of forgiveness must be cultivated within your group such that all those wounded members who join their rank and file will be given an opportunity to experience spiritual healing.

## Step 15: Discern the sons of thunder

While I was growing up, my dad would often characterize me as a motor child. Perhaps I was the proverbial "Energizer bunny" or suffered from some undetectable version of ADHD. But that came in tow with some other bothersome attributes. Mum caught that early. She will still narrate incidents of yours truly crying and banging my head against the wall till my lips turned blue. These temper tantrums were usually regarding not being allowed to have my way, things like "Gimme gimme gimme that candy" stuff.

Be that as it may, by high school, I felt I'd outgrown all that. Maybe getting a brief rendezvous with the Holy Spirit helped, except for one occasion when I overreacted. Some fellow had taunted me with his bullying antics till I'd had it. My retaliation came swiftly, as I overturned all the luggage of my dorm mates. However, since then, I vowed never to get myself into such embarrassment, regardless of what happened.

"You—you'll go blind!" I yelled at some teenagers who had, honest to God, driven me up the wall.

In 1983, I had come into the charismatic renewal movement, and with my little fellowship of stalwarts, we had gathered one morning to pray. Our venue had been contested, for some felt our benefactor had lost his marbles in giving his middle-class home for revival services. They wanted us out. While standing with our eyes shut and hands up in the air during worship, some of "the opposition" had snuck in and carried our seats away. I'd caught it all from the corner of my eye. I was just watching and praying like the Bible says.

Now, I wouldn't let that go, would I? Not when these unsuspecting worshippers in the Spirit would get their behinds bumped on the floor. You guessed right—I gave the naughty bunch a good chase.

At this point, their goodies were packed and ready to go in a jalopy. In other words, I felt apostolic. Maybe I would call down fire from heaven like the Zebedee brothers or curse those rascals blind like Paul. I chose the latter.

"Oh, please, it hasn't come to that yet?" one of those juveniles cried. My visage was stern and unrelenting. He really believed my words were etched in stone.

"We'd only been sent," he pleaded. Some other guy, I guess their leader, tilted his head as though to signal his cohorts. All the chairs were summarily returned, unbeknownst to my group, who were still lost in the Spirit, worshipping.

I quietly took my place within the circle of those singing and praying in tongues. I wondered, *What if some of these fellows actually went blind? Could I have lived with myself? Were my Machiavellian ways justified?* Through the years, I've grown much and wouldn't do that again. I've found the way of love. What I was then was a "son of thunder."

> And James the son of Zebedee, and John the brother of James; and he surnamed them Boanerges, which is, The sons of thunder. (Mark 3:17)

> And when his disciples James and John saw this, they said, Lord, wilt thou that we command fire to come down from heaven, and consume them, even as Elias did? But he turned, and rebuked them, and said, Ye know not what manner of spirit ye are of. For the Son of man is not come to destroy men's lives, but to save them. And they went to another village. (Luke 9:54–56)

Jesus revealed the distinct qualities of true sonship versus "the sons of thunder." The sons of thunder are sons who don't have the spirit of true sonship. The sons of thunder wanted to use the anointing of Elijah without having the spirit of Christ; this meant they would "command fire to come down from heaven, and consume them, even as Elias." But Christ said, "Ye know not what manner of spirit ye are of." The spirit of Elijah, according to the book of Malachi, was originally meant to foster reconciliation between true sons and their fathers.

> Behold, I will send you Elijah the prophet before the coming of the great and dreadful day of the LORD: And he shall turn the heart of the fathers to the children, and the heart of the children to their fathers, lest I come and smite the earth with a curse. (Mal. 4:5–6)

The spirit of Elijah is a spirit of love, prophecy, healing, and reconciliation; John the Baptist embodied that. The angel of the Lord said,

> And many of the children of Israel shall he turn to the Lord their God. And he shall go before him in the spirit and power of Elias, to turn the hearts of the fathers to the children, and the disobedient to the wisdom of the just; to make ready a people prepared for the Lord. (Luke 1:16–17)

Elisha inherited the spirit of Elijah through true sonship.

> And Elisha said, I pray thee, let a double portion of thy spirit be upon me. (2 Kings 2:9)

The last name that Elisha called Elijah before his mantle fell in his hands was "Father." Elisha was qualified through loving, loyal service to use the mantle of his father, Elijah. The sons of Zebedee could only use the mantle of Elijah if they were fathered by him or divinely called to inherit it. In simple terms, it's a wrong spirit to use a mantle you've not faithfully served for or been magnanimously given. You cannot take from God; you can only receive what He gives to you. This wrong spirit on one occasion caused the sons of thunder to solicit for their right to the eternal thrones in glory.

> They said unto him [Jesus], Grant unto us that we may sit, one on thy right hand, and the other on thy left hand, in thy glory. (Mark 10:37, brackets added)

And Jesus said unto them,

> To sit on my right hand and on my left hand is not mine to give; but it shall be given to them for whom it is prepared. (Mark 10:40)

Later on in verses 42 to 45, the Lord explained to them the spirit of true sonship, which is the spirit of loyal servanthood. True sons faithfully serve their fathers in order to inherit greatness from them. However, the sons of thunder have a chaotic spirit; they don't have a calm demeanor. They wrongly mimic "the spirit of Elijah," through wanting to command fire to come down to destroy people (2 Kings 1:9–10).

Obviously, these sons of Zebedee had a spirit that differed from the spirit of Christ who said, "The Son of man is not come to destroy men's lives, but to save them " (Luke 9: 56).

In the case of these disciples, Jesus was their father in the ministry and His spirit was the Spirit of Christ, which is also the Spirit of God. The Spirit of Christ is greater than the spirit of Elijah, for that spirit is identified by its association with humans. The Lord, therefore, in Luke 9:56 turns His disciples' attention from imitating Elijah's spirit unto Himself.

> But he turned, and rebuked them, and said, Ye know not what manner of spirit ye are of. For the Son of man is not come to destroy men's lives, but to save them.

Don't get me wrong—the sons of thunder are faithful sons, yet they have an uncontrolled spirit. This chaotic, uncontrolled spirit causes the sons of thunder to veer from the Spirit of Christ. The sons of thunder must be constantly reined in to prevent the creation of a chaotic scene.

If they faithfully follow the Spirit of Christ and serve Him as true sons, they'll inherit His spirit, which does not destroy by fire but saves men. John Boanerges ultimately became the apostle of love (1 John 4:7).

Salvation is superior to destruction, any day. The Spirit of the Lord in this case is superior to the spirit of the sons of thunder. As anointed as the spirit of Elijah is, it could be tinged with the weakness of man: anger.

Elisha inherited it, and guess what?

> He went up from thence unto Bethel: and as he was going up by the way, there came forth little children out of the city, and mocked him, and said unto him, Go up, thou bald head; go up, thou bald head. And he turned back, and looked on them, and cursed them in the name of the LORD. And there came forth two she bears out of the wood, and tare forty and two children of them. (2 Kings 2:23–24)

The sons of thunder wanted to imitate the spirit of Elijah, for its ability to get infected with human weaknesses appealed to them. The spirit of anointed service, as wonderful as it might seem, must not be poisoned by a chaotic spirit. This destructive and chaotic streak within the spirit of the sons of thunder had the tendency of becoming detached from the Spirit of Christ, their mentor.

From time to time, the sons of thunder became the poster children of a spirit very different from the spirit of their spiritual father. These spiritual detachments are harbingers of infidelity and must be watched.

> Grant unto us that we may sit, one on thy right hand, and the other on thy left hand, in thy glory.

The sons of thunder are those sons who join a ministry and, without having demonstrated a period of loyal servanthood, want the pulpit and the microphone. They're overly ambitious.

They want a place on the platform by any means necessary. The sons of thunder hate humble, loyal service but love to be served. The sons of thunder believe the anointing upon their lives makes them the next major voice in God's kingdom, and those who don't receive their ministry are considered just jealous bigots. The sons of thunder feel too important to serve loyally in the lowly places of God's kingdom.

This narcissistic attitude agitated the members of Jesus's ministry.

> And when the ten heard it, they were moved with indignation against the two brethren. (Matt. 20:24)

The sons of thunder aren't effective team players. How could the sons of an uneducated Galilean fisherman be so conceited? The answer could be found in Matthew 20:20–28.

> Then came to him [Jesus] the mother of Zebedee's children with her sons, worshipping him, and desiring a certain thing of him. (Matt. 20:20, brackets added)

Does that mean their mother was in on all of this?

The name *Zebedee* in the Aramaic meant "abundant portion." Though Zebedee was an uneducated man, he was not poor. He owned a fishing company, worked with his two sons, and gave them out of his abundance whatever they needed.

My parents were great. They were solid believers and mostly resolute, yet their kindness led them to mollycoddle us sometimes. It goes with the parental territory, I guess. Approaches like "Let me give that little brat the chocolate bar to stop this hysteria" can become dangerous to a child, who will grow up with an exaggerated sense of entitlement.

A wealthy father and mother like the Zebedee couple, who could solicit in such a manner for their sons, produce children with unrealistic expectations of life and unchecked egos. Such should be considered a wrong parenting style.

No doubt these young men had their egos inflated by their mother. She backed them in everything, both wise and unwise.

> But Jesus answered and said, Ye know not what ye ask. Are ye able to drink of the cup that I shall drink of, and to be baptized with the baptism that I am baptized with? They say unto him, We are able. (Matt. 20:22)

Their unrealistic expectations of life were a symptom of their ignorance. "Ye know not what ye ask," said Jesus. "Are ye able to drink of the cup that I shall drink of?" he asked them. The Lord was referring to the cup of untold suffering (Luke 22:42), but their unchecked egos were hinged to their lack of understanding of the question. Because of that lack, "They say unto him, We are able."

What did Jesus mean by "ye know not"? He meant "ye know not" that one of you will be killed by the sword in your prime (Acts 12:2). How the reality check did come for their mother Salome in AD 44 was when James Boanerges was beheaded in Jerusalem by Herod Agrippa.

Parents have a responsibility to raise level-headed children. Sons of thunder are raised out of a permissive parentage. What others see in their home as self-serving is seen in theirs as prudent.

Parents who raise egotistic children are sinning, period! Humble children become great men and women in their adulthood.

The principle of meekness and self-effacing attributes must be consistently hammered into the psyche of a growing child.

> And it came to pass, when the time was come that he should be received up, he steadfastly set his face to go to Jerusalem, And sent messengers before his face: and they went, and entered into a village of the Samaritans, to make ready for him. And they did not receive him, because his face was as though he would go to Jerusalem. And when his disciples James and John saw this, they said, Lord, wilt thou that we command fire to come down from heaven, and consume them, even as Elias did? (Luke 9:51–54)

They earlier solicited for the accolades and the podium and now willy-nilly must have their way with these villagers; but should they be denied, they might create a chaotic scene by calling down fire. They cannot handle the rejection. These are the sons of thunder.

*Action:* Your group can't shut its doors to the sons of thunder; however, its members should be on the lookout for the spirit of Boanerges for it has an inflated ego, anger issues, and unrealistic expectations for itself. These attitudes must be discouraged through speaking the truth in love.

# MILESTONE 7

# THE COVENANT

## Step 1: Recognize the unspoken covenant

Understanding the dynamics behind gathering the brethren in a bungalow's yard on November 2014 was *as weird as it comes*. The length of the time we had spent separated and the independence enjoyed by each of us running our ministries, churches, businesses and lives buttressed that point.

After all, we had done fine so far as individuals, hadn't we? Yet, there we sat, clearly trying to fathom our way forward as a group—that is, after making some frantic effort to shove a red herring called the letter under the carpet.

In my view, our "drinking" from the same anointed ministry had something to do with it. That single act of God might have knitted our souls together and somehow could rally us again. It was an unspoken covenant, a strange binding tie.

Without it, our erstwhile leader couldn't have pulled this off. His influence had most certainly cast a long shadow over our varied endeavors through the years.

I looked into a familiar face and whispered, "Hi, it's been a long time." A smile and a nod reciprocated the gesture. This was the kind of custom that got bandied about that evening.

> And it came to pass, when he had made an end of speaking unto Saul, that the soul of Jonathan was knit with the soul of David, and Jonathan loved him as his own soul ... Then Jonathan and David made a covenant, because he loved him as his own soul. (1 Sam. 18:1, 3)

It's important to note in this verse that the knitting of souls preceded the making of the covenant, which was usually visible and audible.

> And Jonathan stripped himself of the robe that was upon him, and gave it to David, and his garments, even to his sword, and to his bow, and to his girdle. (1 Sam. 18:4)

However, this enactment was on a foundation that was hidden from the senses, on the heart-to-heart and soul-to-soul connection. It was the invisible and inaudible dynamic behind the covenant, their unspoken covenant. It was felt by their gut instinct. Group fidelity, trust and unity evolve here.

> So all the men of Israel were gathered against the city, knit together as one man. (Judges 20:11)

The Lord built a little community of disciples out of twelve men with diverse backgrounds and personalities. He managed to keep the group's fidelity going for three and one half years. What was His secret? It was the same invisible bond that existed between Elijah and Elisha, David and Jonathan, and Moses and Joshua. It was a love that is hard to explain in human terms, yet it had a prophetic slant to it. Without a ritual, verbal chemistry or signed contract, they stuck together through thick and thin.

This kind of relationship yields friendship.

> This is my commandment, That ye love one another, as I have loved you. Greater love hath no man than this, that a man lay down his life for his friends. Ye are my friends, if ye do whatsoever I command you. (John 15:12–14)

The Lord isn't done building communes of disciples; He only does it today by the move of His Holy Spirit. He draws individuals together and then knits them as one unit.

> That their hearts might be comforted, *being knit together in love*, and unto all riches of the full assurance of understanding, to the acknowledgement of the mystery of God, and of the Father, and of Christ ... And not holding the Head, from which all the body by joints and bands having nourishment ministered, and *knit together*, increaseth with the increase of God. (Col. 2:2, 19, emphasis added)

By the sovereign act of God, we had all made our peculiar way to the upper room where we became brethren. There the Holy Spirit intertwined our lives into a tapestry of a spiritual movement. According to the apostle

Paul, this was spiritual knitting done with the thread of love. It is an unspoken covenant. It is difficult to tell what initially led Barnabas to seek Saul (Paul) out for the Antioch mission (Acts 11:22).

> Then departed Barnabas to Tarsus, for to seek Saul. (Acts 11:25)

After all, he had a long list of budding evangelists to pick from (Acts 11:20). So why Saul (Paul) in particular?

> And when Saul was come to Jerusalem, he assayed to join himself to the disciples: but they were all afraid of him, and believed not that he was a disciple. But Barnabas took him, and brought him to the apostles. (Acts 9:26–27)

For some mysterious reason, Barnabas trusted Saul (Paul) when no one else did. There was an unspoken covenant between the two evangelists. The secret behind it all was later made obvious by the Holy Spirit.

> As they ministered to the Lord, and fasted, the Holy Ghost said, Separate me Barnabas and Saul for the work whereunto I have called them. (Acts 13:2)

Did you read the words "called them"? The hearts and souls of Paul and Barnabas were knitted by the Holy Spirit's call. An unspoken covenant was cut in their hearts and souls. There was a common spiritual work that lingered in their destinies.

In the case of the brethren, our souls were knitted in the upper room to light the fires of the charismatic renewal around the world. A similar covenant welded together the lives of Charles G. Finney, Daniel Nash, and Abel Carey, launching the second Great Spiritual Awakening (Liardon 2008).

*Action:* Your group must recognize that there is an unspoken covenant between them wrought by the hand of God, that their friendship isn't man-made but God-made. It is their responsibility not to ruin what God had initiated.

## Step 2: Cut the spoken covenant

What people say does in the long run affect how they'll behave. I accidentally recognized this reality while strolling with a protégé of mine.

It's hard to exhume from my memory exactly what he said that day, but it surely did impress me. It's not that I hadn't heard it before, but the capability he showed in saying it as we chatted on the road adjoining a community recreational center startled me. It demonstrated an unwavering conviction, and I loved it.

"Say it again," I said with elation. It was, to the best of my recollection, a statement that revealed the power of the word of faith, so he said it again.

"You've made a very powerful discovery. Never, ever forget it," I said, sounding grave while pointing my finger at him. I had taught many in that port city, much out of the several revelations the Holy Spirit had given me. The revival group he belonged to had come through numerous difficulties and now was at the cusp of something great. Under the shade of a tree, he and I struck a spoken agreement. I had preached it with faith and he had repeated it with faith; a heartfelt covenant had been cut. Jesus might have sensed the same thing when Peter acknowledged Him as the Son of God. The Lord had provoked His disciples to speak, and out of the abundance of the heart, Peter had spoken, "You are the Christ, the Son of the living God."

They both agreed that this was a God thing, and the covenant was cut. Ultimately, Peter went on in spite of his personal challenges to lead the Lord's apostolic team.

My phone's screen lit up and a call came through. "Hello, pastor," the caller said.

"Hello. Please, who is it?" I said because the phone number that had shown up was unfamiliar.

"Daddy, it's me, your son," he said haltingly. It was the young man from the port city. The surprise left me momentarily speechless. I had not heard from him in a while. As a matter of fact, I never even thought of hearing from him anymore after so long. "How are you doing?"

"Fine," he replied. Then he said, "Please, I've started a church in Benghazi, Libya. We're about five hundred in number."

"Son, I always knew you'd do that." I could hear a giggle. The conversation ended quickly, but it set me musing with gratitude. I grinned through my tears.

I was visibly overwhelmed by his fidelity. Was it a surprise, though? It wasn't. Those words of faith spoken under the shady tree cut a covenant to take the vision of the revival to the nations.

Unlike tacit agreements, the spoken covenant is rather overt.

> Ruth said, I entreat me not to leave thee, or to return from following after thee: for whither thou goest, I will go; and where thou lodgest, I will lodge: thy people shall be my people, and thy God my God: Where thou diest, will I die, and there will I be buried: the Lord do so to me, and more also, if ought but death part thee and me. (Ruth 1:16–17)

The Ruth story is one of the most compelling narratives concerning fidelity and covenanting ever told. The fact is, genuine fidelity actually makes no sense to the rational human mind. Fidelity or faithfulness cannot be separated from faith. And true faith is both spiritual and unreasonable. Faith that is based on the visible is never true. For me, Ruth's story depicts all of these qualities of faith and true fidelity.

It's difficult to tell the cause of the tragic circumstances that befell the family of Ruth. Perhaps it was a disease epidemic or plague that hit their community in Moab and hence spared no family. It could also be a gender-related tragedy, for it seems to have claimed the lives of the man Elimelech and his sons, leaving behind only the women in the family. Whatever was the cause, the land of Moab introduced us to the story of Ruth in a situation of death, darkness, pain, loss and brokenness; and Naomi appeared to have borne the brunt of this entire ordeal. In a very short period, she had lost her husband and sons. Her whole life had caved in, and grief had engulfed her very existence. "They [she and her two daughters-in-law] lifted their voice and wept" (Ruth 1:9, brackets added).

Naomi believed that God had dealt unjustly with her. She made some very startling remarks against the Lord.

> The hand of the Lord hath gone out against me. (Ruth 1:13)

The Almighty hath dealt very bitterly with me. I went out full, and the Lord hath brought me home again empty: why then call ye me Naomi, seeing the Lord hath testified against me, and the Almighty hath afflicted me? (Ruth 1:20–21)

It was obvious from her statements that Naomi felt that God had failed her. The unfortunate part of this situation was that these words were rehearsed in the ears of Ruth. They were not faith-building words. They did not foster the spirit of fidelity toward God. Ruth's background did not prepare her to process this through her own faith. She was a Moabitess, and the Moabites worshipped several gods. For if one god failed to meet a need, there were several others waiting in the flanks. Ruth did not need to bother with a God whose worshipper felt maltreated by Him. Moreover, Ruth had come to know the only true God, Jehovah, through her husband's family, and Naomi reflected that. Naomi had been Ruth's inspiration; she had learned about God through her. Now, her faith in her God had totally fallen apart. Many of us come to faith after being inspired by others. We look to these men and women as our heroes. Then, when tragedy strikes and they flounder, we flounder as well.

> And she said, Behold, thy sister in law is gone back unto
> her people, and unto her gods: return thou after thy sister
> in law. (Ruth 1:15)

Naomi made the situation worse for Ruth by encouraging her to revert to her gods. This was not just an option; it was a major temptation. What Naomi was doing was unconscionable. She was calling Ruth and her counterpart, Orpah to relinquish their faith in the only true God. What's strange though is that, Orpah took the bait and accepted this option. Ruth was then left in a woeful dilemma as she watched her colleague, her counterpart, her confidante walk away, back to her gods. You can imagine how lonely this might have felt for Ruth. She had no one to lean on for encouragement. But the decision that Ruth was about to make was to me, the pivot point around which this profound story was to revolve. This is one of the most profound acts of faith known in the Bible. Perhaps it justifies how she, as a woman and a Moabitess, found her story being told unapologetically in a book that had little space for her gender or tribe within its archives, the Bible.

Peering through the darkness of her circumstance with literally nothing to hold on to, she proclaimed her faith. I stand in total awe of Ruth's faith and fidelity. It stands totally unequalled in scripture. What could she do to convince God and her bitter mentor of her unflinching fidelity? She cut a spoken covenant with Naomi.

> Ruth said, I entreat me not to leave thee, or to return from following after thee: for whither thou goest, I will go; and where thou lodgest, I will lodge: thy people shall be my people, and thy God my God: Where thou diest, will I die, and there will I be buried: the Lord do so to me, and more also, if ought but death part thee and me. (Ruth 1:16–17)

One mentor of mine once defined faith as *believing in God in the face of every sense-evidence contradiction*. In this situation, there were several sense-evidence contradictions. In other words, there was enough evidence to prove that fidelity at this stage did not make sense. It was simply nonsensical. Why should Ruth follow the God of a bitter old lady who was ranting words like,

Turn again, my daughters: why will ye go with me? are there yet any more sons in my womb, that they may be your husbands? Turn again, my daughters, go your way; for I am too old to have an husband. If I should say, I have hope, if I should have an husband also to night, and should also bear sons; Would ye tarry for them till they were grown? would ye stay for them from having husbands? nay, my daughters; for it grieveth me much for your sakes that the hand of the Lord is gone out against me. (Ruth 1:11–13)

Ruth demonstrated pure fidelity toward God and Naomi, and pure fidelity does not make sense. There was nothing within the sense realm to offer Ruth the basis for fidelity toward God and Naomi, let alone for cutting a spoken covenant with her.

Her fidelity was very similar to that found within a marriage covenant. It was "till death do us part," for she said, "The Lord do so to me, and more also, if ought but death part thee and me" (Ruth 1:17).

All leaders need associates and followers with the kind of fidelity found within Ruth, those who will cut a spoken covenant with them. Such fidelity cannot be discouraged by contradictions, opposition, persecution, setbacks, abandonment, pain, or hopelessness. And we all know that real life is full of these things. But pure fidelity will cut a spoken covenant and forge ahead in spite of these things till the vision of revival for the local church, fellowship, ministry or group is fulfilled.

*Action:* Your group must conduct covenant services. Individual members can then collectively make a spoken covenant with God and one another for the vision to be fulfilled.

## Step 3: Make the blood covenant

"You should be afraid," the heavily built gentleman said. He was obviously concerned. A former loyalist of the revival group had sought to upend the work by his sinister deeds. He'd been loitering about with this self-serving agenda for a while. Honestly, I couldn't be bothered. After all, it wasn't my call to protect the Holy Spirit's work.

Tragedy had earlier struck that small congregation, and the fidelity of a bunch of them had gone up in the air like confetti. Humanly speaking, there was little I could have done then or could do now. I'll be candid: I had often thought, *What can I do to keep the revival from being discombobulated?* Now, that was a helpless meditation.

Be that as it may, God might have smiled on my helplessness from the balconies of heaven and sent help. "Teach on the covenant, and hold regular services," the Holy Spirit said.

I felt it wouldn't hurt to practice the word, so we did. Heretofore, we had "broken bread" without seeing it as a covenant-making act for the group. Biblically, it is a blood covenant, and this is what the Lord wanted. So we held a series of communion services and had some teaching.

Without much drama, fidelity returned, and the work got stabilized and restored.

Now about that time Herod the king stretched forth his hands to vex certain of the church. And he killed James the brother of John with the sword. And because he saw it pleased the Jews, he proceeded further to take Peter also. (Then were the days of unleavened bread.) And when he had apprehended him, he put him in prison, and delivered him to four quaternions of soldiers to keep him; intending after Easter to bring him forth to the people. Peter therefore was kept in prison: but prayer was made without ceasing of the church unto God for him. (Acts 12:1–5)

This story tells us about how valuable the fidelity of a church is to its spiritual leadership. Herod Agrippa, under the influence of the Jewry, sought to destroy the leadership of the church in Jerusalem. The congregation sat in silence as Stephen was murdered in cold blood by a certain terrorist cell led by Saul (the would-be apostle Paul). Again, they sat watching as Herod beheaded James, a key leader and a pillar within the church. Seeing its paralyzing effect on the church and how pleasurable the martyrdom was to the Jews, Herod undertook to take out Peter also. But he miscalculated his timing.

"Then were the days of unleavened bread," the Passover. This was the exact season of the first New Testament covenanting service (Luke 22:1, 15–21). That night, the communion became the hallmark of the covenant service: the New Testament Passover. *Passover time is blood covenant time and deliverance time* (Exo. 12).

And he took a cup, and when he had given thanks he gave it to them, saying, Drink of it, all of you, for this is my *blood of the covenant*, which is poured out for many. (Matt. 26:27–28 ESV, emphasis added)

Jesus then, knowing the cataclysmic storm this little flock would be subjected to, had welded their fidelity into a blood covenant.

> Then saith Jesus unto them, All ye shall be offended because of me this night: for it is written, I will smite the shepherd, and the sheep of the flock shall be scattered abroad. (Matt. 26:31)

By the power of the blood covenant, the fires of fidelity were stoked and "prayer was made without ceasing of the church unto God for him."

It seemed as if God had waited to see the fidelity of the church so He could respond appropriately. God sent his angel to the prison guarded by four quaternions of soldiers to set Peter free. From a very practical human standpoint, this was in many ways an impossible mission. For "the same night Peter was sleeping between two soldiers, bound with two chains: and the keepers before the door kept the prison" (Acts 12:6).

But the prayer made to God with an intense fidelity prevailed.

> And, behold, the angel of the Lord came upon him, and a light shined in the prison: and he smote Peter on the side, and raised him up, saying, Arise up quickly. And his chains fell off from his hands ... When they were past the first and the second ward, they came unto the iron gate that leadeth unto the city; which opened to them of his own accord: and they went out, and passed on through one street; and forthwith the angel departed from him. (Acts 12:7, 10)

Faithful churches have the awesome capability of praying their leadership out of any situation. Churches must uphold their leaders with their fidelity so the ministry will endure. Many churches have woefully failed in this arena.

> But the land, whither ye go to possess it, is a land of hills and valleys, and drinketh water of the rain of heaven. (Deut. 11:11)

The land or the realm God has called the church to possess is a land or realm with both hills and valleys. Hills are the exalted or elevated places, and valleys are the depressions as we travel through the seasons of life.

According to God, the realm He has called us to possess is characterized by high places and low places, uplifting circumstances and depressive situations, exalted positions and humbling positions. In the ministry of Jesus, He took His disciples to the mountaintop, where they had an exhilarating experience with God's glory (Mark 9). Peter wanted this to be their permanent location, yet the Lord urged them to go into the valley. There, they encountered some devils and demonic manifestations. They saw some failures as well in the valley, yet they stuck together. We need churches that will be covenanted, because there will be high and low seasons that will test their fidelity. We need churches that will keep their covenants or agreements when there are seasons of glorious supernatural manifestations and seasons of demonic circumstances. We need churches that will stay covenanted when they go through those uplifting seasons and realms and still stay covenanted when they go through those depressive spiritual seasons.

*Action:* Your group must conduct regular communion services with particular attention being given to its significance in covenanting its members.

## Step 4: Make the mutual covenant

"There's none faithful among you all like this brother," the leader of the brethren said with such certainty that his words stilled the demeanor of all present. Though we'd known who he was referring to, the comment most certainly surprised us. *Why wasn't it this or that brother but him in particular?* My thoughts raced back and forth. Perhaps he had his own reasons, so it stood uncontested. His words to us seemed the most revered thing next to the Holy Writ.

With the fragmentation of the brethren, our eyes were riveted to the most appropriate choice. And guess who? It was the "most faithful" would-be successor.

> Then all Israel gathered themselves to David unto
> Hebron, saying, Behold, we are thy bone and thy flesh.
> And moreover in time past, even when Saul was king,
> thou wast he that leddest out and broughtest in Israel:

181

> and the LORD thy God said unto thee, Thou shalt feed
> my people Israel, and thou shalt be ruler over my people
> Israel. (1 Chron. 11:1–2)

Our apostolic leader had spoken, and who were we to do the contrary? Hence, a decent majority of we budding leaders did the most commonsensical thing we could envisage, and that was to, one by one, acquiesce to the friendship of "the faithful one." And so he became the leader of the newest revival group in town.

"Let us join our hands as a sign of agreement," he said. That day, in a makeshift chapel—someone's spacious living room—we were called into, his exact words, "a covenant."

*A covenant?* I quizzed myself as we prayed. *Never heard of such, save for Abraham and Moses.* Nonetheless, on such a basis, a revival group was born.

> Therefore came all the elders of Israel to the king to
> Hebron; and David made a covenant with them in
> Hebron before the Lord; and they anointed David king
> over Israel, according to the word of the Lord by Samuel.
> (1 Chron. 11:3)

Can a covenant be made between a pastor and his or her congregation, a leader and his or her followers? Absolutely, if what David did with the elders of Israel was to be a useful example. For a fellowship, ministry, group or local church to be very successful, it will have to enact a covenant between itself and its leader. Israel became very successful in the days of David because they, as a unified entity, entered a covenant with him as their anointed leader. A local church will have to promise faithfulness to its pastor, and its pastor will have to do likewise to his or her congregants. For the covenant to yield its benefits to its parties, there will have to be fidelity. The quality of a congregation is highly dependent on the congregants' faithfulness to their leader or pastor. The quality of a pastor or leader is determined by his or her fidelity to the congregation.

A covenant is imperative because not all have the natural proclivity toward being faithful. For instance, despite the fact that Malachi 2:14 makes it clear that marriage is a covenant between a man and a woman, cheating is commonplace in today's culture, isn't it? It would be wrong as a leader to assume that your followers will take to corporate fidelity as ducks to water.

I read a joke the other day. A group of men were golfing one day, and four of them were on the eighteenth tee. The tee is a cleared space on a golf course from which the ball is struck at the beginning to enter a hole at the very end. A typical golf course has eighteen holes; hence, the eighteenth tee is the final and most important tee of the game. Just when they were ready to tee off, a funeral procession went by, and one of the men stood up straight, took off his hat, and put it over his heart. His golf buddies were stunned. Someone said, "We've never seen anyone ready to tee off and stop to put his hat over his heart to honor a funeral procession. That's amazing." The man answered, "Yeah, she was a great woman. We were married for forty-three years" (Eggerichs 2004). And that could be the summary of some dude's fidelity to his wife of many years.

Infidelity is baggage that many will bring along into any revival group; thus, a covenant is needed to bind their fidelity to the group's vision. Many might miss this, but the Last Supper was simply a good shepherd enacting a covenant with His key leaders. From thence, He had the moral right to demand their unflinching fidelity. A man such as Judas Iscariot got into trouble because he'd made a covenant with his leader yet gave no fidelity to actualize it. His betrayal went against the covenant more than anything else. That night, Jesus saw two of his key leaders, Judas and Peter, act disloyally toward Him, but one was cursed (Matt. 26:23–24) and the other let off the hook. Why? Prior to making a covenant with his leader, Judas Iscariot,

> said unto them [the enemies of Jesus], What will ye give me, and I will deliver him unto you? And they covenanted with him for thirty pieces of silver. (Matt. 26:15, brackets added)

He was cursed because *he came to make a covenant having already "covenanted" with others to betray it.* That was a wicked heart right there. Peter, on the other hand, covenanted with his leader but couldn't anticipate the spiritual warfare ahead or the degree of fidelity it would require. You can call it naïve, perhaps, but not sinister. Jesus foresaw that and interceded for him (Luke 22:31–32).

Right after the communion and Judas's departure, Jesus gives his little flock a critical commandment.

> A new commandment I give unto you, That ye love one
> another; as I have loved you, that ye also love one another.
> By this shall all men know that ye are my disciples, if ye
> have love one to another. (John 13:34–35)

Why would he do that? Those who cut a covenant with a local church, fellowship, ministry or group do so because they "fall in love" with the type of ministry and people there. Love is a key to all covenant relationships. It is then and only then that the congregation can be a blessing to their pastor and he could be a blessing to them. Covenant partners are free to bless each other because they love each other. Those in a marriage covenant are free to bless each other because they love each other. Since God is both loving and faithful (Deut. 7:9), then true fidelity can be produced only when the love between a leader and his followers is evident.

> Let him that is taught in the word communicate unto him
> that teacheth in all good things. (Gal. 6:6)

Fidelity is a product of the love of God (1 Sam. 18:3). It is a divine behavior that proceeds out of love. God is faithful (1 Corin. 1:9), and God is love (1 John 4:8). When God's love is visibly demonstrated in a local church, fellowship, ministry or group, a covenant is enacted among them and demonstrated through genuine fidelity.

Each covenant has its benefits for its parties. During the enactment of the covenant, the parties promise each other benefits. These promises are also called vows; hear the Israelites tell David, "Behold, we are thy bone and thy flesh." Do these words ring a bell? They sound like what Adam told Eve at their wedding in Eden. Ruth said similar words.

> Ruth said, … for whither thou goest, I will go; and where
> thou lodgest, I will lodge: thy people shall be my people,
> and thy God my God: Where thou diest, will I die, and

there will I be buried: the LORD do so to me, and more
also, if ought but death part thee and me. (Ruth 1:16–17)

"Death part thee and me?" Aren't those words in wedding vows?

Every covenant does not yield its benefits automatically to its partners. For example, with the Old Covenant, even though it occurred between Abraham and God, the children of Israel, his seed, were the beneficiaries (Gen. 15:18). Israel had to promise to be faithful to God, and God had to promise to be faithful to Israel (Exo. 19:7–8; Deut. 28:1–8). Israel's faithfulness was demonstrated to God through the circumcision and obeying the Torah. God had to demonstrate His faithfulness to Israel through blessing them. This makes fidelity the secret that activates a covenant. It is also the guarantor of long-term loving devotion.

*Action:* The members of your group must, after a communion service, pledge their love and allegiance to one another, their leader and their vision.

## Step 5: Identify the covenant keepers

I reached deep into my blazer pocket for my phone. Wow—"three missed calls," the notification said. It had been ringing, and I hadn't felt it vibrate at all. Sneaking myself out of the funeral service to sort it out, my eyes became fixated on a signboard. By the curb where I stood, the familiar name of a revival group "yelled" at me. A campus of theirs was in the neighborhood. This ministry had recently seen some nationwide and global success. Nanoseconds of flashback carried me to memory's lane.

"Here, this is the name of the ministry," the man had said, pointing to a word that could sound as cockney to a Martian. "It means 'tears' in my northern dialect," he calmly explained in his inimitable heavy accent. I looked into his eyes, trying to read his thoughts. Having recently graduated from college, his heart was clearly ablaze with the Spirit's fire. Birthing a revival group was obviously the only object within his vision.

My consciousness returned from the 1990s to the present. It was 2015 again, and through the years, the fidelity of the group had been tested to the hilt. Believe you me—it is one thing to birth a child and another to bring it into adulthood. Ministries aren't any different. Through the loss of loved ones and many such thrashings of life that knock the wind out of strong men, their founding members, who were some great friends, had stuck to their tacit covenant—the till-death-do-us-part kind.

Still standing adjacent the Anglican chapel, the realization came that the strength of their fidelity had survived and outlasted pain, discouragement and tragedy. At last they had succeeded. This revival group had made it this far because they were great covenant keepers.

God brings His people together to form local churches, fellowships, ministries, and groups for a reason. God wants strong fellowships, ministries, groups, and local churches so that His presence and glory can be released throughout the earth. Regarding His presence, Jesus said in Matthew 18:20, "For where two or three are gathered together in my name, there am I in the midst of them." Also in Numbers 14:21, God states categorically, "But as truly as I live, all the earth shall be filled with the glory of the Lord." For this reason, God wants strong churches in every corner of the earth.

As stated earlier, churches or groups need to initiate covenants within their rank and file if they are going to be strong enough for God's purposes and plans to be achieved through them.

> Therefore came all the elders of Israel to the king to Hebron; and David made a covenant with them in Hebron before the Lord; and they anointed David king over Israel, according to the word of the Lord by Samuel. (1 Chron. 11:3)

Apostle Peter's experience gives us the notion that covenants are easy to make but difficult to keep. Covenants can be kept only by true fidelity. Anything else will fail.

Every day, men and women enter into covenants for marriages, companies, and churches, yet, as well intended as they may seem, some of these covenants fall apart through divorce, hostile takeovers, and church splits.

People swear, vow, and pledge with forever on their minds, yet these vows are ultimately broken. Why? It is because the covenant partners were never faithful to begin with. The fidelity factor is the covenant-keeping principle. We need covenant keepers to keep our local churches, groups, ministries and fellowships together.

Churches fall apart when the covenant keepers fall apart. For any church to have a great future, its members must be firm believers in covenant keeping. David and Jonathan kept their covenant till death. Loyal people respect covenant keeping. They do not casually enter into covenants. Covenant-minded people, who respect covenant keeping, will build great churches or ministries and greatly advance the cause of Christ. God is faithful; this is the reason He is a covenant keeper. God never breaks His covenants.

> My covenant will I not break, nor alter the thing that is
> gone out of my lips. (Ps. 89:34)

*It only takes a mouth to make a covenant, but it takes character to keep it.*
God is a covenant-keeping God because He is fidelity personified. When we bring loyalty into a covenant, we bring an attribute of God into it, and then the covenant cannot be broken.

> Know therefore that the LORD thy God, he is God, the
> faithful God, which keepeth covenant and mercy with
> them that love him and keep his commandments to a
> thousand generations. (Deut. 7:9)

We cannot have the next move of God in a local church, fellowship, group, or ministry without a covenant-minded people. We need covenant keepers in our church groups and ministries.

*Action:* Your group should follow up their communion services with some bold steps toward keeping their covenant with God, one another, and their leader. Communion services should be moments of renewed tenacity to fulfill their vision.

## Step 6: Deal with the covenant breakers

"This church doesn't know how to love," a man said as though he had premeditated it all for a while. It got me so irritated that I glowered. He'd been such a regular feature in the local church for years that these words hit me from the left field. It was a curveball.

"But you've been a part of this church, haven't you?" I said. We had been ambling along that afternoon on a dirt road and chatting, and in the pit of my stomach, I could sense that something was seriously askew. I made a mental note of his affairs from then on. But honestly, was this really a surprise or the result of my head-in-the-sand attitude?

"Hey, where did you get this guy from?" my friend of thirty-some years asked. He had just concluded a deliverance service with the church that day. This was a few years back.

"You mean—?" I jerked my thumb at the gentleman, our "unloved" brother. He had been in the meeting that afternoon, leading the praise.

"Yep. That guy doesn't have your spirit at all," he added. I'll say that, upon hindsight, he discerned right, didn't he?

For after his not-so-nice comments on the dirt road, we had managed to get along somehow, *the communion services* and all.

I cleared my throat and leaned forward in the seat. "I'm appointing the members of the church board, and I want you on it," I said. Though honest, it might have sounded like a trick suggestion. This was a second discussion on the issue. In the first, he'd asked to take a rain check on it.

"No, I'm afraid I have to decline," he gravely retorted. "The Holy Spirit has told me not to."

*Unbelievable*, I thought. But did I say I'd made a mental note? Afterward, he stealthily left the assembly, not to be heard about for months. Unbeknownst to me, he'd confided in others that some minister had offered him such needed help; the impetus swayed his fidelity, so he broke his covenant.

> This know also, that in the last days perilous times shall come. For men shall be lovers of their own selves, covetous, boasters, proud, blasphemers, disobedient to parents, unthankful, unholy, Without natural affection, trucebreakers, false accusers, incontinent, fierce, despisers of those that are good, Traitors, heady, highminded, lovers of pleasures more than lovers of God. (2 Tim. 3:1–4)

Men and women become traitors only because they become truce-breakers or covenant-breakers. The Greek word translated as *truce-breakers* is *aspondos*, which means, according to *William Mounce's Greek dictionary*, "a person unwilling to make a treaty or covenant." However, *James Strong's Hebrew and Greek dictionary* maintains the meaning "truce-breaker" or "covenant-breaker."

Many churches and organizations that began very well did not achieve their vision. Many showed early prominent signs of greatness, yet after some years, fell apart and became relics of history. A little research I did amazed me by what it turned up. I observed how many great spiritual leaders led great organizations that couldn't survive beyond a single generation. In some cases, the leader, before his death, saw the organization's momentum extinguished; others began to crumble after the leader's demise. In my little observation, without exception, they all began with the great promise of being highly revered institutions someday.

What went wrong, then? What caused the visions to fail? Why did these organizations fail to outlive their leaders?

> So when all Israel saw that the king hearkened not unto them, the people answered the king, saying, What portion have we in David? neither have we inheritance in the son of Jesse: to your tents, O Israel: now see to thine own house, David. So Israel departed unto their tents. (1 Kings 12:16)

David had been in a covenant with the Israelites and their elders during his generation (1 Chron. 11:3).

> Then all Israel gathered themselves to David unto Hebron, saying, Behold, we are thy bone and thy flesh. (1 Chron. 11:1)

Now, in his grandson, Rehoboam's generation, the Israelites had made a 180-degree turn saying, "What portion have we in David? Neither have we inheritance in the son of Jesse."

What went wrong? The recalcitrant behavior of David's grandson and his cohorts had so agitated the nation that they'd broken the Davidic covenant. Unlike David, some leaders aren't that fortunate; the covenants with their followers got broken in their generation.

As we have seen, it takes a covenant between a leader and his followers to develop any level of unity and achieve any level of success. Whenever organizations with great promise fall apart, it could simply be attributed to the lack of covenant keepers. The very opposite of a covenant keeper is a covenant breaker.

According to Romans 1:31, the unsaved person or unbeliever is naturally a covenant breaker. Such a person is "without understanding, natural affection, implacable, unmerciful." Since covenant keeping does not come to us naturally, we will have to be reeducated in it once we become saved. Getting saved does not automatically make us think along the lines of godliness. We have to be taught the ways of godly thinking and godly living. Our minds have to be renewed to understand covenant keeping. Unfortunately, many leaders have failed in this area. They leave this reeducation program to the Holy Spirit. Though I agree that the Holy Spirit is an awesome teacher, He still found it relevant to anoint church leaders to teach their followers the word of God.

Though the church might have its faults, and that is to state it mildly, it is still the pillar and ground of truth. The church is the only known institution for educating the human mind in understanding spiritual and eternal truths.

My wife once became concerned with one gentleman who, after getting saved, got disillusioned with church life so much that he made up his mind to stay at home and read his Bible with the hope that God would teach him His word. There is some growing you can do by yourself, but there is much growing you can do by committing to a local church, fellowship, ministry or group.

> Not forsaking the assembling of ourselves together,
> as the manner of some is; but exhorting one another:
> and so much the more, as ye see the day approaching.
> (Heb. 10:25)

If the believer in a local church needs to keep covenants, then he must necessarily enter a covenant in order to keep it.

How do believers enter a covenant with their local churches, fellowships, ministries, and groups?

> Taking bread, he blessed it, broke it, and gave it to them, saying, "This is my body, given for you. Eat it in my memory." He did the same with the cup after supper, saying, "This cup is the new covenant written in my blood, blood poured out for you. (Luke 22:19–20 MSG)

The Bible is clear that Jesus as a leader, entered into a covenant with His followers through the communion. The communion, as already dealt with in Step 3, is a covenant-enacting principle. There are two elements of the communion—the blood and the bread. Through the blood, Jesus used the words "poured out for you" to represent the sacrifice of a leader for His followers.

Through the bread, Jesus referred to His body, which represents His followers or His church. Throughout the New Testament, the church or followers of Jesus Christ are also referred to as *the body of Christ*. Thus, by communion, we do two things: we enter into a covenant with our leader, Jesus Christ, and we enter into a covenant with His followers, the church. When we drink the wine, which is Jesus's blood, we enter a covenant with him. When we eat the bread, which is Jesus's body, we enter into a covenant with our local church. This is the New Covenant. I am not here dealing with the blood, for that is between Jesus and His church. I am dealing with the bread, which is between the church and its members. The New Covenant deals with the vertical relationship between Jesus, the leader and His followers the church; it also deals with the horizontal relationships among the individual members of the church. This act of the New Covenant is also known as the breaking of bread. The church must break bread often to reenact and renew its covenant with its members. Although, Jesus as a good shepherd by principle, has taught all church leaders through the communion to shed their blood for their followers, this is still exclusively between Him and His church. All leaders of local churches are a part of its membership. This makes the breaking of bread a covenant enactment between a leader and his or her followers. The disciples in the book of Acts broke bread often, and that supposedly included the apostles, elders, deacons, and so on.

Once we enact a covenant as a local church, it then becomes a necessity to keep it. It does not matter how many visions God shows us about our local church; if we will not keep the covenant, the vision will fail. *We need more covenant keepers, not more visions in a local church.* Numerous spiritual leaders can recount many gifted people walking into a church they shepherd, talking about a vision God gave them about the ministry's great future, yet at the least provocation they left without a single explanation.

> Likewise also the cup after supper, saying, This cup is the new testament in my blood, which is shed for you. But, behold, the hand of him that betrayeth me is with me on the table. And truly the Son of man goeth, as it was determined: but woe unto that man by whom he is betrayed! (Luke 22:20–22)

It becomes obvious why Jesus enacted a covenant with His disciples on the night of His betrayal. Betrayal is an act of covenant breaking. Covenant keepers do not betray. No one can be held liable of breaking a covenant if there is no covenant to begin with. Jesus deliberately enacted a covenant with His disciples, so the breaking of the covenant would be obvious. All those who drank the wine as His blood that night had a responsibility to be covenant keepers. All of us who partake of the communion have a responsibility to be covenant keepers.

> Then one of the twelve, called Judas Iscariot, went unto the chief priests, And said unto them, What will ye give me, and I will deliver him unto you? And they covenanted with him for thirty pieces of silver. And from that time he sought opportunity to betray him. (Matt. 26:14–16)

Judas Iscariot, though a disciple, had no business being at that table. The reason was simple—he had already entered a covenant with the chief priests to betray Jesus. He was a two-faced conman.

He was making a covenant he wasn't ready to keep. He set himself up to be a covenant breaker. Judas was placing himself in a tight place, a dilemma. Should he have partaken of the covenant with Jesus, then it would be likely that he would break it later; on the other hand, should he not break the covenant with Jesus, then his infidelity would become obvious to the chief priest. The Sanhedrin would feel duped and come after him. You can only imagine how tense or nervous he might have been that night. Covenant breaking isn't fun.

What is the true purpose of the communion? Is it a ceremonial rite established *only* to remind the church of the sacrifice of Jesus Christ on the cross? No—a thousand times no! I believe it is that and even more. We partake of it to reveal the covenant breakers. It is God's solution for church splits, dissensions, disunity and division.

*Action:* Your group must remind itself repeatedly, especially during its communion services, about the latent potential for covenant breaking and the divine judgment that follows. We'll deal with this in Milestone 8.

## MILESTONE 8

# THE JUDGMENT

## Step 1: Deal with the three factors of divine judgment

A woman collapsed on the floor wailing, "I killed him! I killed him!"

"Wha—what do you mean?" I stammered, gazing with wonderment as she threw her back against the black leather settee and slouched sideways.

My thoughts were reeling out of control. I had just brushed past a gentleman on the stairway who had given me the news in a jiffy. The reality of the tragedy smote me; it felt like a blow to my solar plexus.

"Hey, tell me—what do you mean you've killed him?" I shook her shoulders.

"I killed the brother because his praise and worship ministry was destroying our work."

"What work?" I asked with a grimace, looking into her eyes.

Was she referring to the news I'd heard on the stairway? Last night, the church's praise and worship leader had gone into cardiac arrest and hadn't made it. *Is she serious about this? What kind of assassin might she be?* I thought.

With a desultory look in her eyes, she turned her head upward and said, "I'm a witch." Talk about a double whammy. I knew I had to find every modicum of energy to remain standing. My feet had already developed that jellylike feel, and I fell sideways into the settee. It always jolts one's sensibilities when a young person passes on without any anticipation. He was only twenty-two.

Our conversation in the church office lasted longer than I'd expected. For within minutes, she had managed to regain a regular composure and drawn her beautiful frame up from the floor.

She knew she had to explain her version of the story, especially the witchcraft part. I listened with rapt attention.

In the past few months, we had been close to a church split. The political back-and-forth jostling, with its destabilizing effect, had gone on until we came to a cliffhanger.

The late worship leader, an ardent loyalist of the pastor, had been swayed by the infidelity of a disloyal faction. He verbally revolted. What couldn't be seen as imminent, though, was this calamity. The lady perhaps didn't know the political infidelity going on at the time. But did God know? Yes, He certainly did.

The church's atmosphere had tensed up with strife for a while, "for where envying and strife is, there is confusion and every evil work" (James 3:16); and this was certainly an "evil work."

Taking in her delightful looks, I thought, *Is she a witch for real, a church member?* However, as she sniffed and wept her way through the bizarre story, I became a believer.

In the following months, the church mourned and grieved, observing the fallout of spiritual infidelity. Infidelity is by its very nature a page from Satan's playbook; it's demonic, and most of us never find out till it claims its victim. This young man was a victim of infidelity's judgment.

> For the time is come that judgment must begin at the house of God: and if it first begin at us, what shall the end be of them that obey not the gospel of God? (1 Peter 4:17)

The judgment of infidelity can be very confusing because it's one of the few scenarios in which you find God, the Devil, and man collaborating. Judas Iscariot died of suicide to confirm the human factor in divine judgment, for he "went and hanged himself" (Matt. 27:5) "and falling headlong, he burst asunder in the midst, and all his bowels gushed out" (Acts 1:18). But his death was prophesied by the Holy Scriptures and endorsed by Christ to confirm the divine factor.

> And it was known unto all the dwellers at Jerusalem; insomuch as that field is called in their proper tongue, Aceldama, that is to say, The field of blood. For it is written in the book of Psalms, Let his habitation be desolate, and let no man dwell therein: and his bishoprick let another take. (Acts 1:19–20)

> The Son of man goeth as it is written of him: but woe unto that man by whom the Son of man is betrayed! it had been good for that man if he had not been born. (Matt. 26:24)

Moreover, the Bible states it clearly that he was demonized by Satan. This confirms the satanic factor in divine judgment.

Then entered Satan into Judas surnamed Iscariot, being of the number of the twelve. (Luke 22:3)

In my story, the activities of a disloyal faction and the verbal revolt by the worship leader gave us the human angle. The confessions of a sultry witch gave us the satanic angle. What about the divine angle?

Did God know about the foreboding circumstance—this painful tragedy? He absolutely did. For, "Neither is there any creature that is not manifest in his sight: but all things are naked and opened unto the eyes of him with whom we have to do" (Heb. 4:13).

Then, why did He not stop it? He didn't want to because all His admonishments and His laws are written for us in His holy word.

God judges all infidelity (Heb. 13:4); He's "the Judge of all the earth" (Gen. 18:25). A judge gives all his judgments based on a given law. What law does infidelity break? It is the divine law of covenants. We dealt with this in the preceding milestone.

There are numerous examples in the Bible of people being unfaithful to groups, institutions, agreements, covenants or codes of ethics and the divine judgments that followed.

The following are some divine judgments in the Old Testament.

*1. Poverty and Death*

Adam's Judgment

And the LORD God commanded the man, saying, Of every tree of the garden thou mayest freely eat: But of the tree of the knowledge of good and evil, thou shalt not eat of it: for in the day that thou eatest thereof thou shalt surely die. (Gen 2:16–17)

> And unto Adam he said, Because thou hast hearkened unto the voice of thy wife, and hast eaten of the tree, of which I commanded thee, saying, Thou shalt not eat of it: cursed is the ground for thy sake; in sorrow shalt thou eat of it all the days of thy life; Thorns also and thistles shall it bring forth to thee; and thou shalt eat the herb of the field; In the sweat of thy face shalt thou eat bread, till thou return unto the ground; for out of it wast thou taken: for dust thou art, and unto dust shalt thou return. (Gen. 3:17–19)

## 2. Death by Capital Punishment
Achan's Judgment

And Joshua, and all Israel with him, took Achan the son of Zerah, and the silver, and the garment, and the wedge of gold, and his sons, and his daughters, and his oxen, and his asses, and his sheep, and his tent, and all that he had: and they brought them unto the valley of Achor. And Joshua said, Why hast thou troubled us? the LORD shall trouble thee this day. And all Israel stoned him with stones, and burned them with fire, after they had stoned them with stones. (Joshua 7:24–25)

## 3. Intrafamily Adultery and Murder
David's Judgment

Wherefore hast thou despised the commandment of the LORD, to do evil in his sight? thou hast killed Uriah the Hittite with the sword, and hast taken his wife to be thy wife, and hast slain him with the sword of the children of Ammon. Now therefore the sword shall never depart from thine house; because thou hast despised me, and hast taken the wife of Uriah the Hittite to be thy wife. Thus saith the LORD, Behold, I will raise up evil against thee out of thine own house, and I will take thy wives before thine eyes, and give them unto thy neighbour, and he shall lie with thy wives in the sight of this sun. (2 Sam. 12:9–10)

## 4. Death by Suicide
Ahithophel's Judgment

And when Ahithophel saw that his counsel was not followed, he saddled his ass, and arose, and gat him home to his house, to his city, and put his household in order, and hanged himself, and died, and was buried in the sepulchre of his father. (2 Sam. 17:23)

*5. Death by War and Strife*
Absalom's Judgment

> And Absalom met the servants of David. And Absalom rode upon a mule, and the mule went under the thick boughs of a great oak, and his head caught hold of the oak, and he was taken up between the heaven and the earth; and the mule that was under him went away. And a certain man saw it, and told Joab, and said, Behold, I saw Absalom hanged in an oak. (2 Sam. 18:9–10)

> Then said Joab, I may not tarry thus with thee. And he took three darts in his hand, and thrust them through the heart of Absalom, while he was yet alive in the midst of the oak. And ten young men that bare Joab's armour compassed about and smote Absalom, and slew him. (2 Sam. 18:14–15)

*6. Deaths by a Trans-generational Disease*
Gehazi's Judgment

> But he went in, and stood before his master. And Elisha said unto him, Whence comest thou, Gehazi? And he said, Thy servant went no whither. And he said unto him, Went not mine heart with thee, when the man turned again from his chariot to meet thee? Is it a time to receive money, and to receive garments, and oliveyards, and vineyards, and sheep, and oxen, and menservants, and maidservants? The leprosy therefore of Naaman shall cleave unto thee, and unto thy seed for ever. And he went out from his presence a leper as white as snow. (2 Kings 5:25–27)

*7. Death by the Hand of an Assassin*
Joab's Judgment

> And afterward when David heard it, he said, I and my kingdom are guiltless before the LORD for ever from the

blood of Abner the son of Ner: Let it rest on the head of Joab, and on all his father's house; and let there not fail from the house of Joab one that hath an issue, or that is a leper, or that leaneth on a staff, or that falleth on the sword, or that lacketh bread. (2 Sam. 3:29)

Benaiah went to the sacred tent and yelled, "Joab, the king orders you to come out!" "No!" Joab answered. "Kill me right here." Benaiah went back and told Solomon what Joab had said. Solomon replied: Do what Joab said. Kill him and bury him! Then my family and I won't be responsible for what he did to Abner the commander of Israel's army and to Amasa the commander of Judah's army. He killed those innocent men without my father knowing about it. Both of them were better men than Joab. Now the LORD will make him pay for those murders. (1 Kings 2:30–31 CEV)

## 8. Divine Judgment Followed by an Established Kingdom
Shimei's Judgment

The king said moreover to Shimei, Thou knowest all the wickedness which thine heart is privy to, that thou didst to David my father: therefore the Lord shall return thy wickedness upon thine own head; And king Solomon shall be blessed, and the throne of David shall be established before the Lord forever. So the king commanded Benaiah the son of Jehoiada; which went out, and fell upon him, that he died. And the kingdom was established in the hand of Solomon. (1 Kings 2:44–46)

Divine Judgment in the New Testament
## 1. Death by Suicide
Judas Iscariot's Judgment

The Son of man goeth as it is written of him: but woe unto that man by whom the Son of man is betrayed! it had been good for that man if he had not been born. (Matt. 26:24)

Men and brethren, this scripture must needs have been fulfilled, which the Holy Ghost by the mouth of David spake before concerning Judas, which was guide to them that took Jesus. For he was numbered with us, and had obtained part of this ministry. Now this man purchased a field with the reward of iniquity; and falling headlong, he burst asunder in the midst, and all his bowels gushed out. (Acts 1:16–18)

*2. Premature Death*
Ananias and Sapphira's Judgment

And Ananias hearing these words fell down, and gave up the ghost: and great fear came on all them that heard these things. (Acts 5:5)

*Action:* Your group must constantly remind its members of the harsh judgment of spiritual infidelity. The power to start or stop infidelity is ultimately with humans.

## Step 2: Respond to the different strokes of divine judgment

Have you ever heard some folks say, "Knowledge brings accountability, and accountability brings judgment?" Many within the charismatic movement, such as the brethren, used to say that.

A call had just come through from one of our international campuses. It was impromptu, a habit they had acquired of getting in touch. Not that it bothered me, but on this day, it was bad news. An elder of their congregation had passed on.

"What happened?" I asked, calmly trying to collect my thoughts as best as I could.

"He had testicular cancer," the caller said, sounding forlorn. He had been his pastor in that city.

"Daddy, we prayed and prayed."

"I see," I said, sighing heavily. I thought about the several occasions he had called and passed the phone on to an elder. Though I had never seen him in the flesh, those calls helped us reasonably connect.

He interjected my train of thought and said, "Daddy, I had warned him about his abuse of the church's funds." I shuddered, hearing that.

"I told him many times that such behavior was dangerous."

"And he didn't listen?" I asked, sensing the precariousness of the situation. *Did he repent or did he not, before dying?* I felt the pathos the pastor had been through. He'd tried for months to nurse him back to health, but inevitably, his best hadn't worked out.

Without question, God judges financial infidelity. Ananias and Sapphira saw this clearly. All of this was avoidable. God would have overlooked it if he had been a novice, as in Acts 17:30, which says, "these times of ignorance God overlooked." The elder should have listened.

And the Lord said, Who then is that faithful and wise steward, whom his lord shall make ruler over his household, to give them their portion of meat in due season? Blessed is that servant, whom his lord when he cometh shall find so doing ... And that servant, which knew his lord's will, and prepared not himself, neither did according to his will, shall be beaten with many stripes. But he that knew not, and did commit things worthy of stripes, shall be beaten with few stripes. For unto whomsoever much is given, of him shall be much required: and to whom men have committed much, of him they will ask the more. (Luke 12:42–43, 47–48)

"For unto whomsoever much is given, of him shall be much required." This is a very important rule that defines the magnitude of divine judgment. God does not judge us humans in the same way we judge one another. Most of us tend to judge one another with the same rod or paint everyone with the same paintbrush. Just because an individual church, group, fellowship, or ministry member commits an action of marital infidelity does not make his or her local church a licentious congregation. Yet that is what we do; we say, "You know thus-and-so goes to so-and-so church but has been sleeping around with these number of men, so her church has got to be a backslidden one." Such hasty generalization does not fit into God's method of judging people.

> And shall make him of quick understanding in the fear of
> the Lord: and he shall not judge after the sight of his eyes,
> neither reprove after the hearing of his ears. (Isa. 11:3)

According to this messianic prophecy, Jesus will never judge things from the natural or human standpoint or by the use of His natural senses. A careful examination of Jesus's words in Luke 12:47–48 indicates that there are different levels of infidelity, so there are also different magnitudes of divine judgment. In judging the level of faithfulness of each servant, the Lord gave each of them different stripes. The one "which knew his lord's will, and prepared not himself, neither did according to his will, shall be beaten with many stripes. But he that knew not, and did commit things worthy of stripes, shall be beaten with few stripes" (Luke 12:47-48).

Through the years, I've come to believe that there's an element of truth to the saying. The more knowledge you would entrust to a person, the more responsibly you would expect that person to behave and the greater the punishment you would mete out to such an individual should he or she run afoul of his or her responsibilities. In the natural world, judges will judge juveniles who commit crimes differently from adults who do the same thing, based on this rule. God is no different in this regard.

> For he that eateth and drinketh unworthily, eateth and
> drinketh damnation to himself, not discerning the Lord's
> body. For this cause many are weak and sickly among
> you, and many sleep. For if we would judge ourselves, we
> should not be judged. But when we are judged, we are
> chastened of the Lord, that we should not be condemned
> with the world. (1 Corin. 11:29–32)

In these verses, the apostle Paul is dealing with the nature of divine judgment as it pertains to the local church at Corinth. His assertion was that, because certain of the church folk there had abused the sacredness of the communion, they had been judged by the Lord. Now, how did the Lord judge them? "But when we are judged, we are chastened of the Lord." The Greek word *translated* as "chastened" is *paideuo,* which means "to educate, discipline and punish." This implies that when the Lord judges an individual, He educates, disciplines, or punishes him or her. In the case of the Corinthian church, the Lord seems to have punished them. How did He do it? "For this cause many are weak and sickly among you, and many sleep." The Basic English translation of the Bible puts it this way: "For this cause a number of you are feeble and ill, and a number are dead." Thus, Paul ties these issues of physical weakness, sickness, and death to divine judgment or punishment. Why did the Lord use three types of punishment for the Corinthian congregation? It is simply because of the relative nature of divine judgment.

> I write unto you, little children, because your sins are forgiven you for his name's sake. I write unto you, fathers, because ye have known him that is from the beginning. I write unto you, young men, because ye have overcome the wicked one. I write unto you, little children, because ye have known the Father. (1 John 2:12–13)

The apostle John in his writing divides his target audience in the local church into three groups: the little children, the young men, and the fathers. On the surface, it might look like he is dealing with biological groups, but he is not. He tags each group to specific spiritual achievements, which are not necessarily associated with biological persons. The fathers are tagged to knowing "him that is from the beginning," the little children are tagged to their sins being "forgiven ... for his name's sake" and knowing "the Father," and the young men are tagged to having "overcome the wicked one." In this, we can safely conclude, that we are dealing with spiritual persons because you do not "overcome the wicked one" simply by being a young man or woman.

The apostle John was writing to spiritual "little children," "young men," and "fathers." These are groups with three levels of maturity. For clarity's sake, let me put it this way: they are the spiritually immature, the maturing, and the mature. The immature are "little children" or babes, the maturing are "young men," and the mature are "the fathers."

When the entire local church in Corinth got infected with infidelity (1 Corin. 5:1–6), God decided to judge the congregation but only based on the rule of *relative judgment*. My safe guess was that He judged these groups differently based on their level of spiritual maturity and knowledge. The punishment had three levels of intensity based on three levels of maturity. Though John's categorization wasn't based on the rule of relative judgment, the Lord punished the immature with the *few stripes* of physical weakness, the still maturing with *more* stripes of physical sickness and the mature or more responsible, with the *many stripes* of premature death.

This is the way divine judgment is meted out to a congregation; it's on different levels based on people's level of maturity. My educated guess is that, God punished Ananias and Sapphira with premature death because they had a much higher level of maturity than the ordinary believer in the first century Church.

> Not many of you should become teachers, my brothers, for
> you know that we who teach will be judged with greater
> strictness. (James 3:1 ESV)

The Greek word translated in the verse as *strictness* is *krima*; it means "judicial sentence" or "the execution of justice." The teacher, or "the more knowledgeable," will have a severer judicial sentence or condemnation.

*Action:* Decisive actions must be taken against members caught in situations of infidelity. The provision of options to either exit the group or repent would be an appropriate way to enforce change and avoid the severity of divine judgment.

## Step 3: Run on the purpose of divine judgment

The crowd cheered and jeered amid catcalls and whistles. The high decibel of their sound yanked me out of the world of sleep. "Joe Tex! Joe

Tex! Joe Tex!" they yelled in unison. For good reason, I was instantly plunged into a feeling of gut-level nervousness. I reminisced by seeing that name on a poster, "Joe Tex for sports president."

It was the voting season in my college hall, and some aspiring ones were vying for the sports presidency. Our praise and worship leader was among them. His nickname was Joe Tex. I figure you'll now know why I was concerned.

He was this stout bloke with the physique of a boxer, but he was great in his ministry. The ongoing revival in our fellowship had benefited hugely from him. However, at the dining hall–turned–convention center, a gaggle of undergrads had gathered to hear his manifesto. The sonority of his voice ratcheted up in me that edgy sensation.

I'd felt this way for a while, and he knew about it. My counseling hadn't helped dissuade him. I thought my frustration had reached its apogee.

"God, this sports position will distract him, and what would become of his ministry or this revival?" I prayed.

*Don't worry. I'll handle him,* the still, small voice of the Holy Spirit spoke. I had the choice of either believing or doubting. That wasn't easy. It was a gray area, and I couldn't relax, particularly on my bed that evening. His voice came on the speaker again, and they roared, "Joe Tex! Joe Tex! Joe Tex!" His cue soon ended, and others had theirs. That didn't interest me.

Morning came, and he strolled into the auditorium's basement for prayer. He had a chip on his shoulder, giving him an air that said, *I'm the next sports president of my hall and there isn't anything you can do about it.*

I recalled the Spirit's words and breathed easy.

Needless to say, voting day arrived. Joe Tex was gung ho that day. His great moment was near.

Would I let that bother me? I didn't. The balloting ended, and an uneasy hush fell across the hall. He was visibly absent from our prayer sessions. I wondered.

But campus news travels at lightning speed.

"Are you the only stranger in Jerusalem?" one guy from the fellowship said.

"He didn't win?" I had asked about the result, only to be slapped with the news. "How did that happen?" I was strangely elated and curious.

"They voted and he lost … by one vote."

"By just one vote? Only one?" I said.

Ouch, that did most certainly hurt!

The Lord had surely undertaken to judge swiftly in this matter.

The next day, I made it a point to visit and commiserate with Joe Tex. He was appreciative and might have taken that as an olive branch. Sheepishly, he pussyfooted into his role, with all of his shoulder chips gone and a new look of reverence lighting up his eyes.

That is the purpose of divine judgment, isn't it? It restores reverence to the recalcitrant.

> And Ananias hearing these words fell down, and gave up the ghost: and great fear came on all them that heard these things … And great fear came upon all the church, and upon as many as heard these things. And by the hands of the apostles were many signs and wonders wrought among the people; (and they were all with one accord in Solomon's porch. And of the rest durst no man join himself to them: but the people magnified them. And believers were the more added to the Lord, multitudes both of men and women.) Insomuch that they brought forth the sick into the streets, and laid them on beds and couches, that at the least the shadow of Peter passing by might overshadow some of them. There came also a multitude out of the cities round about unto Jerusalem, bringing sick folks, and them which were vexed with unclean spirits: and they were healed every one. (Acts 5:5, 11–16)

The purpose for all forms of judgment against infidelity is to restore the fear of God in the church. Infidelity takes root in the absence of reverence for God and his authority. It's in this vacuum that men are demonically inspired to desert the ministry, rebel against leaders, abuse the coffers, split the congregation, sexually molest the innocent, and deceive their superiors. When Ananias and Sapphira were judged by God, "*great fear came on all* them that heard these things" and "*great fear came upon all* the church." The fear of God became tangible wherever people went.

With the fear of God came a new level of reverence for God's delegated authority figures—the apostles. As a result, "by the hands of the apostles were many signs and wonders wrought among the people;" "and of the rest durst no man join himself to them: but the people magnified them." The apostles were "magnified" or held in such high esteem that they became larger than life. In a global church visibly permeated by the attitude of the Egyptian, which considers the shepherd as an "abomination," a series of divine judgments will be the only cure. Divine judgment in both pulpit and pew can plunge the global church into a season of reawakening. In this season of restoration, the church will "magnify" its leadership as it was in the first century.

When the fear of God swept across "all them that heard these" through divine judgments (and this means as far as its news went), *everyone* magnified the local church leaders, "and believers were the more added to the Lord, multitudes both of men and women." There was significant church growth because people both far and wide highly esteemed the "men of God" of their day. When the demonic virus of infidelity is expunged from every nook of the global church, then certainly a new season of spiritual awakening is upon us.

In Milestone 10, we'll explore the rewards reaped from the restoration of reverence.

*Action:* Your group, like the apostles, must confront forthrightly the attitudes of infidelity and irreverence that might infiltrate their morals. Zero tolerance must be demonstrated for such ethics.

# THE CHANGE

## Step 1: Pray and supplicate

My upper room experience at Caprice had drilled deeply into me a view that all true change should have a supernatural antecedent. In this, groups aren't very different from individuals. Prayer should be at the heart of all genuine change.

It was 1990, and I found myself in Nashville, Tennessee. There, on Bordeaux County's Eatons Creek Road, a little enthusiastic church group needed a change. I advocated my view: prayer.

"Brother Sagoe, we're gonna have a shut-in," Dr. Alex said. As the pastor of the fellowship, it seemed he had caught the vision.

With the two elders on board, the time of consecration took off that summer. It was a sunny July morning, I recall. The quartet plunged into long, uninterrupted sessions of tongue-speaking. The synergy was there. Minutes turned into hours and hours into days and nights. The red carpet of the sanctuary became our bed. Their idea of a shut-in was a hunger strike for Jesus with occasional bathroom and water breaks.

Saturday evening arrived. As for myself, I had been plugged into the Holy Spirit so much so that time had whisked by me that afternoon.

We looked at one another realizing the magnitude of the achievement. I said, "Whew! We've just been through praying for three days." Our fidelity had steeled us for this.

> These all continued with one accord in prayer and supplication, with the women, and Mary the mother of Jesus, and with his brethren. (Acts 1:14)

Being inspired by the Lord's vision, the disciples labored continuously "in prayer and supplication." This was their season of uninterrupted hard work. Fidelity kept the 120 disciples in prayer and supplication for seven unbroken days. Fidelity to the Lord's command to wait in Jerusalem turned the upper room from a stuffy, self-imposed prison into a prayer closet for bombarding the gates of heaven. They were hungry for a Holy Ghost outpouring.

At Eatons Creek road, the change did begin, albeit slowly. The tipping point was finally reached when the Holy Spirit used Robert Scales's visit as a catalyst for collective repentance. He was a young evangelist in the Tennessee area who had gotten turned on for the Lord. In the sanctuary, our services began with little space and got filled till there was none.

I left Bordeaux that September with a settled sense of the momentum. The fellowship was going somewhere. Dr. Alex and I met many years later, and that which began hadn't yet ceased. Thank you, Lord.

The following can be a possible prayer format your group can use. It was paraphrased from Ezra 9:7-15:

O, my God, we are ashamed and cannot lift up our faces to thee, our God: for our corruptions are increased over our head and our infidelities have grown up unto the heavens. Since the days of our fathers have we been in a great corruption unto this day; and for our untrustworthiness our church, fellowship, ministry, and clergy have been delivered into the hand of demonic entities of the land, to be murdered, attacked by sickness and disease, and poverty, to the confusion of our faces, as it is this day.

And now for a little space of grace had been shown from the LORD our God, to leave us a few people to escape this situation, and to give us a place to stand in your holy presence, that our God may lighten our eyes, and give us a little reviving in our spiritual bondage.

For we were slaves of sin; yet our God had not forsaken us in our bondage, but had extended mercy unto us in the sight of the principalities and powers to give us a reviving, to set up the Church of Jesus Christ, and to repair its spiritual desolations thereof, and to give us divine protection from demonic invasion. And now, O our God, what shall we say after this? For we have forsaken your spiritual direction, which you have commanded by your servants the prophets, saying,

the land, unto which your go to possess for the Kingdom of God, is an unclean land with the filthiness and abominations, which have filled it from one end to another. Now therefore do not conform to their moral standards nor seek their ill-gotten wealth forever: that you may be strong, and eat the good of the land, and leave it for an inheritance to your children forever.

And after all that is come upon us for our unfaithfulness, and for our great rebellion, seeing that you our God has punished us less than our corrupt motives and actions deserve, and has given us such salvation by the blood of Jesus; should we backslide and disobey your directions, and join in affinity with these worldly abominations? Would you not be angry with us till you have consumed us, so that there should be none to escape?

O LORD God of Israel, you are righteous: for we have escaped many of your judgments, as it is this day: behold, we are before you in our trespasses: for we cannot stand before you because of this. Amen.

This is the result.

> Now when Ezra had prayed, and when he had confessed, weeping and casting himself down before the house of God, there assembled unto him out of Israel a very great congregation of men and women and children: for the people wept very sore. (Ezra 10:1)

It is noteworthy that the genuine prayer and repentance of a few from spiritual infidelity can transform a whole congregation. The power resident in this gesture must not be underestimated.

*Action:* Your group must pray and fast for change.

## Step 2: Fight the spirit of Egypt

"You don't like speaking against men of God, do you?" He spoke with an attitude of mellowed amazement. The conversation he had pitched had somehow dovetailed into finger-pointing of some clergy. I wouldn't have any of that. Most rookies in ministry have no clue how dicey some church-life situations can be. I wouldn't take the critique of a general from a sergeant. If you can't honor the man, in fairness you should at least revere his experience.

Coming into this discovery wasn't as decorous as it might seem. I jaywalked into it, spiritually speaking.

*Don't speak that way again about my son!* I knew that voice; it was the Holy Spirit. I'd misspoken that evening, going on a tirade against one bishop's supposed indiscretions. As I drove on, God spoke so loudly I was visibly shaken behind the wheel.

*Never speak that way again about my son*, he said with the same deep vocal intonation, *for when no one wanted to go, he went.* Some folks might profess being delivered from bad habits through exorcism, but in that car, the voice I heard cured me from my irreverence and branded into me the fear of God. It transformed my worldview to see that, regardless, God stands by His people. I got it that day, never to forget.

God spoke through the prophet Malachi, declaring,

> Behold, I will send you Elijah the prophet before the coming of the great and dreadful day of the LORD: And he shall turn the heart of the fathers to the children, and the heart of the children to their fathers, lest I come and smite the earth with a curse. (Mal. 4:5–6)

This prophecy reveals that, before the coming of the day of the LORD, there will be a spiritual breach between the fathers and their children that will require healing. Moreover, according to this prophecy, the persistence of this breach will cause the Lord to smite the earth with a curse. In many places in the Old Testament, these Hebraic expressions do not necessarily mean that God will cause a curse but rather that He will permit it to occur.

How would the curse occur? The spirit of Egypt has an agenda, and it is to separate fathers from their sons, flocks from their shepherds, and pastors from their congregations. This separation will produce spiritual impoverishment, when the flocks and sons go without the life-enriching messages of their shepherds and fathers. Every form of impoverishment is a curse in the eyes of God.

How would the separation occur? Separation comes through irreverence by seeing the shepherds as an abomination.

> And it shall come to pass, when Pharaoh shall call you, and shall say, what is your occupation? That ye shall say, Thy servants' trade hath been about cattle from our youth even until now, both we, and also our fathers: that ye

> may dwell in the land of Goshen; for every shepherd is an
> abomination unto the Egyptians. (Gen. 46:33–34)

The spirit of Egypt is the spirit or attitude that considers the true shepherd as an abomination. In the Hebrew language, the word *pastor* is synonymous with the shepherd of a flock. In the New Testament, the word *pastor* refers to the spiritual shepherd or overseer of spiritual sheep or a church. The word *abomination* in the Hebrew means "disgusting." Biblically, the Old Testament shepherd is a shadow of the New Testament pastor. The Egyptian has a condescending attitude toward true shepherds, such that he despises them. I call this attitude *the spirit of Egypt.* The spirit of Egypt wants to end the move of God with a curse. The spirit of Egypt is against the upcoming revival in your group, fellowship, ministry or local church. The spirit of Egypt wants to reproduce the curse that prevailed in Israel before the ministry of Jesus Christ.

> But when he saw the multitudes, he was moved with
> compassion on them, because they fainted, and were
> scattered abroad, as sheep having no shepherd. (Matt. 9:36)

This is the kind of picture of a curse that the spirit of Egypt seeks to achieve within the body of Christ. Flocks without shepherds are easy prey for the wolves in sheep's clothing (Matt. 7:15). The spirit of Egypt has an agenda to destroy the spiritual sons (Exo. 1:11–12) and the next spiritual generation. It has an agenda to cut off the spiritual sons from the spiritual life flowing from their fathers.

How will the spiritual sons be cut off? You will have to believe the spiritual father that shepherds and inspires you with the spoken word in order to prosper or advance in your generation. But the spirit of Egypt wants to plant in the flock an attitude of irreverence toward their shepherds and fathers.

When did this begin?

> And Noah began to be an husbandman, and he planted
> a vineyard: And he drank of the wine, and was drunken;
> and he was uncovered within his tent. And Ham, the

father of Canaan, saw the nakedness of his father, and told
his two brethren without. And Shem and Japheth took a
garment, and laid it upon both their shoulders, and went
backward, and covered the nakedness of their father; and
their faces were backward, and they saw not their father's
nakedness. (Gen. 9:20–23)

The spirit of Egypt could be genealogically traced to Ham, the father
of Mizraim, the father of the Egyptians (Gen. 10:6). It is a spirit that
reveals the "nakedness" of the spiritual fathers of the land (Gen. 9:20–22).
This mockery and irreverence was contrary to the spirit of reverence
and love that resided within Shem and Japheth, the spirit that "covers a
multitude of sins;" for reverentially, they "went backward, and covered the
nakedness of their father; and their faces were backward."

Whenever reverence for a shepherd or father breaks down, a spiritual
breach develops in his relationship with his flock and spiritual sons. Due
to this breach, the flow of spiritual revelation and anointing from the
spiritual fathers to their sons is impeded. The breach is developed when
the shepherds and fathers feel their sons' and flocks' infidelity.

And Noah awoke from his wine, and knew what his
younger son had done unto him. And he … cursed. (Gen.
9:24–25)

Do you see the relationship that exists among irreverence, the curse
and the breach? The infidelity and irreverence of sons or flocks are felt
through their disrespect.

The following is a typical example:

I wrote unto the church: but Diotrephes, who loveth to
have the preeminence among them, receiveth us not.
Wherefore, if I come, I will remember his deeds which
he doeth, prating against us with malicious words: and
not content therewith, neither doth he himself receive the
brethren, and forbiddeth them that would, and casteth
them out of the church. (3 John 1:9–10)

This is how spiritual life in the next generation of spiritual sons will be snuffed out—through the irreverence or disrespect of shepherds. This is spiritual murder, an infanticide. Diotrephes was committing mass homicide of spiritual sons.

In Milestone 8, we saw how the spirit of Egypt's causing a breach between a worship leader and his shepherd made it possible for his life to be extinguished.

> And the king of Egypt spake to the Hebrew midwives, of which the name of the one was Shiphrah, and the name of the other Puah: And he said, when ye do the office of a midwife to the Hebrew women, and see them upon the stools; if it be a son, then ye shall kill him. (Exo. 1:15–16)

It'll produce a curse that will smite the earth because the next generation of sons of God or spiritual seed-bearers will be extinguished.

The solution is as follows:

> But the midwives feared God, and did not as the king of Egypt commanded them, but saved the men children alive. And the king of Egypt called for the midwives, and said unto them, Why have ye done this thing, and have saved the men children alive? And the midwives said unto Pharaoh, Because the Hebrew women are not as the Egyptian women; for they are lively, and are delivered ere the midwives come in unto them. Therefore God dealt well with the midwives: and the people multiplied, and waxed very mighty. And it came to pass, because the midwives feared God, that he made them houses. (Exo. 1:17–21)

We need evangelical leaders who will be the "Shiphrah and Puah" movement of today, those who will not obey the bidding of the spirit of Egypt but rather will be spiritual midwives who would help usher in the next move of sons of God or spiritual seed-bearers.

The "Shiphrah and Puah" movement will also preach the uncompromising word of God to save the next generation of spiritual children. They "saved the men children alive." God will deal well with these "midwife" leaders who fight the spirit of Egypt through their reverence of God.

"But the midwives *feared God*, and did not as the king of Egypt commanded them." The weapon of the spirit of Egypt is irreverence of the shepherds, but the counter weapon of "Shiphrah, and Puah" is reverence for God and His people. Whereas one comes with an attitude of irreverence, the other counters it with the fear of God or reverence. This is the key to trans-generational impartation: it helps pass on the revival and life-giving message from one generation to the next.

*Action:* Your group must make it their culture to not speak evil of anyone. They must fight irreverence toward their leadership by cultivating the attitude of reverence toward God and His people.

## Step 3: Heal the breach

The man I met was this six-foot-two or so hunk of a man. His frame towered over me as he offered his hand for a shake. I reciprocated, feeling in its firmness the strength of his grip. I would later find out that he'd been great at college football, his ambitious career being cut short by injury.

"Hi, welcome to Nashville," he said with a smile.

"Hello," I responded meekly, completely overwhelmed by what I'd seen so far in the Music City. Sizing him up, I got myself a view. *This should be a nice guy.*

And so, life at Eatons Creek Road began. Meeting usually in the evenings when Bible study or prayer sessions were held, the garage-turned-chapel gave me an idea that, in many ways, America isn't very far from Africa in church-survival tactics.

The pastor who had introduced us was an African man, a Ghanaian-born professor of Fisk University. We'd often banter in Fanti, a mother tongue we shared. This usually left the confident, self-assured elder out of the loop. He perhaps thought we'd been running circles around him. With time, this kind of chemistry might have irked him. Though he was an African American, the tongue of my continent to him sounded much like the language of aliens from Pluto. But, try as he could, he felt offbeat with his mimicry. He distanced himself completely. And I could sense some acrimony.

They might have had their own issues in that little assembly, but my presence seemed to have exacerbated them. In the following months, I did my best to allay his fears. On this day in particular, I had not the slightest clue of how bad his angst had gotten. One day service was being held, and he wasn't present. *It could be anything*, I supposed. Out of the serene blue, I heard screams from the sanctuary. *What?* My mind raced, and so I tried to find out. There was some controlled helter-skelter in there surrounding the pastor's dad who lay supine on the floor.

The doleful eyes of Miss B, the church secretary, looked at me. "What's the matter?" I asked.

"He suddenly collapsed. An ambulance is coming over," she spoke, emoting very much like myself.

"Pastor has a speaking appointment," she added. "Could you please take the schedule?"

"Oh no, I'm not sure. I'm not mentally ready for such," I said.

She drew close, held my upper arm, and whispered, "But you're spirituality equipped, Brother Sagoe."

So, on to the Baptist church I went. The preaching took off with a greater anointing than I'd anticipated. But somewhere in the middle of my flow, my eyes picked up on a burly man taking his seat on a back pew. I proceeded to conclude.

While exiting the hall, I finally figured the visitor out. It was the elder. *What is he doing in here?* I thought.

"Hey, great service," he said. "Please let me drop you off." Somewhere during the drive to Bordeaux, he broke the silence.

"You know, I was on my way to Atlanta for a business meeting," he said as he swallowed. "I knew about this meeting. The pastor and I were invited together, but I couldn't be bothered," he added, accelerating the speed.

Having turned onto Eatons Creek, he intimated, "God spoke to me on the way, so I turned. I know you're a true man of God because you spoke word for word what He told me on the way." My message that evening, you might guess, was on the love of God.

Going forward, the elder's attitude totally transformed. The acrimony evaporated. Riding in town one day after a successful deliverance session, we all belly laughed as the presence of God filled that car. The breach had been healed.

> Behold, I will send you Elijah the prophet before the coming of the great and dreadful day of the LORD: And he shall turn the heart of the fathers to the children, and the heart of the children to their fathers, lest I come and smite the earth with a curse. (Mal. 4:5–6)

How does one become a spiritual father? The natural father is the natural seed-bearer, and by it he fathers a child. Thus the one who carries the spiritual seed of the word then automatically becomes the spiritual father. Regardless of gender, should a person sow the seed of the word into the heart of another person, the born-again experience will make him or her the spiritual father. A female in this way can also say, "But ye know the proof of him, that, as a son with the father, he hath served with me in the gospel" (Phil. 2:22).

How does one become a spiritual child? Out of this seed, a new generation of spiritual children will be reproduced. The apostle Paul called his spiritual seed "my gospel," and by it all his spiritual children were reproduced (Rom. 16:25).

Spiritual children are not only the product of the spiritual seed carried by their spiritual fathers, but also are nourished by the same person into spiritual manhood.

> My little children, of whom I travail in birth again until Christ be formed in you (Gal. 4:19).

All fathers have the responsibility to sow the seed or sperm that produces a child and then raise that child into adulthood. Paul uses the word *again* to indicate a second effort. The first effort produces a spiritual baby, but the second effort produces a mature believer. There is a travail involved in this as well (Gal. 4:19).

How is the spiritual breach developed? The spirit of Egypt seeks to bring spiritual death into the lives of spiritual sons. This worldly spirit uses materialism and secular philosophies to bring spiritual death into the hearts of spiritual sons.

> For Demas hath forsaken me, having loved this present world, and is departed unto Thessalonica. (2 Tim. 4:10)

> Ye adulterers and adulteresses, know ye not that the friendship of the world is enmity with God? whosoever therefore will be a friend of the world is the enemy of God. (James 4:4)

The spirit of Egypt mocks the teaching of the fathers, so the faith of spiritual children will be aborted. At the Mars Hill, the spirit of Egypt was in full force. "And when they heard of the resurrection of the dead, some mocked: and others said, we will hear thee again of this matter" (Acts 17:32). The spirit of Egypt uses the secular philosophies of the day to counter the message of the spiritual fathers, so their spiritual sons will abort their confidence in the revelation of God's word. In Athens, it was the Epicureans and Stoics who demonstrated the spirit of Egypt.

> Then certain philosophers of the Epicureans, and of the Stoicks, encountered him. And some said, What will this babbler say? other some, He seemeth to be a setter forth of strange gods: because he preached unto them Jesus, and the resurrection. (Acts 17:18)

The spirit of Egypt seeks to *counter* and *ridicule* the spiritual fathers via their media and secular education so their spiritual sons will despise them. They seek to drive a wedge between the spiritual fathers and their sons so that the blessing of the move of God will not continue into the next generation. "The generational gap" experience pointed out by sociologists in the 1960s is a very dangerous trend when it comes to spirituality. Spiritual children need the blessing and wisdom of spiritual fathers.

What is the fear and concern of the spirit of Egypt? The spirit of Egypt wants to bring a curse into the earth because it is threatened by the recent multiplication of spiritual children in the earth. It is threatened by the growth of the evangelical revival movement worldwide.

*Action:* How can a breach in the group get healed?

He shall turn the heart of the fathers to the children, and
the heart of the children to their fathers. (Mal. 4:6)

This implies that your group should take the necessary steps toward
reconciling offended individuals or factions. The offended must pray for
those who had despitefully used them with a heart of forgiveness. The
offender must repent, confess his or her offense, render apologies, and offer
restitutions to the offended.

In Milestone 7, we saw that the breach between spiritual fathers and
children can be permanently healed by the covenant.

## Step 4: Initiate fatherly transference and impartation

There is a point within every family when the possessions of the father
must change hands. At this juncture, the baton of the father gets handed
from one generation to the next. Words of wisdom, revelations, and the
anointing of the spiritual fathers fall within this paradigm.

I had been in prayer for hours one morning and for some reason
couldn't let up at the usual time.

*Call Johnny and lay your hands on him. I have to make a special deposit
into his life*, the voice said. It was the Holy Spirit.

The young man had been living with my wife and me for a while. I
therefore groggily stood up and found my way to the bedroom door.

He had been doing some ironing in the hallway when the knob turned.
I hastily got the door ajar for a peep-through. Staring at him from within,
I might have startled him.

"Please come," I said, beckoning from my position at the entrance. He
cut off the power on the socket and walked toward me. Sensing a surge of
God's power on me, I stepped forward into the living room and laid my
hands on his forehead, saying, "The Lord told me to impart this anointing
into you."

The shock of it all knocked him backward and onto the floor. He tried
to get back on his feet but took a few stumbling steps forward as though
intoxicated and then swooned onto the concrete.

He lay there for a while—I can't remember exactly how long. When
he finally came to, his reddened eyes glanced in my direction as he strode

into the guest room like a bumbling drunk. We both agreed on one thing after that day: that his life was never the same. He had received something that he had never before experienced. It completely changed him, for from then on, his anointed ministry began.

The prophet Samuel took a vial of oil and poured it on Saul's head, saying,

> And the Spirit of the LORD will come upon thee, and thou shalt prophesy with them, and shalt be turned into another man. (1 Sam. 10:6)

How can this be actualized to transform your fellowship, church group, ministry, band or team?

> Moreover he said, I am the God of thy father, the God of Abraham, the God of Isaac, and the God of Jacob. And Moses hid his face; for he was afraid to look upon God. (Exo. 3:6)

When God revealed Himself to Moses at the burning bush, He did so as a trans-generational God. Therefore it was His idea to be the supernatural binding tie between the generations. The spiritual faith of Jacob was to be tied to the faith of his father, Isaac, and Isaac's was to be tied to the faith of his father, Abraham. It was God's idea for the faith demonstrated in Him to be passed down through the generations. In this way, God becomes a trans-generational God. The generational gap concept does not originate with God. It was introduced by something foreign to the nature of God—the spirit of Egypt. But there is a clause: without the fidelity of a new generation to the older generation, the generational gap cannot be avoided.

> And the things that thou hast heard of me among many witnesses, the same commit thou to faithful men, who shall be able to teach others also. (2 Tim. 2:2)

The divine mysteries and anointing entrusted to one generation must be transferred to the next in order for spiritual truths to endure within the body of Christ. But without the existence of "faithful men" within the global church, the Most High God will cease to be a trans-generational God. His vision will be truncated by a generation of infidels.

God has poured out in these last days His supernatural power and anointing upon all flesh, and lots of people worship every day in the houses of worship where this anointing is being released, people who want it in their lives. Despite this, there are many who worship in anointed churches without walking in the anointing that flows there. The man of God, Moses, had a church called the Church in the Wilderness (Acts 7:38), but the anointing for serving the congregation there rested upon him "alone."

> And it came to pass on the morrow, that Moses sat to judge the people: and the people stood by Moses from the morning unto the evening. And when Moses' father in law saw all that he did to the people, he said, What is this thing that thou doest to the people? why sittest thou thyself alone, and all the people stand by thee from morning unto even? (Exo. 18:13–14)

While Moses, the father of the church, was highly anointed, the people of his church remained un-anointed. God's original intention was for His people never to be un-anointed; the anointing was to be poured upon all flesh. The anointing of the fathers was meant for the sons—that is their divine inheritance. Hence, something has got to happen to change this situation. The sons of the house must share in the anointing of their fathers. How can this transference of anointing get done so the sons will cease to remain un-anointed?

To answer this question, we will have to closely examine why God anoints the fathers in the first place. God anoints the fathers to serve the sons of the house with blessings, deliverance, healing, restoration, prosperity, and so on. This service to the sons is the burden of the fathers. This is the burden of the Lord for His people, which He has shared with the fathers of these houses of worship—burdens of serving God's sons with His word, healing, deliverance, leadership, and guidance. Jesus said to the congregation at Nazareth,

> The Spirit of the Lord is upon me, because he hath
> anointed me to preach the gospel to the poor; he hath
> sent me to heal the brokenhearted, to preach deliverance
> to the captives, and recovering of sight to the blind, to set
> at liberty them that are bruised ... And he began to say
> unto them, This day is this scripture fulfilled in your ears.
> (Luke 4:18, 21)

This was Jesus's local church since He was a child, and it was His custom or habit to read the scriptures to them (Luke 4:16). However, on this day, the Lord stood to bear the burdens of ministry under an anointing of the Holy Spirit. Every consecrated ministry and house of worship has its burdens and responsibilities, and the purpose of the anointing is to strengthen the father to bear it. The anointing is the supernatural power that strengthens men to bear the burden of the Lord with Him. God pours out His anointing upon the fathers so they can bear this burden without collapsing under its weight.

However, the sons need to inherit the anointing of the fathers so they can also serve their generation with honor and dignity, but the anointing cannot be inherited without its associated burden, for it only comes to strengthen a person to bear a burden. So a son who wants to share in the anointing of the father of his house must be ready to share in the burden upon his shoulders. God calls the sons to share in the anointing because He wants them to share in a burden—the burden of financing the ministry, praying for the vision to succeed, growing the congregational size, and serving the baby Christians.

> And the Lord said unto Moses, Gather unto me seventy
> men of the elders of Israel, whom thou knowest to be the
> elders of the people, and officers over them; and bring
> them unto the tabernacle of the congregation, that they
> may stand there with thee. And I will come down and
> talk with thee there: and I will take of the spirit which is
> upon thee, and will put it upon them; and they shall bear
> the burden of the people with thee, that thou bear it not
> thyself alone. (Num. 11:16–17)

The Bible says that God instructed Moses to call seventy of his church elders to their chapel—"the tabernacle." These seventy were men who were ready to share in carrying the burden upon Moses. God then took the anointing that was upon Moses "alone" and poured it upon the seventy men, and because it was a prophetic anointing, they prophesied without ceasing. When the anointing upon the father descends upon the sons, they will be able to do the same thing that he does.

This is the system by which God will pour out His Spirit upon all flesh in these last days. Thus, anyone who wants to flow in any anointing must be ready to bear the burden upon the house of the fathers; for the anointing is for the carrying of burdens for growing churches, healing the sick, delivering the oppressed, preaching and prophesying the word, financing the vision, and so forth. Jesus said that "The harvest is truly plentiful but the laborers are few" (Mat. 9:37); thus, the few laborers need to step up to receive the anointing upon the fathers to strengthen them to perform the burden of doing the plenteous work.

*Action:* Your group must have retreats organized specifically for the impartation of faith and their leader's anointing. In exchange, the members of the fellowship must collectively agree to be faithful to their vision.

## Step 5: Keep the unity of the Spirit

> These all continued with one accord in prayer and supplication, with the women, and Mary the mother of Jesus, and with his brethren. (Acts 1:14)

The Lord's vision became the rallying point for all the disciples. The vision welded all their agendas into "one accord." It was a supernaturally engineered unity, forged through one vision. The vision of the Lord swallowed up all their personal goals until nothing mattered except what the Lord wanted.

The disciples no longer felt fidelity to their individual goals, but to the Lord's vision, for its light had blinded their eyes to any hidden, personal agenda. They were loyal with one accord.

> Men and brethren, this scripture must needs have been
> fulfilled, which the Holy Ghost by the mouth of David
> spake before concerning Judas, which was guide to them
> that took Jesus. For he was numbered with us, and had
> obtained part of this ministry ... For it is written in the
> book of Psalms, Let his habitation be desolate, and let no
> man dwell therein: and his bishoprick let another take.
> (Acts 1:16–17, 20)

They had dealt with the infidelity in their midst. Judas was history, and the hubristic attitude of the Zebedee brothers had been quelled. A new day had begun; it was time for teamwork.

It was early morning at the basement of our college auditorium, and the revival group that met there had largely put some unfortunate infidelities behind it. Dear brother Joe Tex was back in the fold, and some new faces had replaced certain absences. We had reformed, and much seemed like we were ready to take on the world.

"I saw the same thing," one sister said in her usually inspired but stoic manner. A brother had seen a vision of a dark being standing over a light-skinned lady with a dagger in hand. Though others in the circle had seen it as well, the image meant nothing more than an elusive apparition of some demon. We "bound" devils as our regular pastime in that basement—big deal. This would have been waved off as one of the numerous visions that highly spiritualized minds see, save that it had struck a mysterious note with me. My lovely auntie, who had been hospitalized for surgery, was in a fight for her life. The description fit her well.

*What am I going to do?* I thought. The last thing I wanted was to betray her privacy. Those of my college hall knew her particularly well. She had been their bursar, after all. I began shivering. I didn't have much time to make up my mind, so I owned up.

"Hey, that's my auntie you saw in that vision. She's gravely ill and in hospital for surgery."

With their hands held tightly in a circle, they glanced at one another.

"I think God wants us to pray for this woman," one rather shy fellow said. The agreement was unanimous and immediate. We weren't only seeing the same things; we were sensing the same things in that tunnel-like underground space. There was synergy there.

The group attacked that diabolical being like a pack of wolves prayerwise. Thankfully, my auntie got pulled out of that quagmire by an unseen hand and lived long enough to see me graduate. The power of God did the impossible.

A story is told of the largest, strongest horses in the world—Belgian draft horses. Each horse can pull at most eight thousand pounds. Two Belgian horses that are in harness but strangers to one another can pull twenty to twenty-four thousand pounds together. As a team, they can pull not twice as much but *thrice*. The weird thing is that, when the two are raised, trained and teamed to think as one, the unified pair can pull thirty to thirty-two thousand pounds—almost four times what they could pull on their own (Ramsey 2011)!

The principle is called synergism. By definition, the simultaneous actions of separate agents working together have a greater total effect than the sum of their individual efforts. More can be done in a team effort than can be accomplished solo. In order for the principle of synergism to work like it should, there has to be teamwork or unity.

This is what the devil seeks to disrupt. Be it through Judas's pernicious ways or the disrespectful and irreverent attitudes of the spirit of Egypt, he has eyes set against teamwork, synergy, cohesion and unity. Why? Because he knows very well that he'll stand no chance when the upcoming tsunami of God's power is unleashed in your fellowship, ministry, group, or local church.

Endeavouring to keep the unity of the Spirit in the bond of peace. There is one body, and one Spirit, even as ye are called in one hope of your calling; One Lord, one faith, one baptism, One God and Father of all, who is above all, and through all, and in you all. (Eph. 4:3–6)

How do we endeavor *to keep the unity of the Spirit?* By maintaining the principles practiced in Milestone 7—the covenant.

***Action:*** Your group must endeavor by any means necessary to keep the unity of the Spirit. The tactics of the devil must be discerned and fought before they interrupt the teamwork, synergy, cohesion, and unity of the group.

# THE REWARD

## Step 1: Rise as a servant

"Do you have anything to share?" My mumbling of those words to that little group barely yielded anything. The campus leader had failed to turn up that early morning, and none felt appropriately equipped to fill his seat. And so it seemed.

They each shook their heads in turn as I approached and singled them out for a response. I had taken it upon myself to make this request person after person, basically because this had been the order: prayer, prophecy, then teaching—every day.

I slumped into my seat, wondering what I was going to do. Then I guess I had a moment of realization: *I'll teach one of those revelations the angel of the Lord had taught me.* After my first supernatural encounter in the basement, I had had these morning angelic visitations in my room. They were as regular as clockwork.

"Can I please share some little thing that I have?" I glanced around the circle. Their nods affirmed the gesture.

To think, I was the Johnny-come-lately among that little flock who had found the effrontery to sit in for their leader, might seem chesty with a cursory look. But I'd found myself in previous months, a frequent companion of his. It wasn't an accident, for in my second week among them, I had nominated myself to perform the ushering duties, arranging chairs and stuff like that. Perhaps he had taken note of that and found it most beneficial to co-opt my services. I felt honored and loved it. After all, he carried a peculiar teaching anointing on his life, and this proximity was my privilege. Martin felt that way too, and I'd been supernaturally swept into another world as he taught on my first day.

I would have assumed that such would be the status quo (my offering these ushering services each dawn), till this day in question came. It is hard to explain what it was exactly, save that this unusual presence descended on me barely five minutes into my delivery and sucked me out of my body.

I mysteriously found myself out of my body, standing two yards away, watching me teach. It made a lot of sense to read from the apostle Paul: "whether in the body I do not know, or whether out of the body I do not know, God knows—such a one was caught up...." (2 Corin. 12:2). I returned to consciousness with my audience staring, completely spellbound, I suppose. From then, I began to teach consistently like the campus leader, exuding an anointed ministry akin to his. Through offering him my menial services, something he had might have rubbed off on me. I was eternally grateful.

> And it shall come to pass in the last days, saith God, I will pour out of my Spirit upon all flesh: and your sons and your daughters shall prophesy, and your young men shall see visions, and your old men shall dream dreams: And on my servants and on my handmaidens I will pour out in those days of my Spirit; and they shall prophesy: And I will shew wonders in heaven above, and signs in the earth beneath; blood, and fire, and vapour of smoke. (Acts 2:17–19)

According to the prophecy of Joel, God was going to pour out His Spirit upon all kinds of people. In the prophecy, God refers to the entire human race as "all flesh." He categorizes the human race into three specific groups: the old men and young men; sons and daughters; and servants and handmaidens. The first group is defined by their age, the second group by their gender, and the third by their social role. The category I want to focus on at this moment is the third, the one that deals with a social role. The prophecy is referring particularly to the social role of a servant. The menservants and the handmaidens, as people of the opposite gender, both perform the same social roles. They are all servants. God was going to baptize the servants with His Spirit. The last days are going to be the season of the servant. If God was going to pour out His Spirit upon servants, then our churches should be full of them. According to the apostle Paul, he served God with his spirit (Rom. 1:9). Jesus portrayed servanthood by donning the attire of a servant to wash the feet of His disciples (John 13:4–9). We must all be servants. It is a critical part of our Christlikeness. Paul calls himself a servant of Jesus Christ. Paul was a servant of Jesus Christ called to be an apostle (Rom. 1:1). Epaphras was also a servant of Christ. In a way, we must all be servants of Christ. I've seen multitudes of men and women who had received the outpouring of the Spirit upon their lives and did not make much out of it. And there are those who desire to come under the unction of the Holy Spirit and do great things in the Lord's name but do not understand that what they're thirsting for is actually the portion of servants. The anointing is the portion of servants. There is a reason that servants will particularly attract God's anointing in these last days. The reason we can quickly point out is fidelity. The Bible in several places ties the social role of a servant with the attitude of fidelity: "It is required in stewards that a man be found faithful" (1 Corin. 4:2). It is expected of servants that a man exhibits the character of highest fidelity. If God was going to pour out His Spirit upon us, then we would need to be faithful stewards or trustees of His anointing.

According to the Lord in Matthew 24:45, there are only two levels of ministry within His household. The first level is made out of servants, and the second represents masters or leaders. The understanding that this scripture gives us, is that the level of a master or leader is higher than a servant. Therefore, a servant must necessarily be promoted in order to become a leader or master. Servants must rise to the level of leadership. Churches will have all their future leaders rising from within their rank and file. It is totally unbiblical for a church to expect its leadership to be imported from somewhere else. The leadership of each church must be homegrown.

Whenever God seeks for a leader to lead His people, where does He set His eyes? When King Saul failed the test of fidelity, God immediately began looking for a new leader for His people. A day came when God instructed the prophet Samuel to fetch Him a king from among the sons of Jesse the Bethlehemite. When Samuel arrived at the house of Jesse, his mission was declared as a prophetic service to be held there. Jesse paraded his sons before Samuel to receive his prophetic ministration. The word of the Lord to Samuel was to identify during this time the future leader of Israel. God rejected every one of them. This most likely left Samuel bemused. Ultimately, he quizzed Jesse about all of his sons and realized that one of them, the shepherd boy among them, had been left out. His name was David. When David arrived, Samuel was immediately instructed by the Lord to anoint him as king over Israel. The question is, what did God find in this ruddy shepherd boy? The psalmist gave us a clue in Psalms 89:20: "I have found David my servant; with my holy oil have I anointed him." God found in David a "servant." He was the servant among his brethren; he cared for the sheep.

God cannot claim to have found David till He had sought him out. Finding only follows the act of seeking. Whenever God is looking for a leader, He looks within the demography of servants. Joseph served as a slave boy in the house of Potiphar before he was promoted to be an overseer and then the prime minister over Egypt (Gen. 39:1–6). Joshua was first called a servant of Moses before he became a leader over Israel. "And Joshua the son of Nun, the servant of Moses, one of his young men" (Num. 11:28). David served under King Saul as a musician before he was noticed as a captain over God's army (1 Sam. 16:22–23). "Elisha the son of Shaphat, which poured water on the hands of Elijah" (2 Kings 3:11). Elisha was Elijah's servant.

Why was God seeking for a servant in particular? This was because David was to be anointed to serve his generation (Acts 13:36). We cannot serve God's anointing to our generation till we are truly servants in attitude. David's posture as a servant positioned him to be anointed. He therefore became an anointed servant. It is critical to note that, right after this prophetic service, David returned to care for the sheep in the wilderness. It is there that he tested the fresh anointing against the lion and the bear and defeated them (1 Sam. 17:34–37). This showed that, although he was a servant, the anointing of the Lord upon him was still a formidable essence against any opposition. God first identified David as a servant, yet anointed him to be ruler or leader over His people (1 Sam. 16:1). The anointing came to set David the servant on a path to promotion. In Matthew 25:21–23, the Lord gives us further insight into his mode of selection, into how His servants are selected for leadership. He refers to the servant He is seeking for as having two essential qualities: being both good and faithful. In the Lord's eyes, fidelity is a good human quality. In other words, a good servant should be a faithful servant. One cannot come without the other. According to the scripture, the servant is only good because he is faithful over a few. God identified David when he was still a faithful servant over a few sheep (1 Sam. 17:28). The principle, therefore, is that if we demonstrate fidelity over a few, then God will find us and anoint us to be leaders over many. The servant should demonstrate a consistent sense of duty over a few. He should demonstrate his fidelity in the days of small beginnings so he will qualify to be anointed as a leader over a multitude.

Ultimately, when God found a servant within Joshua, He marked him as the future leader of the Israelites. But this future leader was not going to become anything by his effort; God was going to *make him.*

> His lord said unto him, Well done, thou good and faithful servant: thou hast been faithful over a few things, I will make thee ruler over many things: enter thou into the joy of thy lord. (Matt. 25:21)

How was God going to "make" Joshua a great leader over the Israelites?

> And the Lord said unto Joshua, This day will I begin to magnify thee in the sight of all Israel, that they may know that, as I was with Moses, so I will be with thee. (Joshua 3:7)

The word *magnify* was translated from the Hebrew word *gadal.* It means "to exalt, grow, develop, nurture or glorify." God made Joshua, Moses's servant, a leader by growing, developing, nurturing, exalting, and glorifying him. This means that no spiritual leader is self-made, for they are all God-made. The role of the servant is to serve with pure fidelity and then leave his or her development as a leader to God. In the right season, God will exalt and glorify the servant "in the sight of all."

In these last days, God's eyes are going to and fro in the earth to identify servants. For servants who have exhibited true fidelity *over a few,* He will pour out His Spirit upon them to be leaders *over multitudes.* The last days is the season of servants. It is the season for the rise and promotion of faithful servants. I can see a fresh outpouring of supernatural rain coming. I can see on the supernatural horizon the rain clouds gathering. Though this rain will be poured upon "all flesh" and in no way would be discriminatory, it is the loyal servants of God's household who will rise among the nations to oversee the multitudes that will be touched by His Spirit. Let the faithful servants of God's house be still loyal to the Lord, who will see their labor in secret and will anoint and promote them to the places of great leadership and notoriety. The next Billy Graham, Oral Roberts, T. L. Osborn, or Kenneth E. Hagin may be found today, perhaps serving as an usher or cleaning the toilets of his or her place of worship.

> Therefore, my beloved brethren, be ye stedfast, unmoveable, always abounding in the work of the Lord, forasmuch as ye know that your labour is not in vain in the Lord. (1 Corin. 15:58)

*Action:* Your group must realize that their mantle or anointing rests on the shoulders of their leader, and through faithfully serving him, they like Elisha can tap into it for themselves. This would be their reward.

## Step 2: Plug into God's reward system

> Then answered Peter and said unto him, Behold, we have forsaken all, and followed thee; what shall we have therefore? And Jesus said unto them, Verily I say unto you, That ye which have followed me, in the regeneration when the Son of man shall sit in the throne of his glory, ye also shall sit upon twelve thrones, judging the twelve tribes of Israel. And every one that hath forsaken houses, or brethren, or sisters, or father, or mother, or wife, or children, or lands, for my name's sake, shall receive an hundredfold, and shall inherit everlasting life. But many that are first shall be last; and the last shall be first. (Matt. 19:27–30)

The apostles "have forsaken all and followed" Jesus's ministry across the land of Israel. It had been a while since Peter and his colleagues left their families, houses, boats, and vocations to faithfully serve the multitudes alongside Jesus. There were moments when Peter's "brethren, or sisters, or father, or mother, or wife, or children" felt forsaken by him. The families of these apostles did not see much of them, especially during certain occasions. The question Peter asked was, "What shall we have therefore?" Was it worth the effort and the trouble?

Jesus knew what Peter was talking about. Hence, He did not beat about the bush. He therefore explained to him how God's reward system operates. There were two dimensions to it: the eternal dimension and the earthly dimension. The eternal dimension will provide specific eternal rewards, and the earthly dimension will provide earthly rewards.

Regarding the eternal rewards, the Bible says,

> Ye which have followed me, in the regeneration when the Son of man shall sit in the throne of his glory, ye also shall sit upon twelve thrones, judging the twelve tribes of Israel ... and shall inherit everlasting life. (Matt. 19:28)

These apostles will inherit endless life and sit on twelve eternal thrones, judging the twelve Israeli tribes.

The earthly rewards were described as, "Every one that hath forsaken houses, or brethren, or sisters, or father, or mother, or wife, or children, or lands, for my name's sake, shall receive an hundredfold" (Matt. 19:29). These apostles will receive a hundredfold of everything they forsook to follow the Lord. These were the rewards of their fidelity.

The eternal rewards were to be received in the hereafter for the spiritual ministry offered faithfully to the Lord. The earthly rewards were to be received in the here and now for the spiritual ministry offered faithfully to the Lord.

Now, I would not bother you with the hereafter, but I will venture into the here and now. Jesus and Elisha taught us about the earthly rewards of fidelity being twofold: first, the anointing of the Holy Spirit, and second, material possessions (Step six will address this).

"Do you remember that miracle?" I asked. It was July 2016, in a wooded neighborhood adjoining a college campus, and I had met with a member of an erstwhile evangelistic team I had led. He was a visiting professor from Wilfrid Laurier University, still animated all these years about the things of God—totally sold out to serving Him.

I was referring to an event that had happened in 1988: "There comes the Holy Spirit!" I had bellowed across the room. With my index finger, I pointed to an invisible spot on the right side of the podium; the attention of both students and staff was guided and became magnetized to the space as though they had seen what I had visualized. The teenagers had rallied up to the front when the altar call was made, eager and yearning to make a connection with God.

This is what we had been praying for: an unusual encounter with the Holy Spirit. It had been weeks since the evangelistic team began fasting in anticipation of this meeting. We had been invited for the service by the high school. Its boarding campus was the pearl of this sleepy mountaintop township, nestled within a forested elevation.

They had been kind enough to have housed the group in some guest house hidden behind their masters' bungalows. We had not slept much. The night had been passed praying and groaning in tongues. Time flew past us like cabooses.

In the school's chapel that morning, loud shrills and shrieks of over fifty juveniles had coincided with our expectation. Their eyes had been riveted for a few seconds to that invisible direction, anticipating some supernatural visitation.

It sounded like a hurricane, if I recall accurately. A strange mix of wind and heat invaded the hall. These wards were surprised as much as we were, for they moaned like the Holy Spirit's presence was cutting through their entrails. Then, without warning, they began to throw up whatever they had eaten that afternoon.

*Good gracious!* I thought. Puke was everywhere. It took quite a while for the commotion to subside. Relieved that it was all over (the cleanup and all), we began to take their testimonies. Numerous unbelievable healings and deliverances had occurred. Our fidelity had paid off. Our reward was that a girl who was previously blind in one eye had begun seeing in both. Her mates were elated. "What shall we have therefore?" (Matt. 19:27).

It had been decades since that event, and every member who served faithfully on the team had moved on to sterling achievements, some into ministries spanning the globe. Their fidelity had been rewarded by God.

> But without faith it is impossible to please him: for he
> that cometh to God must believe that he is, and that he is
> a rewarder of them that diligently seek him. (Heb. 11:6)

*Action:* The members of your group must be ready to forsake all and follow the move of the Holy Spirit if need be. Their fidelity must bring them to the point of being sold out to serving the Lord. By this they'll plug into God's reward system.

## Step 3: Receive the outpouring of the Spirit

"A man in white approached me and told me all my sins are forgiven," the young girl said demurely. She'd been bamboozled, and her demeanor for some thirty minutes had been a catatonic-like state. These were the first words she'd uttered after the overwhelming experience, wondering where she was.

This had been one of the mightiest baptisms of the Spirit I had ever witnessed. The Holy Spirit's power had descended that afternoon on the crowd of students like a massive torrent of supernatural rain. They were as startled as I was.

The evangelistic team had faithfully participated in a prayer and fasting chain. In some cases, it could run uninterrupted for seventy-two hours.

I had broken the group up into several pairs, with each assigned a specific time slot on the roster. They had given the program their utmost fidelity, running their shifts with such enthusiasm that I felt challenged and honestly grateful.

Standing before my young audience, I had wondered whether their number was worth my while. The journey to that part of the country had been long, tiring, and difficult. For all of our troubles, the altar call had yielded only sixty persons, many fewer than I had anticipated. We were used to larger responses to our efforts.

*Isn't it too late to bother about it?* I thought, brushing it off.

Then, without warning, the outpouring came, catching us off guard. Joel's prophecy said, "And it shall come to pass in the last days, saith God, I will pour out of my Spirit upon all flesh" (Acts 2:17). However, very few realize the degree of fidelity required in its actualization. With all due respect, the evangelistic team had paid its dues in this regard.

Jesus said, "But ye shall receive power, after that the Holy Ghost is come upon you" (Acts 1:8). The Holy Ghost had "come upon" the little crowd, and they had received power that surpassed their estimation, for heaven could not deny such united, loyal, focused, sustained, around-the-clock prayer.

In similar historic circumstances, the fidelity factor had proved itself time and again. On the day of Pentecost, the Jewish Harvest Festival, the gates of heaven were opened, and the mighty rushing wind of the Holy Spirit stormed into the upper room. The heavenly tongues of fire set the place alight with glory. The awaited promise of the Father had finally come. The Spirit filled up those 120 disciples till they spoke in strange languages (Acts 1:15; Acts 2:1–4).

At this milestone, the continued unbroken fidelity of these disciples had birthed tangible results and rewards. They will never see it the same way again.

The Jerusalem upper room experience gives us today a vital model for every fellowship, ministry, group, or local church to follow. The lesson we had learned from it is that the outpouring of the Holy Spirit awaits every group that will respond positively to the nine critical milestones we've journeyed through.

On a high school campus, a young man strolled toward me with one of our team members and struck a conversation.

"I can recall every word you spoke that day in your message," he said in such an upbeat way that I got tickled. It's been a little over a decade since my group received that outpouring with those high school converts in the hinterlands, and this gentleman was one of them.

"Really?"

"Yes," he answered, nodding enthusiastically. He had become a leader of a Christian group that had invited me to speak in their institute.

"All those people saved that day have become pastors and leaders," he added. Truly, the realization pleasantly shocked me. But didn't Jesus say, "Ye shall receive power, after that the Holy Ghost is come upon you: and ye shall be witnesses unto me" (Acts 1:8)?

If He did, then what the heck was this surprise about if they had become "witnesses" unto Him? Fidelity had yielded its reward, and I'm thankful.

*Action:* Your group must conduct frequent Holy Spirit baptism services for their new converts, backing it up with intense preparation in prayer and fasting. This will open "the floodgates of heaven" over the group. In this, I'll recommend my book *The Law of Manifestation* as very useful (Sagoe-Nkansah 2015).

## Step 4: Possess the double portion

If anyone feels like he or she would never fit into a specific mold, I can attest that I easily relate to that.

"I don't know how to place you and the kind of ministry you have. There are different dimensions to your calling," the man said. It sounded like what he'd witnessed was a potpourri of diverse anointing. I'd never realized that the dear brother had been checking me out. As a matter of fact, I had on several occasions felt that way too—like some spiritual eclectic act.

Since that dawn when the teaching mantle fell on me, I had plunged serendipitously into certain ministerial expressions that had me frankly puzzled. I had thought I was called to teach only because of the fluidity of biblical revelations, but then I wasn't sure anymore.

The Holy Spirit had swept through an all-night service in a strange way years later. Without a clue, prophetic revelations had begun pouring out with the same fluidity as the teaching anointing. Try as I could, stymieing the flow seemed the hardest thing to do, so I let it be, as one revelation after another got uttered.

*What in the world is going on with me? I have never considered myself prophetic,* I thought, reflecting on that morning.

I'll be candid; it took me several years to ultimately get a grip on that occurrence. My conclusion is that the mantle that fell on me in the basement was my double portion. I had unconsciously tapped into a mixture of teaching and prophetic mantles, probably through my service to the campus leader and other spiritual mentors. Denying that was hard.

And it came to pass, when they were gone over, that Elijah said unto Elisha, Ask what I shall do for thee, before I be taken away from thee. And Elisha said, I pray thee, let

> a double portion of thy spirit be upon me. And he said,
> Thou hast asked a hard thing: nevertheless, if thou see me
> when I am taken from thee, it shall be so unto thee; but
> if not, it shall not be so. (2 Kings 2:9–10)

1. "Elijah said unto Elisha, Ask what I shall do for thee." Elijah was provoking Elisha to place a request that had been provoked by his unflinching and unconditional loyalty. True fathers can only be provoked by genuine loyalty. Elisha was a provoker who used fidelity as his tool.

2. "I pray thee, let a double portion of thy spirit be upon me." You can't reject the spirit of a father and inherit it at the same time. Elisha wanted the spirit of Elijah so badly that he unconditionally embraced it when the sons of the prophets had distanced themselves from it. "The sons of the prophets went, and stood to view afar off: and they two stood by Jordan" (2 Kings 2:7).

3. "Thou hast asked a hard thing." Those who take the hard road of unflinching fidelity to their spiritual father will be qualified to ask for the "hard things."

4. "And fifty men of the sons of the prophets went, and stood to view afar off: and they two stood by Jordan" (2 Kings 2:7): The double mantle of fathers are things that are hard to get, these are what the sons of the prophets failed to achieve.

Note: This ratio is significant; Elisha was the only one who inherited Elijah's twofold mantle or spirit, amid fifty sons of the prophets who didn't. The ratio is 1:50. For every 51 sons that will follow a man of God, only one will inherit his twofold anointing. Reason? It's "a hard thing."

5. "Thou hast asked a hard thing: nevertheless, if thou see me when I am taken from thee, it shall be so unto thee; but if not, it shall not be so." Only true sons inherit the double portion of their father's legacy. As a result of this, it is only true sons who see themselves at the end of their fathers' season in ministry. To do this, they'll need to travel with him for the entire season. This is a hard thing to do.

Spiritual hobos, bastards, and vagabonds do not have in them the long-term fidelity to inherit the double portion of any mantle whatsoever, for somewhere down the line they will betray the journey.

Question: Are you a spiritual vagabond, hobo or bastard; or are you a true son?

6. "He took up also the mantle of Elijah that fell from him, and went back, and stood by the bank of Jordan; And he took the mantle of Elijah that fell from him, and smote the waters, and said, Where is the LORD God of Elijah? and when he also had smitten the waters, they parted hither and thither: and Elisha went over. And when the sons of the prophets which were to view at Jericho saw him, they said, The spirit of Elijah doth rest on Elisha. And they came to meet him, and bowed themselves to the ground before him" (2 Kings 2:13–15).

The "sons of the prophets" had remained behind at Jericho, but Elisha's fidelity to Elijah had prodded him on to Jordan. Between Jericho and Jordan was the "extra mile" accessible only to men of fidelity. Was this extra mile worthwhile?

Absolutely.

Elijah "took his mantle, and wrapped it together, and smote the waters, and they were divided hither and thither, so that they two went over on dry ground" (2 Kings 2:8).

Elisha "took the mantle of Elijah that fell from him, and smote the waters, and said, Where is the LORD God of Elijah? and when he also had smitten the waters, they parted hither and thither: and Elisha went over" (2 Kings 2:13).

Elisha came into possessing something that fifty others had failed to obtain because it was "a hard thing." It was the ability to do the same thing that his superior had done: "they [the Jordan] parted hither and thither," and more so "a double portion" of Elijah's spirit, mantle, or anointing rested on him. "The spirit of Elijah doth rest on Elisha."

"…when the sons of the prophets which were to view at Jericho saw him, they said, The spirit of Elijah doth rest on Elisha. And they came to meet him, and bowed themselves to the ground before him" (2 Kings 2:15). The rewards of fidelity for Elisha were twofold: first, Elisha was submitted to by fifty others who had failed their fidelity test; and second, he went on to perform a double of the miracles that his superior had.

Just as much as individuals, groups can collectively possess their double portion. Joel prophesied,

Be glad then, ye children of Zion, and rejoice in the
LORD your God: for he hath given you the former rain
moderately, and he will cause to come down for you the
rain, the former rain, and the latter rain in the first month.
(Joel 2:23)

*Action:* Your group should arise through fervent fidelity to the Lord's
direction and their apostolic father to possess "the former rain and the
latter rain" of the Holy Spirit. As individuals also, its members can possess
a double portion of their leader's anointing.

## Step 5: Walk in the acts of the Holy Ghost

The congregation that night gathered around and cheered. The
fascination with the gentleman's feet was obvious in their looks.

One fellow who had been invited to our service that evening had one
leg that was longer than the other. He had gotten extra height added to
one shoe to even out his walk. Till then, I had never found the bravado to
grow a leg, given that God had never used me in creative miracles. But the
little harbor city ministry had been faithfully crying to God for months.
We desperately wanted a move of His Spirit in our midst.

As the man limped forward, the audience didn't know what to expect.
Their laid-back attitude showed in their body language.

"Can you please sit on this table and stretch your legs?" I asked. As he
obediently moved, I could feel the heat of the anointing in my feet. They
seemed to be on fire. We measured his limbs to confirm the disparity.
Surely, it was shorter by three quarters of an inch.

"In the name of Jesus, I command you to grow," I said. His shorter leg
jerked uncontrollably, and then his body shuddered. Realizing the bizarre
activity, I asked him, "What do you feel in your leg?"

"I can feel something is—is happening in there," he stammered with
trepidation. Suddenly, his leg gave an added jerk, only it was stronger this
time. Slowly, it lengthened, edging closer to being on par with the other.

"Look, it is growing!" I yelled. This got the others leaping out of their
seats. Sheer curiosity had an upper hand in turning their passivity around.

Ultimately, the jerking and shivering subsided, and both feet lined up equally.

"Please get down and walk," I implored.

His perfect gait was obvious as he strode back and forth. We had just witnessed the miraculous extension of bone tissue. Fidelity had paid its price, and the long nights of consistently pressing into God had been rewarded. God was using us.

> But without faith it is impossible to please him: for he
> that cometh to God must believe that he is, and that he is
> a rewarder of them that diligently seek him. (Heb. 11:6)

The book of the Acts of the apostles was written by the evangelist Luke to document the acts of the Holy Ghost during the first century of the church's history. It reveals the Holy Spirit in His true element, as He moved with the disciples to fulfill the Lord's vision for every creature under heaven.

> ... the gospel, which ye have heard, and which was
> preached to every creature which is under heaven; whereof
> I Paul am made a minister. (Col. 1:23)

Though it was the passion of the Holy Spirit to see all men saved, it took His association with the disciples like Paul to see God's vision accomplished. God had to depend on man to make his acts known in the earth.

> What? know ye not that your body is the temple of the
> Holy Ghost which is in you, which ye have of God, and
> ye are not your own? (1 Corin. 6:19)

The body of man is the temple of the Holy Ghost. The Holy Spirit is the driver, yet man is His vehicle. He needs the human body as the vehicle of His supernatural acts "for ye are the temple of the living God; as God hath said, I will dwell in them, and walk in them; and I will be their God, and they shall be my people" (2 Corin. 6:16); for the Gospel to have reached every creature on earth required the reliability of the driver as well as the vehicle.

The success of the vision depended on two sides: the God-ward side and the man-ward side. All people of faith do not question the infallibility of God, yet practically speaking we do have enough reason to question the infallibility of man. God is perfect in all that He does (2 Sam. 22:31).

Should the mission of the first-century church have failed, it would have been from the man-ward side and nowhere else. But since it didn't, it tells much concerning the dependability of the human vehicles the Holy Spirit used then. This dependability is what we choose to call the fidelity factor.

The fidelity factor was then and is now the critical key to the success of any mission. It guarantees the reliability of God's human instrument.

Down through the centuries, an uncountable number of missions that the Holy Spirit initiated failed simply because the fidelity of man fell apart. Jesus's own mission was thrown into temporary disarray because of the infidelity of man. Judas Iscariot and Simon Peter were the main culprits.

> Behold, the hour cometh, yea, is now come, that ye shall be scattered, every man to his own, and shall leave me alone: and yet I am not alone, because the Father is with me. (John 16:32)

Every organization, be it a local church, fellowship, ministry, or group, that is determined to achieve its mission must know how to manage the fidelity of its members. Whether it does that or not will establish its failure or success. God has no problem in using, growing, and prospering organizations; rather, His challenge is how to find the loyal people to use, and whenever He finds them, He brags on them, for they will by His grace get His job done. They will reach the unreached with His miracles, signs, and wonders.

> And he said, Hear now my words: If there be a prophet among you, I the Lord will make myself known unto him in a vision, and will speak unto him in a dream. My servant Moses is not so, who is faithful in all mine house. (Num. 12:6–7)

God had no choice other than to rely on the fidelity of Moses to achieve His mission in Egypt and to build the vision of His house. Men of fidelity are special in the eyes of God. The challenge of God has become the challenge of every leader called by Him. The fallen human nature has made fidelity a rare human trait. Thus, every fellowship, ministry, group, or local church endeavoring to walk in the acts of the Holy Spirit has to clearly understand the fidelity factor in order to trust the right people. Why? So its mission doesn't suffer. Fidelity is at the root of every corporate success story.

*Action:* Your group must completely yield itself in fidelity to the vision that God has for its community, town, city, or nation. This is so it will be successfully used by the Holy Spirit to demonstrate His acts to suffering humanity.

## Step 6: Walk in the secret of wealth trusteeship

"You've come home quite early today," I said calmly with surprise to Adelaide, my wife. Our agreement was to take turns caring for the children, and my shift was to end at dusk, right before embarking to church for the evening service. She managed a smile. In the morning, we had run out of finances, only it was rock bottom this time. Figuring things out was my call, but honestly, I'd been tottering at my wits end.

"God has provided," she said softly.

"How?" I asked, looking up.

A brother we had not heard from in a while had unexpectedly paid her a visit at the office. It had been years since he and I partook in several revival groups. The most memorable was at the college basement. Our recollections were mutual.

Taking her seat on the wooden armchair, she faced me to explain.

"He said God had told him and his wife this morning to begin paying your salary," she responded.

"Really?"

"Yes, and he brought with him the first payment."

My heart almost missed a beat. Obviously, God had been watching over us. He had assigned His trustees to fund the ongoing revival and supply my need. In my bedroom, I went on my knees and tearfully thanked Him. In the following years, fidelity gingered this God-revering couple to stick to their guns for us. They gave faithfully out of their need.

As the mission grew, I watched with amazement as they simultaneously moved from their two-bedroom rented apartment into one pretty sizable mansion. Standing in the front yard of the tall, whitewashed edifice, I inhaled and took it all in. I had observed that they no longer drove their secondhand cars but had begun buying straight-from-the-showroom vehicles. This was a God thing.

Their financial loyalty to the revival in the port city had certainly raked in huge dividends. The Holy Spirit had led them into a secret, that same ancient mystery He'd handed down to all the trustees of wealth.

> Every man according as he purposeth in his heart, so let him give; not grudgingly, or of necessity: for God loveth a cheerful giver. And God is able to make all grace abound toward you; that ye, always having all sufficiency in all things, may abound to every good work. (2 Corin. 9:7–8)

Ever since man by disobedience fell in the Garden of Eden, he has been spiritually separated from God and fallen short of His glory.

> Behold, the LORD'S hand is not shortened, that it cannot save; neither his ear heavy, that it cannot hear: But your iniquities have separated between you and your God, and your sins have hid his face from you, that he will not hear. (Isa. 59:1–2)

Adam ran and hid as God's presence stepped right into the garden. Satan had already won him over to sign away his rights and deed (Luke 4:6).

Man was now suffering from sin-consciousness and shame. Later, he was visibly banned from the Garden of Eden due to his rebellion (Gen. 2–3). The separation of man from God produced spiritual death (Eph. 2:1–2).

God has from then longed for the return of man into His presence (Gen. 6:3). God is the eternal source of spiritual life; hence, separation from Him degenerates into spiritual death. If the separation from God causes spiritual death, then reconciliation to God results in spiritual life. "For with thee is the fountain of life: in thy light shall we see light" (Ps. 36:9).

God's vision was therefore to have all of His estranged children who had become slaves and children of Satan to be freed and returned to be His again.

> And the LORD said, My spirit shall not always strive with man, for that he also is flesh: yet his days shall be an hundred and twenty years. (Gen. 6:3)

At Calvary, the blood of God's Son Jesus Christ was shed to deem man a legal temple of God's Holy Spirit.

> Forasmuch as ye know that ye were not redeemed with corruptible things, as silver and gold, from your vain conversation received by tradition from your fathers; But with the precious blood of Christ, as of a lamb without blemish and without spot. (1 Peter 1:18–19)

We can therefore say that man in His most depraved state is currently owned by God.

> What? know ye not that your body is the temple of the Holy Ghost which is in you, which ye have of God, and ye are not your own? For ye are bought with a price: therefore glorify God in your body, and in your spirit, which are God's. (1 Corin. 6:19–20)

God's vision is therefore to have His redeemed property returned to Him. To achieve this vision, God has always looked for men and women He could work with. When God finds the men and women He can work with, it is only because He trusts them and they, therefore, become His trustees.

> I have found David my servant; with my holy oil have I anointed him: With whom my hand shall be established: mine arm also shall strengthen him. (Ps. 89:20–21)

God has unfathomable wealth both in the natural and the supernatural realm. To these trustees, God entrusts His natural and supernatural wealth. Both the natural and supernatural wealth of God are tied to His blessing.

> The blessing of the LORD, it maketh rich, and he addeth
> no sorrow with it. (Prov. 10:22)

God told Abraham,

> I will make of thee a great nation, and I will bless thee,
> and make thy name great; and thou shalt be a blessing.
> (Gen. 12:2)

In this verse, we see that, when God found Abraham, He decided to make Him a channel of both natural and supernatural wealth—"a blessing." Abraham was to become a trustee of God's blessings.

What is the purpose for God to entrust these trustees with natural and supernatural wealth? It is to facilitate the vision of God.

> And I will bless them that bless thee, and curse him that
> curseth thee: and in thee shall all families of the earth be
> blessed. (Gen. 12:3)

This is God's vision that "all families of the earth be blessed." Fidelity feeds on divine visions, and visions live off of the fidelity of people. Every time faithful people surround a vision from God, they cause it to come alive.

> And the scripture, foreseeing that God would justify the
> heathen through faith, preached before the gospel unto
> Abraham, saying, In thee shall all nations be blessed.
> So then they which be of faith are blessed with faithful
> Abraham. (Gal. 3:8–9)

I cannot find God entrusting His trustees with wealth that has no bearing on His vision for having His lost children return to Him. God's vision is to "justify the heathen through faith" and bring eternal life to mankind. But man is not an owner of natural wealth, for God said,

> The silver is mine, and the gold is mine, saith the LORD
> of hosts. (Hag. 2:8)

Humans are just trustees of the natural wealth of God's earth. When God calls a person the trustee of His wealth like He did "with faithful Abraham," He calls him or her to be a distributor of His entrusted wealth. The purpose of this distribution is to facilitate God's vision for bringing His lost sons and daughters into a relationship with Him.

The principle is simple: God tests the faithfulness of man to His vision by asking Him to distribute the little that he or she has to fund it. This was the case of a wealthy young ruler Jesus met.

> Now when Jesus heard these things, he said unto him,
> Yet lackest thou one thing: sell all that thou hast, and
> distribute unto the poor, and thou shalt have treasure in
> heaven: and come, follow me. (Luke 18:22)

In the opinion of God, human wealth is little as compared to His. What humans obtain from this evil world system through their toil and sweat is called by Jesus Christ "unrighteous mammon."

> If therefore ye have not been faithful in the unrighteous
> mammon, who will commit to your trust the true riches?
> (Luke 16:11)

Unrighteous mammon is money as we know it; it is the culmination of all the currencies known to mankind. Money in itself is not unrighteous but the human system within which it flows is unrighteous. It is hard to tell what the money we possess in our wallets may have been used for; it might have been used for patronizing the services of a call girl, and right after it leaves our hands, it might be used to purchase some cocaine. The unrighteous mammon we possess in the bank is in God's eyes "little." It is never enough, for the apostle Paul calls it "uncertain riches."

> Wilt thou set thine eyes upon that which is not? for riches
> certainly make themselves wings; they fly away as an eagle
> toward heaven. (Prov. 23:5)

But according to Malachi 3:10, God wants to make humans trustees of His wealth, which there is not enough room to contain. God wants to promote humans from the "little" to much, from lack to overflow. If the man will faithfully distribute his little unrighteous mammon as God wants it, such that God's vision is brought into reality, then God will make him His trustee and entrust him with much wealth. God promotes people to be His trustees by honoring their faithful distribution of the entrusted wealth. In other words, the fidelity factor is at the heart of financial prosperity. When people faithfully invest their unrighteous mammon into funding God's vision, God makes out of them trustees of His fabulous wealth.

As has already been said, the money that flows in this perverse world system is called unrighteous mammon. The "true riches" that Jesus talks about are the opposite of unrighteous mammon. Notice that Jesus never refers to unrighteous mammon as true riches. If unrighteous mammon is counted as the opposite of true riches, then, in Jesus's view, it is actually a form of false riches. Jesus in Mark 4:19 mentioned the deceitfulness of riches. Whereas the false riches operate in this world system, the true riches belong to another world—the heavenly world. Jesus calls the true riches the treasures in heaven. To God, the true is "up" there and the false is "down" here. The real is "up" there and the uncertain is "down" here.

> Lay not up for yourselves treasures upon earth, where moth and rust doth corrupt, and where thieves break through and steal: But lay up for yourselves treasures in heaven, where neither moth nor rust doth corrupt, and where thieves do not break through nor steal. (Matt. 6:19–20)

Now, there are two kinds of treasure or wealth: that which is on earth and that which is in heaven. The earthly treasure is uncertain because it is corruptible wealth and can be stolen; the treasure in heaven is incorruptible wealth and cannot be stolen.

James speaks along the same line, describing the nature of false wealth.

> Your gold and silver is cankered; and the rust of them shall be a witness against you, and shall eat your flesh as

it were fire. Ye have heaped treasure together for the last
days. (James 5:3)

How we distribute the false wealth or unrighteous mammon to finance
God's vision will determine whether God will entrust us with the true and
heavenly wealth or not.

When Jesus met the rich young ruler, He asked him to distribute his
unrighteous mammon to the poor. The rich young ruler wanted eternal life,
which to Jesus was very much a part of the treasure in heaven. According to
the prophet Malachi, when the windows of heaven open, then the heavenly
blessings will be poured out. These blessings should necessarily be a part of
the treasure in heaven. The treasure in heaven—eternal life and heavenly
blessings—encompasses everything that money can and cannot buy. These
blessings reproduce the kind of wealth that cannot be destroyed by the evil
system of the world because it is rooted in God.

> The blessing of the LORD, it maketh rich, and he addeth
> no sorrow with it. (Prov. 10:22)

The apostle Paul calls the blessing that reproduces wealth, the grace
of God.

> And God is able to make all grace abound toward you;
> that ye, always having all sufficiency in all things, may
> abound to every good work. (2 Corin. 9:8)

We cannot buy these heavenly blessings with money, for they are the
blessings of the Lord. We cannot buy this grace with money, for it is the
grace of God.

> And I will bless them that bless thee, and curse him that
> curseth thee: and in thee shall all families of the earth be
> blessed. (Gen. 12:3)

God said all the families of the earth shall be blessed with the
blessings of Abraham. The blessings of Abraham caused both natural and
supernatural wealth. The servant of Abraham knew something about this

wealth-producing blessing when he said, "And the LORD hath blessed my master greatly; and he is become great: and he hath given him flocks, and herds, and silver, and gold, and menservants, and maidservants, and camels, and asses" (Gen. 24:35).

There is a designated blessing for every man, woman, and family. In other words, in God's economy, no family has any reason to be poor. This wealth-producing blessing is our dream, our vision, our destiny. This blessing belongs to us; it was designated for our families through Abraham. It is in heaven for our possession. It is a part of the true riches, which is our own by reason of our redemption.

Now, how do we qualify to own this designated wealth-producing blessing? Jesus told us a secret.

> And if ye have not been faithful in that which is another man's, who shall give you that which is your own? (Luke 16:12)

We are looking for that which is our own, that which belongs to us—our blessings, our dream, our destiny, our vision. Therefore, we must be faithful in what belongs to another individual. This is a universal mystery; we must faithfully sow into another person's dream before we can reap a harvest of realizing our own. *If we do not demonstrate the necessary fidelity required for someone to realize his or her dream, our own dream will remain unrealized.*

You can pray and cry all you want about your dream, vision, or destiny and still turn out a failure. The vital secret here is to faithfully act to commit your acquired financial wealth—the unrighteous mammon—to making another's vision or dream a reality. Then, providence will move in your favor to materialize your dream or vision.

When this universal secret is applied in our relationship with God, then nothing can stop great things from happening to us. When we invest our limited financial resources—our unrighteous mammon—into making God's dream come true, God will move heaven and earth to give us a manifestation of our dreams or visions.

How we faithfully distribute the unrighteous mammon we have to make God's dream real will qualify us to be trustees of the true riches, the treasures in heaven, the grace of God, or the designated blessing. If we use the unrighteous mammon to fund God's vision or dream to bring His children back to Him, He promises to give us what belongs to us—our dream, our vision or our destiny. In Matthew 6:33 Jesus brings up the principle when He says,

> But more than anything else, put God's work first and do what he wants. Then the other things will be yours as well. (CEV)

God will expedite the fulfillment of your dream through His blessing and His grace.

Why will a person fail to be promoted or prosper? Why will a person fail to obtain the blessing and grace that money cannot buy—the true riches?

Why will people fail to see their dreams fulfilled? It is because they fail to distribute their unrighteous mammon to fund God's dream. But why will they not distribute it? The word of God explains that they trust in uncertain riches rather than God. When the trustees begin to trust in the unrighteous mammon, their lives will depend on it and hence they will be reluctant to distribute. This was the problem of the rich, young ruler. He missed God's will, eternal life, his ministry, his promotion, and true riches because he was not willing to distribute to the poor his unrighteous mammon.

*Action:* Your group must create the opportunity for God to make its members trustees of His wealth. Their fidelity must be demonstrated through funding their vision of revival and human salvation.

# EPILOGUE

# HUMANS, THE KEY FIDELITY PLAYERS

It was E. M. Bounds who once said, "Men are God's method" (Bounds 1983). Not the organization, fellowship, group, ministry, or local church, but the men.

"I have a wonderful surprise for you," my friend John said in an upbeat kind of way. There was a twinkle in his eyes that got me wondering. John was a dear friend, and his coming across town to surprise me seemed rather thoughtful.

"And I can't disclose who it is, but you've got to come along with me," he quickly added. As we drove through town that afternoon in his car, my mind went into its own overdrive motion.

*Urgh! I dislike surprises.* But I hastily settled on an opinion. Navigating through some unfamiliar suburb to a large storied house, I had my gut-instinct suspicions.

"Oh, my brother! Long time no see!" the apparent "surprise" said with open arms. My hunch nailed it; it was Dr. Alex with his usual jolly-good-fellow kind of attitude. His hug conveyed that I'd been sorely missed. We had a lot of catching up to do. It had been years since I had left Eatons Creek Road for my home country.

Bringing me up to speed on his ministry, I got excited due to what had come of our labor together. The church had purchased a twenty-some acre landed property on the Ashland City Highway, and was encountering rapid church growth while engaged in an ongoing building project.

"Wow, Alex! You've done great!" I said.

"You know, I have a proposal. Why not come over with me to the States?" he said. It jostled my frame of mind. I hadn't seen this coming. I had a new group going in the port city then who hung on my every word. For months they had been trusting in my leadership, and revival was in the air—we were that close. My thoughts divulged the faces of the members.

*How will they feel? Will they survive my absence? Will bailing out of the revival now be God's will?* I thought.

I hate pressured decision making, but I didn't want to take a rain check. I needed to be forthright, so I leaned forward in my seat and gazed at the floor. "Alex, I appreciate your wanting me over, but I'm sorry. I've got to stick with my little group for now." Frankly, choosing between an obviously burgeoning ministry in the States for a fledgling group in a third-world country was colossally difficult.

My response stung him, and he sat back amazed. He honestly felt that he had heard from God. I felt otherwise; God was depending on my fidelity.

The day of Pentecost was predestined by God. It was the day of the Jewish Harvest Festival. The Jews had, throughout their history, celebrated this festival without truly realizing its prophetic significance. When the prophet Joel declared his vision of Pentecost, it was hard for his audience to determine the true prophetic interpretation of what he had said, but Jesus did. He pointed to the place within the Jewish timeline that it would occur.

> For John truly baptized with water; but ye shall be baptized
> with the Holy Ghost not many days hence. (Acts 1:5)

The words "not many days hence" indicate Christ's pointing to the Harvest Festival and reconciling it with Joel's prophecy. The apostle Peter taught the awestruck Jewish crowd this important connection by saying, "This is that which was spoken by the prophet Joel" (Acts 2:16). This Harvest Festival is that which was spoken by the prophet Joel. But since Adam, God had never been successful with anything in the earth without human cooperation. To flesh out His vision, Jesus needed a bunch of people who would stick it out together for the "not many days hence." He needed the fidelity of mortal man to commit to a divine cause. The Holy

Spirit was coming to the planet for good, and human history would never be the same again.

But when biblical historians recite the Pentecostal phenomenon that occurred in the Jerusalem upper room, they usually do so by side-stepping the role that fidelity played in this event. This is the fidelity factor. The fact that God's plan is critically interwoven with human fidelity during its execution makes this factor an understated reality, in my opinion.

As history has borne this out, it took God wooing the fidelity of a reluctant prince turned shepherd to pull off one of the most epic deliverance operations of all time. God needed Moses's fidelity so badly that no excuse of his could dissuade Him.

Many authors who have written books about the power of prayer in setting the fires of spiritual revival have paid little attention to the fidelity factor. In Charles Finney's outstanding ministry, it took the fidelity of his associates Daniel Nash and Abel Carey to groan in prayer for days and nights till revival spread across the land like blazing fire on a grassland (Liardon 2008). I want to posit that without the fidelity factor, all the intercessory prayer efforts that have characterized all the modern-day revivals, be they Pentecostal or charismatic, would have failed. If we want to see another Great Awakening, speakers, authors, and leaders need to hammer on the subject of fidelity to a divine cause. I personally don't think we have done enough in this area of Christian conduct.

In studying the history of the Azusa Street Revival, it became apparent that specific acts of spiritual infidelity played a major role in the demise of the Apostolic Faith Mission that emerged out of it. Certain dissenting measures taken by some associates of the mission, like Florence Crawford, Clara Lum, and William H. Durham, destabilized the fidelity of the congregation to its leader, William J. Seymour (Cauchi 2004).

In spite of all of this, it is significant to note that the fidelity factor has suffered some element of abuse by certain unscrupulous and misdirected elements within church history. It is unfortunate to witness multitudes of well-meaning loyalists being led astray into deception and destruction by cults. The apostle Paul declared that,

> Also of your own selves shall men arise, speaking perverse things, to draw away disciples after them. Therefore

watch, and remember, that by the space of three years I ceased not to warn every one night and day with tears. (Acts 20:30–31)

The year 1993 brought the death of David Koresh along with seventy-five members of his sexually deviant, prophetic, cultish church, the Branch Davidians. This occurred during a standoff with the FBI. In 2000, the orchestrated mass murder of 778 members of the Movement for the Restoration of the Ten Commandments (a doomsday cult) occurred in Uganda. In cases and events like these, the group members stick loyally to their leader's instruction even when certain red flags become very apparent. These were strange leaders, and the average believer must be trained to discern certain worrying signs. As laudable as membership fidelity is, it can go seriously askew.

To mention human fidelity as an element necessary only for the advancement of a spiritual movement is to limit its relevance to life inside the church. The dynamic that occurred within Jesus's inner circle is typical of any that occurs every day in some ministry, fellowship, group, or local church somewhere. Thus, testing followers or colleagues with the aim of measuring their fidelity is of utmost importance to a spiritual leader or worker who wants his or her group to step into the upcoming move of the Holy Spirit. The fidelity factor should be imperative to the development of any human resource management model.

In a nutshell, those of us who want to lead successful organizations or be "known in the gates" when we sit "among the elders of the land" (Prov. 31:23), must know how to measure the fidelity in our own hearts and in the hearts of others.

# WORKS CITED

Abotsi, Maureen. 2013. "Tema Pastor Facing a Sodomy Trial Proven to Be HIV Positive." *GhanaNation*. http:// http://www.ghanagrio. com/news/13094-tema-pastor-facing-a-sodomy-trial-proven-to-be-hiv-positive.html.

Barnes, Albert. "Albert Barnes' Notes on the Whole Bible." http://www. studylight.org/commentaries/bnb.html.

Blair, Leonardo. 2014. "'Yes We Eat Grass and We're Proud of It,' Say Congregants Who Were Convinced by 'Miracle' Working Preacher." *Christian Post*. Accessed September 9, 2016. http://m.christianpost. com/news/yes-eat-grass-and-were-proud-of-it-say-congregants-who-were-convinced-by-miracle-working-preacher-112400/.

Bounds, E. M. 1983. *Power through Prayer*. New Kensington, PA: Watchmaker Publishing, Whitaker House.

Cauchi, Tony. "William Seymour and the History of the Azusa Street Outpouring." *Revival Library*. http://www.revival-library.org/ pensketches/am_pentecostals/seymourazusa.html.

Eggerichs, Emerson. 2004. *Love and Respect*. Nashville, TN: Thomas Nelson.

Foxe, John. 2001. *Foxe's Book of Martyrs, Updated to the 21st Century*. Orlando, FL: Bridge-Logos.

"Jim Jones." 2016. *Wikipedia*. https://en.wikipedia.org/wiki/Jim_Jones.

Kubi, Vincent. 2013. "Jailed Pastor in Fresh HIV Scandal," *Modern Ghana*. https://www.modernghana.com/news/493037/1/jailed-pastor-in-fresh-hiv-scan.html.

Liardon, Roberts. 1996. *God's Generals*. New Kensington, PA: Whitaker House.

Liardon, Roberts. 2008. *God's Generals: The Revivalists,* New Kensington, PA: Whitaker House.

Ramsey, Dave. 2011. *EntreLeadership.* Brentwood, TN: Howard Books.

Roberts, Oral. 1999. *Seed-Faith 2000.* Tulsa, OK: Oral Roberts Ministries.

Sagoe-Nkansah, Dr. S. 2015. *The Law of Manifestation,* Maitland, FL: Xulon Press.

Shakarian, Demos, John Sherrill, and Elizabeth Sherrill. 1975. *The Happiest People on Earth.* Old Tappan, NJ: Fleming H. Revell.

Thomas, Anthony. 2014. *Secrets of the Vatican.* February 25. http://www.pbs.org/wgbh/frontline/film/secrets-of-the-vatican/.

The International Churchill Society. (1954, November 9). *Resources, Quotes, Famous Quotes and Stories.* Retrieved February Wednesday 1st, 2017, from The International Churchill Society Website: http://www.winstonchurchill.org/resources/quotations/499-famous-quotations-and-stories

Wesley, J. (1791, February 24). *Letter to William Wilberforce.* Retrieved February 1, 2017, from The United Methodist Church Website: http://www.umcmission.org/Find-Resources/John-Wesley-Sermons/The-Wesleys-and-Their-Times/Letter-to-William-Wilberforce

Printed in the United States
By Bookmasters